Literature Is *Back!*

Using the Best Books for Teaching Readers and Writers Across Genres

CAROL J. FUHLER · MARIA P. WALTHER

SCHOLASTIC

New York • Toronto • London • Auckland • Sydney
Mexico City • New Delhi • Hong Kong • Buenos Aires

Dedication

To Dick, for your continued quiet support, and to our sons and
their wives, who have planted and nurtured the love of reading
in our grandchildren. *C. J. F.*

To Lenny, because we make a great team, and to our
daughter, Katie—you are the best! *M. P. W.*

Credits: Page 142: Figure from Shanahan, T., and Shanahan, S. (May 1997). "Character Perspective Charting: Helping Children to Develop a More Complete Conception of Story." *The Reading Teacher*, *50*(8), 668–677. Reprinted with permission of the International Reading Association.

Page 211: "April Rain Song" from THE COLLECTED POEMS OF LANGSTON HUGHES by Langston Hughes, edited by Arnold Rampersad with David Roessel. Copyright © 1994 by The Estate of Langston Hughes. Reprinted with permission of Alfred A. Knopf, a division of Random House, Inc.

Page 213: "Flight Practice" from HUMMINGBIRD NEST by Kristine O'Connell George. Copyright © 2004 by Kristine O'Connell George. Reprinted with permission of Harcourt, Inc.

Page 226: "Clickbeetle" from THE LLAMA WHO HAD NO PAJAMA by Mary Ann Hoberman. Copyright © 1976 by Mary Ann Hoberman. Reprinted with permission of Harcourt, Inc.

Page 227: "Song of the Train" from ONE AT A TIME by David McCord. Copyright © 1966 by David McCord. Reprinted with permission of Little, Brown and Co.

Every effort has been made to find the authors and publishers of previously published material in this book and to obtain permission to print it.

Editor: Gloria Pipkin; Production Editor: Dana Truby; Copy Editor: Eileen Judge

Cover design by Maria Lilja; cover photo by Somos Images/Veer

Interior design by Holly Grundon

Interior photographs by Maria Walther and Iowa teachers

ISBN-13: 978-0-439-88875-2

ISBN-10: 0-439-88875-1

Copyright © 2007 by Carol J. Fuhler and Maria P. Walther

All rights reserved. Printed in the U.S.A.

1 2 3 4 5 6 7 8 9   40   12 11 10 09 08 07

Contents

Acknowledgments

A heartfelt thanks goes to:

♦ Our colleagues and our students: The lessons and teaching strategies found in our book have been enriched by reflective conversations with fellow educators and the knowledge gained from spending time with our learners. Maria thanks her "Tuesday Night Team" members, especially Katherine Phillips, Sue Lambert, and Mary Blessing, newcomers Kellie and Sarah, those who have been part of this innovative group of teachers in the past, and the hundreds of first graders who have shared her love of books.

♦ The teachers and their willing students who were so eager to show you how much they liked reading and writing: Michael Brancato, a third grader at May Watts School in Naperville, Illinois, for your brilliant essay; Amanda Skeffington and her fourth graders at Beaver Creek Elementary School in Johnston, Iowa; Nicole Artist and her third graders at the same school; Katie Milani and her fifth-grade class at Garner-Hayfield Elementary School in Garner, Iowa; and the students at Gwendolyn Brooks Elementary School in Aurora, Illinois. Our book is so much richer for these authentic contributions.

♦ Our fellow book lovers at Anderson's Bookshop in Naperville, Illinois—Jean Getzel, Jill Brooks, Jan Dundon, and award-winning author Sally Walker—who have nurtured our passion for children's literature and strive to keep teachers up to date on the latest stellar titles.

♦ The following publishers for generously sharing hot-off-the-press titles with us: Candlewick Press, Boyds Mill Press, Houghton Mifflin, and Scholastic.

♦ Gloria, our editor, because words cannot express our gratitude for your upbeat attitude, your positive comments, and your passion for books.

♦ Lenny Walther, our at-home graphics guy, who patiently scanned book covers, created figures, and is always willing to add just one more book.

♦ Our families, who had to peer over or walk around stacks of books to find us and who kept things running smoothly while we sat for hours, days, weeks, and months with our fingers tapping away on our laptops.

♦ The amazing design team at Scholastic, who truly made *Literature Is Back!* sing: Dana Truby, production editor; Holly Grundon, superb designer; and Ray Coutu, supervising editor. To Susan Kolwicz for her marketing genius. Also, thanks to Terry Cooper and Lois Bridges for welcoming us into the Scholastic family.

Literature Is Back!

Foreword

Reading *Literature Is Back!* brought back two memories. First, the book transported me to my childhood visits to the library. Two blocks from our apartment building in the Bronx, the public library was the high point in my life. As I read about different genres in Fuhler and Walther's text, I found myself back in that small room in the basement of a New York City project, sitting on the tile floor, surrounded by piles of fairy tales, realistic novels, or picture books. I can still hear Mrs. Schwartz, the children's librarian, reading to me and a small group of friends from *Mary Poppins* and *The Secret Garden*. And then, after browsing through every book I pulled from the shelves, I'd choose the stack to check out and carry home to read by myself or have my mom or dad read to me. Through elementary and junior high school, I'd walk to the library twice a week, anticipating leafing through books and, once there, savoring the time I had to decide which books I wanted most. I can still smell the mustiness of that library, feel the chill of the steel shelves, and hear Mrs. Schwartz's warm, raspy voice reading to us.

Now, leap forward to my first year of teaching in Gainsboro, Virginia, a small, rural town surrounded by rolling hills and mountains. For my class of 30 sixth graders, I had one set of grade-level basal readers, even though only five could read the basal. *Literature Is Back!* could have spared me the struggles that year as I scoured area libraries for materials! The good news is that this book, filled with riches about different literary genres and teaching ideas for each genre, can save teachers' lives today and give children memories about reading and listening to stories similar to mine.

Recently I was at a state reading conference at which teacher after teacher expressed frustration over being required to use a grade-level basal with the entire class. When I suggested that teachers use the basal with grade-level readers but find texts on similar genres at instructional reading levels that met the needs of other students, again and again, I heard, "But I don't have the time." Every classroom teacher can relate to that comment, and that's why I believe that every classroom teacher and school librarian will find this book invaluable. That's why I recommend that every teacher and librarian own a copy of *Literature Is Back!*

At this point, I'm sure that you're wondering why I staunchly believe this is a must-have professional resource. First, *Literature Is Back!* does so much more than offer annotated lists of books. Fuhler and Walther, both teachers, fully understand what teachers need and want, and they've packed their book with teaching ideas for reading and writing that address the needs of primary and intermediate teachers. As I read the first chapter, the authors hooked me with their passion for literature and reading. This chapter grounds readers in the world of children's books by reviewing literary elements and providing a structure for student book talks, then moves to discussing the power of reading aloud to primary and intermediate grade students.

The chapters that discuss literary genres contain two parts. The first part is a refresher course on the structure of picture books, traditional literature, fantasy and science fiction, realistic fiction, historical fiction, nonfiction, and poetry. Here, Fuhler and Walther share an annotated list of their favorite titles and reproducibles with guidelines that will enable you to evaluate books in a specific genre and choose the finest for your students. In the second part of each chapter, you'll explore a sampling of books neatly organized in a chart—books for teaching the genre, along with thumbnail summaries of teaching ideas. Next, both authors steep you in outstanding and easy-to-implement mini-lessons for reading and writing in the genre in primary and intermediate grades.

The closing chapter discusses, in depth, the role of children's literature in the classroom. Some of the beneficial ideas you'll find here are a reading conference form to use with students; an excellent explanation of "gradual release of responsibility"; a strategy that helps learners integrate reading, writing, thinking, and discussing; a list of professional books for further study; and a chart of the characteristics of proficient readers and writers.

What makes *Literature Is Back!* such a treasure is that you, like me, will return to chapters and sections of the book to ground yourself in a specific genre. Then, with Fuhler and Walther as your guides, you can find the best books to reach every reader and writer in your classroom where they are and gently move them forward with joyful and successful reading and writing experiences.

—Laura Robb

Introduction

We simply cannot resist a good book. Whether it is a picture book, a novel, or nonfiction, we savor every delectable title. In thinking back over our years of teaching to life in our classrooms today, neither of us can remember being able to teach without a book nearby. In her first-grade classroom and in her work with teachers across the country, Maria is continually searching for the best titles to teach reading and writing strategies. Her classroom brims with a multitude of books. In Carol's middle-school classroom, regardless of students' abilities, pertinent picture books, novels, and nonfiction titles were at the tips of her fingers. That didn't stop at the university level, where she still carries a stack of irresistible titles to undergraduate and graduate classes.

What do we do with all of these books? Both of us use wonderful children's literature to read aloud, regardless of the ages of our listeners. We reach for exemplary titles to teach, model, and practice research-based reading strategies across the grades and age levels. When it comes to writing instruction, we count on many an author to help us unlock the craft and illuminate techniques. Who better to model character development, the impact of style, or the use of figurative language? Beyond the classroom, you will still find us getting lost in the enticing world of books, which never grows old.

This kind of book-generated excitement is what we want to share with you. The chapters in this book will help you to use the rich body of children's literature to its fullest potential. Join us as we look at how children's literature is essential for literacy instruction, highlighting the different genres and underscoring what makes them unique. Each genre chapter includes background information and practical ideas for teaching key literacy skills and strategies. Found in the sections titled The Reading Connection and The Writing Connection, primary or intermediate lesson ideas can be used as is or adapted to dovetail with your district standards. If you are teaching the genre of fantasy and are searching for a reading lesson idea, simply turn to The Reading Connection in Chapter 4. If poetry is an area of focus, Chapter 8 is the place to begin your search. These suggestions are not intended to be add-ons to a bursting curriculum. Instead, they are meant to energize lessons you currently teach to truly invite learning.

Together we will sample some of the best titles available. Some are old favorites and some are exciting new ones that you will surely want to consider. When you're ready, refer to the numerous collections of irresistible titles to match all readers with just the right books so that they read, and then read even more.

Whether you are savoring or searching, we invite you to join us on our journey through the genres of children's literature. We hope that our enthusiasm will inspire you, that our suggestions will help guide you, and that you, too, will pass the joys of reading and writing on to your students, your colleagues, and your administrators. Share the message: *Literature Is Back!*

Chapter 1

Why Children's Literature Is Essential

FOR LITERACY INSTRUCTION

Children's literature—it can brighten a day, add breathing space to a hectic schedule, broaden one's knowledge about a topic of interest, and offer solace in times of need. No matter what our age, it pleases us, humors us, teaches us, and validates us as human beings. Life inside and outside the classroom takes on an added richness through reading great books, one title after another. Whether fiction, nonfiction, poetry, or prose, books

> "Literature is a kind of golden string that can place us in contact with the best minds in every period of history, the wisest, the tenderest, the bravest of all who have ever lived. And it can do this for children, if only we can help them to grasp hold of it. We recognize that children's literature is a part of the mainstream of all literature, that one literature experience builds on the last one, provided children can see the connections and are helped to wind them into a ball."
>
> (Charlotte Huck, 1982, p. 315)

(presented through a variety of artistic media and meticulously chosen words) are an integral part of the literacy curriculum. Books are meant to be savored, whether as read-alouds or during independent reading. They are perfect vehicles for teaching primary, elementary, and even middle-school students the essential skills and strategies that successful readers and writers employ. Filled with potential, children's literature can invigorate your teaching and inspire your learners, and ought to be common classroom fare for every child. It is tragic that it is not. Those children who relish books and have ready access to them are fortunate indeed.

As teachers, it is our responsibility and our joy to share the wonderful world of children's literature with all of our students. We wish you well as you infuse your days with fine books.

A Quick Look Back at Children's Literature

Over time, the field of books for children has expanded from initial offerings of nursery rhymes, folk and fairy tales, and moralistic stories to include a myriad of fiction and nonfiction selections. With over 389,000 children's titles currently in print, it is essential for teachers to be able to select the best and most appropriate for their use (Bogart, 2007). Because there continue to be more books published each year, it becomes a dizzying prospect to determine which of those should become an integral part of classroom life. In order for you to make judicious decisions, it will help to review what children's literature is and then to learn what distinguishes a good book from those that are not as noteworthy.

Children's Literature Defined

Children's literature includes a collection of books—fiction, nonfiction, and poetry—written particularly for readers from infancy to age 14 (Mikkelsen, 2000; Tomlinson & Lynch-Brown, 2002). This collection contains a variety of genres, formats, and styles, including picture books, traditional literature, fantasy, science fiction, poetry,

> The best children's books carefully define characters, represent fine examples of diverse writing styles, include exemplary interpretations of the theme, and present information in a clearly organized manner.
>
> (Galda & Cullinan, 2006)

contemporary realistic fiction, historical fiction, and informational books. As a classroom teacher, you have the exciting opportunity to introduce readers to a sampling from each of these categories.

The following pages will look more closely at children's literature, examining the characteristics of a good book and discussing how those characteristics tie in to what readers like. We will highlight the value of children's literature and underscore why it should be at the heart of your literacy program. In addition, we will reinforce and endorse the absolute necessity of setting aside ample time every single day to read aloud to your students. There is much to celebrate in the world of children's books and the promise they hold for your literacy curriculum. We begin that celebration with this chapter.

What Makes a Good Book?

If you ask a young child to tell you what a good book is, she probably cannot tell you, but she will eagerly show you. Off in a flash and back as quickly, she might hand you *Goodnight Moon* (Brown, 1947) or *Brown Bear, Brown Bear, What Do You See?* (Martin Jr., 1992). If you look at her closely, you will see a hopeful look in her eyes: Perhaps you'll read to her? Pose the same question to a kindergartner or first grader, and he may tell you it is the book his teacher is currently reading. It might also be *The Waterfall's Gift* (Ryder, 2001) or *Chicka Chicka Boom Boom* (Martin Jr. & Archambault, 1989). Grabbing the first book, he will proudly show you where a tiny insect is cleverly hidden on each page. If you stand still long enough, he and a few classmates may even recite the finger-snapping refrain from *Chicka Chicka Boom Boom*.

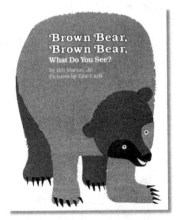

Young children enjoy hearing books read again and again.

This enjoyment of literature is infectious, isn't it? Certainly we can say that a good book is well loved by its readers. But there is more to it than that.

An intermediate-grade reader might tell you a good book is a classic. From her desk, one seasoned reader pulls out *The Secret Garden* (Burnett, 1962). She remembers having it read to her when she was younger. Her classmate recommends *Hatchet* (Paulsen, 1987). Without a doubt, survival stories are the best. Another friend chimes in that she likes Lemony Snicket's A Series of Unfortunate Events because she loves to be just a little bit frightened. A classmate scoffs at the quality of those books. His top-ranking choice is Wilson Rawls' (1996) *Where the Red Fern Grows*. He admits that it's a little sad, though. Now the definition of a good book includes classics, adventure, and mass-market popular series books. What would we, as teachers, usually say?

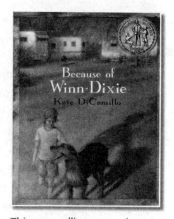

This compelling story gives readers much to discuss.

When asked about good books, we look for fine writing along with believable characters to whom our students can relate. We often pick a powerful or compelling story that gives readers something to talk about when the book is finished (Leu & Kinzer, 2003). Sometimes we want a title that is lighter but still written by a knowledgeable and skilled author. We suggest *Dear Mrs. LaRue: Letters From Obedience School* (Teague, 2002) or the rhythmic *Seven Spunky Monkeys* (Koller, 2005) for younger children. For books that give intermediate-grade readers something to discuss, we think *Because of Winn-Dixie* (DiCamillo, 2000) or Louise Erdrich's (1999) *The Birchbark House* are titles that exemplify that criterion. Is everyone right?

In a sense, they are. What could be regarded as the qualities of a good book will vary between critical and not so critical readers. Some authorities stick by the quality of writing as displayed in Katherine Paterson's (1978) *The Great Gilly Hopkins* or Jerry Spinelli's (1990) *Maniac Magee*. Students often endorse general appeal and reach for books in popular series like Junie B. Jones, The Magic Tree House, or Captain Underpants. Let's consider the qualities that experts look for in an outstanding book and balance those with a reader's possible choices. The experts look to literary elements, the fundamentals of distinctive writing. As we review the elements, we will highlight exemplary, illustrative titles and offer teaching ideas galore.

The Literary Elements

Plot

Rebecca Lukens (2007) explains that plot is tied to the element of possibility that exists in a story. It involves a sequence of actions and reactions that are carefully chosen to tell the tale best. A well-conceived, original plot holds everything together as the story moves through its conflicts, suspense, excitement, and the tension in action that reaches a climax, and then settles down with an eventual resolution. Even in quieter stories, there must be some tension. The test of a well-written, believable plot is that you get caught in the just-one-more-chapter mode. The book is simply too irresistible to put down.

In addition, when setting the pace of the story, writers decide upon the *narrative order*, the order in which events of the plot will unfold. The most common choice is a *chronological* or *linear order,* where one event naturally follows another. A second option writers use is an *episodic* plot. In this case, each chapter is a different story or episode in a character's life. The chapters may also be linked by a common theme. Appealing examples of stories with episodic plots are Arnold Lobel's Frog and Toad series or *Wind in the Willows* (Grahame, 1961). For young readers just beginning to transition to chapter books, these are especially comfortable books to read.

When writing for older readers, authors may interrupt the chronological sequence of events by using *flashbacks*. This is a way to inform the reader of events that occurred before the first chapter of the book. Flashbacks enable the writer to fill in additional background to shed light on what is currently happening. For instance, in Cynthia Rylant's (1992) *Missing May*, 12-year-old Summer's memories of her Aunt May interrupt the ordered events, providing additional information about this special aunt. Readers in the primary grades have trouble following such jumping back and forth in time and events, which is why flashbacks are more commonly found in books for older readers.

One final choice that writers may employ is *alternating plots*. In this case, there is more than one main character. Each character tells his or her part of the story in alternating chapters. For instance, in Chapter 1 of *Flipped* (Van Draanen, 2001), Bryce explains the early days of his relationship with Juli Baker by stating, "All I've ever wanted is for Juli Baker to leave me alone. For her to back off—you know, just give me some space" (p. 1). Chapter 2 begins with an ecstatic Juli, "The first day I met Bryce Loski, I flipped. Honestly, one look at him and I became a lunatic. It's his eyes. Something in his eyes. They're blue, and framed in the blackness of his lashes, they're dazzling. Absolutely breathtaking" (p. 11). You can already see trouble coming from the opening lines! Switching back and forth between characters, each voice rings true as they tell their own interwoven tales in a memorable book appropriate for mature upper-grade readers. See the chart that follows for ideas to help you model, discuss, and teach different plot structures.

Alternating plots are used in this memorable book.

Introducing Plot in the Primary Grades	
Type of Plot/ Suggested Books	**Teaching Ideas**
Chronological Plot Structure *Alexander and the Terrible, Horrible, No Good, Very Bad Day* (Viorst, 1972) *Rattletrap Car* (Root, 2001)	Work together to create a "Map of the Characters' Day" (see figure below). After reading, draw or write about the main events in sequence. Once you've modeled this activity, provide children with opportunities to do it on their own.
Episodic Plot Structure Henry and Mudge, Mr. Putter and Tabby, and Poppleton series by Cynthia Rylant George and Martha series by James Marshall	Play Episode Charades. Read aloud one of these popular series books. Divide students into small groups, one for each chapter/episode in the book. Each group prepares a quick dramatization of their episode and presents it to the class. The class then tries to guess which episode they are dramatizing.
Alternating Plot Structure *Once Upon a Cool Motorcycle Dude* (O'Malley, 2005)	To demonstrate the different voices and plots in this book, find an enthusiastic male and female reader to read it aloud to your students.

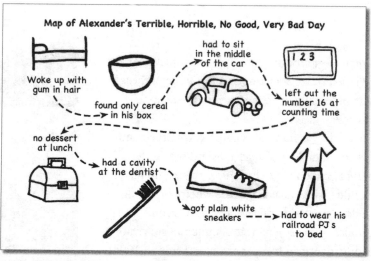

A map of Alexander's day

Teaching About Plot in the Intermediate Grades

Type of Plot/ Suggested Books	Teaching Ideas
Chronological Plot Structure *Hill Hawk Hattie* (Clark, 2003) *Hattie on Her Way* (Clark, 2005)	Chronological order reveals more than the order of events. It is an effective way to show how a main character grows or matures from the beginning to the end of a story. Have students use a character map to plot the changes in Hattie as the story evolves. Discuss the findings with an eye to the role that chronology plays in quality character development.
Episodic Plot Structure *Sideways Stories From Wayside School* (Sachar, 1978)	After reading about each of the unique teachers and children, have students work in pairs to create a "new kid" for Wayside School. At the same time, teachers may choose to write about an unusual teacher. Both teachers and students will be writing a short episode for a sequel. Polish and place episodes in a class book.
Alternating Plot Structure *The Wanderer* (Creech, 2000)	Students pick a character to follow throughout the book, then write journal entries as if they were that character. Ask students to reflect periodically on the events that have occurred as if they were writing at the end of the day.

Conflict

There are as many as four different kinds of conflict involved in a well-developed story. Sometimes two or more of these conflicts occur, especially in novels for intermediate- to upper-grade readers.

When the conflict is internal, a battle within the main character, it is an example of *character-against-self*. In the picture book *Ira Sleeps Over* (Waber, 1972), young Ira has an internal conflict when he can't decide whether to bring his beloved teddy bear to his first sleepover. A second type of conflict, *character-against-nature*, is common in survival tales. It is readily identified in *Brian's Winter* (Paulsen, 1996), in which Brian continues his struggles to survive in the Canadian wilderness after a plane crash. He faces the harsh

Holes contains character-against-character conflict.

Canadian winter with its intense cold, the need to winterize his home and his clothing, and the necessity of finding food. The third type of conflict is *character-against-character*. In this case, the main character may be at odds with an adult, a sibling, or a peer. For example, in the Harry Potter series, Harry is constantly on guard against his nemesis, evil Lord Voldemort. The final type of conflict is *character-against-society*. In the beautifully illustrated picture book, *The Trouble With Henry: A Tale of Walden Pond* (O'Neal & Westengard, 2005), Henry David Thoreau faces the ridicule of the townspeople who favor material wealth and the expansion of factories over preserving nature. They find Thoreau's concerns for the environment and love of solitude in his cabin on Walden Pond to be laughable.

The Great Kapok Tree has a character-against-nature conflict.

Introducing Conflict (Problems) in the Primary Grades

Type of Conflict	Suggested Books	Teaching Ideas
Character-Against-Self	*Ira Sleeps Over* (Waber, 1972)	As you read these books aloud to your students, make a chart titled "Stories Have Different Kinds of Conflicts/Problems."
Character-Against-Nature	*The Great Kapok Tree* (Cherry, 1990)	Across the top of the chart list the four different types of conflicts/problems. After reading each book, discuss which type(s) of conflict occurred in the story. List the title of the book under the appropriate heading. Refer to this chart during writing workshop to remind students of the different types of conflicts they may choose to include in their own stories.
Character-Against-Character	*Beany and the Meany* (Wojciechowski, 2005)	
Character-Against-Society	*Old Henry* (Blos, 1990)	

Teaching About Conflict in the Intermediate Grades	
Type of Conflict/ Suggested Books	**Teaching Ideas**
Character-Against-Self *The Sign of the Beaver* (Speare, 1983)	As you read aloud, chart Matt's conflicts on an overhead or chart paper. Next to each conflict write how he resolved it and what events led to his decision. Model how to use evidence from the text to support your thinking. Assess students' understanding when they apply this activity to a book of their choice.
Character-Against-Nature *Wild Man Island* (Hobbs, 2002)	As students read this or other books exemplifying this type of conflict, have them list the ways in which nature creates conflict. Periodically meet as a whole class to discuss findings.
Character-Against- Character *Holes* (Sachar, 1998)	Using this or another title in a whole-class read-aloud, model the use of a two-column chart that lists the characters in one column and the conflicts they create in the second column. Discuss how this type of conflict moves the story along.
Character-Against- Society *Number the Stars* (Lowry, 1989)	Create a bulletin board that examines the key types of conflict. Once students have completed a novel of their choice, have them use 3" x 5" note cards to write title, author, and type of conflict they discovered plus an example. Color-code cards according to the type of conflict. Post under the appropriate type of conflict on the bulletin board. Review the board, having students share their contributions.

Characterization

When examining characterization in a picture book, you and your students will be looking at the development of the characters' personality, behaviors, goals, desires, and accomplishments. In chapter books or novels, which allow the author more time to develop a character, the characters should be multidimensional and well rounded, showing both strengths and weaknesses. The author helps us to know characters in a number of ways: through a description of their appearance, their conversations, their thoughts, their actions, the comments of the author (or narrator), and their interactions with other characters (Galda & Cullinan, 2006). In Avi's (1994) *The Barn*, we "eavesdrop" on Ben's reactions as he tries to communicate with his father who has had a stroke:

Suddenly all my anger rushed together within my chest. It was as if I had been struck by a musket ball. Why had he done this? It was a cruel thing he had become, and I felt a hatred for it. He had abandoned us when we needed him. He had become a child when we were children...

"Father!" I screamed in annoyance. "If you mean yes, you must close your eyes!"

And then—he did.

When I realized he had given me an answer, I was so stunned I burst into tears (pp. 38–39).

By studying this 9-year-old's feelings, you can get a sense of the determination to build his father's dream barn despite nearly insurmountable odds. Next, consider this example of how other people's comments can reveal tidbits about a main character. See what you can learn about *Sadako* (Coerr, 1993) in the early pages of the book:

"Mother, may we go ahead to the Peace Park?" Sadako asked.

"Yes, Sadako chan," her mother answered. "Go slowly in this heat!" But the two girls were already racing up the dusty street.

Mr. Sasaki laughed. "Did you ever see Sadako walk when she could run, hop, or jump?" (unpaged)

If the author has done a masterful job, we get to understand these characters so well that it seems as if we know them. It's as if they are a classmate, a friend, or a neighbor down the street. When an author has given us enough information about characters so that we form a reading relationship with them, she has created *round characters*.

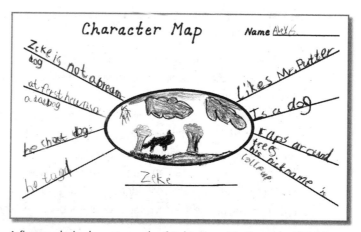

A first grader's character web of Zeke from *Mr. Putter and Tabby Walk the Dog* (Rylant, 1994).

In addition to believable main characters, books are peopled with secondary characters. They are as follows:

- *flat characters*: found in many a folk and fairy tale. They have limited development.

- *stereotypical characters*: flat characters that represent a group of characters like those handsome princes who rescue one princess after another or characters that fit the role of a typical mother.

- *static characters*: remain much the same from the beginning to the end of a tale. As with the others, readers don't get to know them well.

All of these can complete the cast of characters and may be necessary to the action and events, but they are not memorable.

For younger readers who are just beginning to learn about characters, start by exploring books in which they can get to know the character through descriptions of their appearance, actions, and other concrete traits. A character web (see figure, page 17) is an effective tool for identifying character traits. See page 19 for a few books and ideas to get you started.

The criteria for excellent characterization, then, include characters that are multidimensional, round, and also dynamic. In the latter case, these believable people or animals grow and change to a degree throughout the story. In the process, many become part of a select group of almost-real people who live on in our literary memories.

Try This! Collecting Convincing Characters

Challenge students to pay careful attention to how the author has created a believable character. While reading independently, students use sticky notes to mark instances when the character is revealed through description, conversations, actions, author's comments, or interactions with other characters. Encourage them to jot down evidence from the text to support their thinking. Once the book has been completed, students use their gathered evidence to write a brief summary of how the character was developed. Character development summaries can be added to writer's notebooks for future reference. For additional lesson ideas in working with characterization with intermediate-grade readers, please see Chapter 5, Contemporary Realistic Fiction.

Teaching About Character in the Primary Grades

Suggested Books	Characters	Teaching Ideas
Tough Boris (Fox, 1994) 	Boris von der Borch 	This book is wonderful for introducing character because Mem Fox uses only six words to describe Boris. After reading, create a character web with the six words (see example at left), then ask students to tell you six words to describe the principal, P.E. teacher, student teacher, etc. Consider using Fox's repetitive sentence pattern to do a shared rewriting of the text (see left).
Henry and Mudge: The First Book of Their Adventures (Rylant, 1987)	Henry and Mudge	After reading, model creating a character web for students describing Mudge. Students then work with partners to create a character web for Henry.
Strega Nona (dePaola, 1975a), *Big Anthony and the Magic Ring* (1979) and other titles in this series.	Strega Nona Big Anthony Bambalona Strega Amelia	The Strega Nona series is an excellent way to show young readers how an author can create a series of books based on the literary element of character. In each book, dePaola introduces and helps the reader get to know a new character.

Setting

You already know that the setting of a story is the time and place in which the tale unfolds. It may be either *incidental* or *integral* to the story. In the first instance, the setting is merely a backdrop for the story, as is typically seen in traditional literature. The phrases "Once upon a time" or "In a country far, far away" give very little information about when or where the story takes place. That is perfectly appropriate for tales where the action is of paramount importance, quickly carrying the reader from the beginning to the end. It is also effective when the author wants readers to have the opportunity to create the details of place in their own imagination. In other stories, however, the setting is more likely to be *integral*. In this case, it is essential to the action, events, and the characters, who are influenced by the time and place in which the story is staged. Whenever the setting is integral, the author gives us plenty of help in visualizing the time and place. Finally, the setting should add credibility and depth to a story (Jacobs & Tunnell, 2004).

A book with an integral setting.

One example of an incidental setting can be found in Carolyn Crimi's (2005) *Henry and the Buccaneer Bunnies.* The story is set somewhere on the "high seas," with no particular time or sea designated. Aboard the "crickety" old ship, the *Salty Carrot*, readers meet Captain Barnacle Black Ear, a notably bad bunny brute. While he has his share of problems, the biggest one is his disappointing, book-reading son. Eventually that son redeems himself in his sea-loving father's eyes when he saves the day because of information gleaned from a book.

For a change of pace, older readers will chuckle their way through *A Long Way From Chicago* (Peck, 1998), a perfect title to assess the impact of an integral setting upon a story. This story takes place in a sleepy Illinois town somewhere between Chicago and St. Louis. The time period is one summer during the Depression. The carefully crafted details help us create scenes in our mind, giving us the feeling that we've been there, and we're not likely to forget the visit. The story simply would not be the same if it were set in another time and place.

Theme

Rebecca Lukens (2007) tells us that the theme of a story is its idea or central meaning. It typically involves an author's observation about society or human nature. Themes usually include establishing relationships, seeking moral values, learning to accept oneself and others, respecting authority, coping with a variety of situations, and growing up (Norton, 2003). You and your readers will find that themes can be *implicit*, in that you have to dig a little to find them, or *explicit*, those that are quickly apparent. The implicit theme that emerges from *A Day's Work* (Bunting, 1994) is that one should be honest and take pride in a good day's work. The explicit theme that ends *Giraffes Can't Dance* (Andrede, 1999) is that we can all be successful if we follow what it is that makes us unique. You will find a closer inspection of theme and its role in the genre of fantasy in the intermediate reading lesson in Chapter 4.

Try This! **Thinking About Theme**

Create a classroom chart titled "Thinking About Theme." Post the chart where students have easy access to it. For the primary grades, pick a collection of picture books with various themes. Read them aloud and discuss the author's message or purpose. Record the title, author, and theme on the chart. For the intermediate grades, choose one or two read-alouds. After you've explored various themes, students can contribute to the chart by adding books they've read independently. Periodically review the chart and discuss common themes that might be emerging.

Style

Style involves the writer's choice and arrangement of words, phrases, sentences, and paragraphs. It looks more at how a writer uses words than what she says in the process. One way a writer can work with words is by using imagery, a tool to paint pictures in the mind of a reader. When imagery works effectively, the readers' senses are involved, such as seeing the hot sun melting an ice cream cone, tasting the rain on the tip of the tongue alongside the main character, smelling the freshly baked bread, or feeling the itchy coarseness of woolen clothing against their skin. Activating the readers' senses brings the book to life.

Then, authors work with the sound of their words. They apply literary devices like similes and metaphors to compare one thing to another, or use exaggeration to make a point. Writers might try alliteration, the repetition of initial consonants, or onomatopoeia, words that sound like their meanings. They will focus on rhythm, working with the words so that they flow as they add richness to their text. The sounds of language may be taken for granted when they seem to be used so effortlessly, but they are one of the pieces of the element of style that is important to evaluate. Literary devices such as these will be further examined in Chapter 8, which highlights poetry.

Pick up a standard dictionary and thumb through it. You will quickly recognize that authors have a phenomenal choice of words at their disposal when they write. It is a reflection of their talent that they can select just the right words and arrange them in exactly the right way to tell their stories.

Try This! ## Sentence Fluency in Action

These writers have the same reservoir of words, yet look how differently they use them. One can easily see how clearly word choices and sentence fluency reflect each writer's style.

Primary Grades

My Little Sister Ate One Hare (Grossman, 1996). Grossman's catchy repetitive rhyming text invites young listeners to read along:

> My little sister ate 3 ants.
> She even ate their underpants.
> She ate 2 snakes. She ate 1 hare.
> We thought she'd throw up then and there.
> But she didn't.

Intermediate Grades

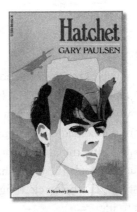

Hatchet (Paulsen, 1987). Paulsen uses repetition along with crisp wording and varying sentence length to create suspense:

> He was stopped. Inside he was stopped. He could not think past what he felt. All was stopped. The very core of him, the very center of Brian Robeson was stopped and stricken with a white-flash of horror, a terror so intense that his breathing, his thinking, and nearly his heart had stopped. Stopped . . . (p. 12)

Try This! **Teaching About Style**

Regardless of the grade you are teaching, you can help your students develop an ear for style by collecting and sharing samples from your favorite authors. Have children listen for the sounds of interesting words, the flow of language, and the way the sentences weave together. Take time to discuss why the style works well with the story. Once older learners are familiar with the elements of style, they can work with their peers to find other books to add to the collection. Invite them to pick a particularly good example of their chosen author's style, practice reading it, and then take turns sharing the excerpts within their group. Volunteers might want to read their samples to the whole class as you celebrate excellence in applying the elements of style. You might try these sample texts that paint a picture with words.

Primary Grades

Hello Ocean (Ryan, 2001). Ryan uses the senses when vividly describing the ocean:

> I see the ocean, gray, green, blue, a chameleon always changing hue. Amber seaweed, speckled sand, bubbly waves that kiss the land… (unpaged)

Intermediate Grades

Mariel of Redwall (Jacques, 1991). Jacques paints a vivid word picture of this tranquil setting for his readers:

> Trudging silently along beside Traquin, the mousemaid had her first view of Redwall Abbey. She liked what she saw. With the dusty brown path running across its front, the late afternoon sunlight played over the structure, giving it a faded rosy glow. Behind the stout outer wall with its battlements and ramparts, she could see the high spired Abbey roof, flanked by lower sloping ones, peaceful and serene, standing homely and solid with the summer green forest at its back. (p. 79)

Point of View

Point of view is actually a part of style but is easier to examine on its own. It is the position the author takes to tell her story. One common approach is the *first-person narrative*. The voice readers hear from this perspective is "I." Thus, if I were telling my story, readers would be seeing the events in the story only through my eyes. In the process, I would also be describing events, actions, and the perceived feelings of others around me from my subjective point of view.

Two examples of first-person narrative to share with intermediate-grade readers are *A Time for Andrew: A Ghost Story* (Hahn, 1994) and *The Wolf's Story* (Forward, 2005). In *A Time for Andrew*, Andrew is visiting his aunt when he inadvertently encounters ghostly Drew, a young ancestor. The boys change places in time so that Drew can receive medical attention for his diphtheria. Once healed, however, he does not want to return to 1910, leaving Andrew in a frightening situation. On a lighter note, the point of view is very clear in *The Wolf's Story* as Wolf recounts his version of what really happened to Little Red Riding Hood. Younger readers have long been tickled with *The True Story of the Three Little Pigs* (Scieszka, 1989), another natural title to teach first-person perspective.

Another perspective to teach is the *omniscient* narrator. Here, the story is told in the third person, and the narrator is all knowing, telling the readers about all of the characters' feelings, thoughts, and ideas using words like *he*, *she*, and *they*. In this case, the reader is learning about the main character through the eyes of the writer. A picture book example is *Faraway Home* (Kurtz, 2000). The narrator shares Desta's worries when she learns that her father will have to travel to Ethiopia to be with his mother who is ill. What if he likes it better in the village where he was a child? Will he ever come home?

The short novel *Simeon's Fire* (Clinton, 2005) is a perfect example of a third-person narrative. Readers learn about Simeon's thoughts as he goes through his farm chores; hear his father, Daat, planning the day's haying and other tasks; and then overhear the voices of the men who set the family's barn on fire. The all-seeing narrator describes events that center around the values of a hard-working Amish family and the destructive forces of prejudice that impact their lives. In these examples the reader is inside the minds of the major characters in each book. He is well aware of the surroundings at all times because of the author's choice of point of view.

Design and Layout

One final aspect to investigate when assessing the quality of a book is the design and layout. Jacobs and Tunnell (2004) suggest evaluating the following items: Look at the cover. Is it inviting? How do the endpapers add to the visual quality? Are there color-coordinated endpapers or do they have a design that ties in to the story? In *Kidogo* (McGrory, 2005), for instance, the beginning endpapers show and name all of the larger

East African animals in the book. These particular characters make Kidogo feel small and insignificant. In a creative wrap-up to the story, the endpapers identify all of the characters who make him feel just the right size. Thus, well-designed endpapers invite the reader to step into or extend the story.

Other items to note are the width of the margins, the size of the type and the style selected, the position of the page numbers, and the spacing between the lines of text. In addition, with picture books, check the placement of the text. In some cases, chunks of text are interspersed with the illustrations, paragraphs may move from the top of a page to the bottom of the next page, or the book may be wordless. Overall, you are asking yourself about the visual appeal.

After reading through the preceding paragraphs, you can see there is a great deal of care that goes into a book that falls into the "exceptional" category. The journey to discovering what is good and what does not earn that rating should be filled with many a book and many a varying opinion from your students. May your classroom be filled with lively defenses of what should earn high rankings as students justify their decisions and refine their critical-thinking skills in the process.

Try This! | **Using "A Critic's Review" to Organize Student Book Talks**

Apply the knowledge of literary elements by having upper-grade students complete A Critic's Review, on page 26. They might complete a review periodically, selecting books they think are especially well written. Keep sheets in a reading corner folder or in a folder on the desktop of the classroom computer. After completing A Critic's Review, a student can give a five-minute book talk on that title. At that point she can issue a "Critic's Challenge," inviting classmates to read and review the book. Once someone accepts the challenge, the readers can gather for a short, critical discussion to compare and contrast their observations.

A Critic's Review

Directions: Use this sheet to review a book you think is well written. Give a brief book talk. Then challenge classmates to read and review your book, too.

Title: _____ Author: _____

How would you describe the plot? Type: Chronological _____ Episodic _____ Alternating _____ Use of flashbacks? _____ Examples from text:	**How would you describe the character?** Multidimensional _____ Round _____ Dynamic _____ Flat or static _____ Stereotypical _____ Examples from text:
What is the main conflict? character-against-self _____ character-against-nature _____ character-against-character _____ character-against-society _____ Examples from text:	**What is the main theme?** Implicit? _____ Explicit? _____ Examples from text:
How would you describe the author's style?	**What point of view does the author use?** First person _____ Third person/omniscient _____
Share your thoughts on the design and layout of the book.	**What is your overall assessment of the book?**

The Power of the Read-Aloud

Is a read-aloud one of the highlights of your day? If you queried your students, they would probably say it is one of theirs. One after another, researchers endorse the fact that "the single most important activity for building the knowledge required for eventual success in reading is reading aloud to children" (Anderson, Hiebert, Scott, & Wilkinson, 1985, p. 23). This means reading to students across the grades and onward. Do not shortchange older students who still enjoy hearing a story read well, whether it is a picture book suited for an older audience or a well-crafted, fast-paced novel (Farris, Fuhler, & Walther, 2004; Huck et al., 2004).

Joe, a third grader, gives his book talk.

What the Research Says:
The Top 10 Reasons to Read Aloud

1. Prepares children for literacy learning and helps them acquire essential literacy skills.

2. Develops an interest in reading and fosters a positive attitude toward reading.

3. Promotes general language development and broadens vocabulary knowledge.

4. Increases reading achievement.

5. Positively influences writing as it introduces various genres and different styles and triggers ideas for writing.

6. Provides opportunities for social interaction in response to a book.

7. Enables readers of all abilities to enjoy a story.

8. Presents an enthusiastic adult who is a wonderful reading model.

9. Highlights the pleasures of reading and motivates children to read on their own.

10. Expands and deepens one's knowledge base.

(Trelease, 2006; Huck et al., 2004; Galda & Cullinan, 2003, 2006)

Take a minute to think about the impact of this information: Marilyn Adams (1990) states that if a child is read to for 30 to 45 minutes each day from the time he is 6 weeks old, he will enter the first grade with "1,000 to 1,700 hours of storybook reading—one on one with his face in the books" (p. 85). What a solid foundation upon which to build upcoming literacy skills! If a child is not that fortunate, primary teachers must fill in that missing piece by reading aloud as often as three or four times a day.

Reading Aloud in the Primary Grades

Jim Trelease (2006) has practical tips for teachers to make the most of the time they spend reading aloud with their students. Check to see how many of these are already in place in your classroom.

- Plan on repeated readings of predictable books. Children love to hear a favorite title read again and again.

- Set aside a designated time for reading aloud every day so that children can anticipate these special times.

- Read several times a day whenever possible.

- Vary the subject matter of your readings. Along with fiction, enjoy poems, songs, and lots of nonfiction.

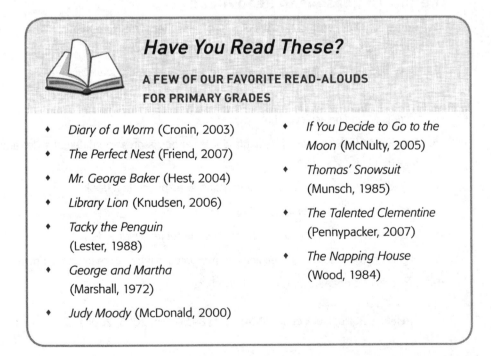

Have You Read These?

A FEW OF OUR FAVORITE READ-ALOUDS FOR PRIMARY GRADES

- *Diary of a Worm* (Cronin, 2003)
- *The Perfect Nest* (Friend, 2007)
- *Mr. George Baker* (Hest, 2004)
- *Library Lion* (Knudsen, 2006)
- *Tacky the Penguin* (Lester, 1988)
- *George and Martha* (Marshall, 1972)
- *Judy Moody* (McDonald, 2000)

- *If You Decide to Go to the Moon* (McNulty, 2005)
- *Thomas' Snowsuit* (Munsch, 1985)
- *The Talented Clementine* (Pennypacker, 2007)
- *The Napping House* (Wood, 1984)

- Divide longer stories into two sessions, especially at the beginning of the year.

- Always tell the children the title, the author, and the illustrator, no matter how many times you read the book.

- Group the children to be certain that everyone can see the pictures. Spend a few minutes showing the pictures so that listeners have time to take them in. You are strengthening visual literacy skills as you do so.

Along with the suggestions above, periodically select a book that will make the readers stretch intellectually. Children can "listen up" to a book. One caution is that you should not choose a title that is above your students' emotional level. For example, while *Hiroshima No Pika* (Maruki, 1980) is a picture book, it is about the bombing of Hiroshima. With its abstract but still graphic illustrations, and content about dropping the atomic bomb, it could be disturbing fare for lower-grade readers. The book would be much better placed in an upper-grade classroom, perhaps as a part of a social studies unit.

Reading Aloud in the Intermediate Grades

When you read aloud in the intermediate grades, Trelease (2006) and other noted authorities suggest that you choose books that both you and your students will enjoy. If you like it, your enthusiasm will show. As motivation to read dwindles in the intermediate to upper grades, this enthusiastic endorsement of reading can catch apathetic readers unawares and reel them right back into the reading fold. If you find that your students are not engaged in a novel, set it aside, and try another title. Maybe students will be ready for it later in the year. If not, those who were interested can continue reading the title on their own. As you plan, keep the following suggestions in mind.

- Create a comfortable reading atmosphere.

- Sit where students can easily see you. Even though you may be reading a novel with no pictures to see, listeners still want to see you.

- Plan your reading advantageously, choosing a suspenseful part of the chapter at which to stop, leaving the audience hanging until the next read-aloud session.

- Start each read-aloud session with a question or two about what has happened up to that point to get the students back into the story. This is also a quick check to see whether the class understands the story.

- Even upper-grade readers enjoy an appropriate picture book. See Chapter 2 for a list of picture books for older readers.

Because you are still reinforcing broad reading, vary the materials you read aloud and include poetry and nonfiction in the mix. A word, or two, of advice: Don't choose only books that have won awards when making your selections. Some award-winning books are superb to read individually but are not the right choice for reading aloud. You will know what will work if you like it and know that this year's class will enjoy the title, too. Finally, don't read right up until the bell rings and class is dismissed. Save some time after each reading session to chat together about the book. This time enables students to learn from one another as they share their reactions. It also is one way to deepen individual responses to a book.

In addition to the general support given to reading aloud, think of its value to students who struggle with reading. It is the one time of day when they can sit back and enjoy a story without struggling one word at a time to get through a sentence. They hear the rhythm of well-constructed sentences and can practice visualizing the story in their minds. Second language learners benefit enormously as well. They have yet another opportunity to hear the English language used correctly. Furthermore, they can match words with the pictures in the text. They can also better understand what happened in the story by listening to their classmates' discussions. All in all, read-aloud time is relaxing, enjoyable, educational, and thought provoking—a time when an author's words can fill the classroom and the minds of the listeners. And who knows the long-term impact of those words?

Have You Read These?

A FEW OF OUR FAVORITE READ-ALOUDS FOR INTERMEDIATE GRADES

- *A Week in the Woods* (Clements, 2002)
- *Sahara Special* (Codell, 2003)
- *The Tale of Despereaux* (DiCamillo, 2003)
- *Rose Blanche* (Gallaz & Innocenti, 1985)
- *Fireboat: The Heroic Adventures of John J. Harvey* (Kalman, 2002)
- *A Year Down Yonder* (Peck, 2000)
- *Esperanza Rising* (Ryan, 2000)
- *The Invention of Hugo Cabret* (Selznick, 2007)
- *Zachary's Ball* (Tavares, 2000)
- *Charlotte's Web* (White, 1952)

The Role of Children's Literature in the Classroom: What the Research Says

Charlotte Huck (1982) is a master at explaining the value of children's literature, both for its use in the classroom and for its effect on children's lives. She believes it:

- ♦ develops compassion by educating the heart as well as the mind
- ♦ helps children entertain new ideas and develop insights they never had before
- ♦ stretches the imagination—creating new experiences, enriching old ones
- ♦ develops a sense of what is true and just and beautiful (p. 317)

Other researchers explain that being surrounded by a variety of books and supported by teachers and parents in their use of them is paramount in children's acquisition of literacy, as important as oral language is in learning to talk (Galda & Cullinan, 2003).

Richard Allington (2002) underscores the fact that the more children read, the better they become at reading. So the adage "Practice makes perfect" works with reading as well as other areas of our lives. Along those same lines, time spent in independent reading has a measured impact on gains in reading achievement (Anderson et al., 1985). When you give children an opportunity to reread books they love, to listen to books in the listening center on audiotape, and to read with parents at home, or when you invite upper-grade children to read with lower-grade readers, the time spent with good books is time well invested.

Additionally, by using children's literature, teachers and students can improve the application of effective reading skills and strategies as it affords more authentic opportunities to practice. When a new skill is introduced and taught within the context of a great book, then practiced within the context of other appealing books, that learning sticks (Fuhler, 2000; Leu & Kinzer, 2003; Pressley, 2000; Tunnell & Jacobs, 1989).

As a teacher, you know that children broaden their learning when they are exposed to excellent fiction and nonfiction. This is especially true when they have an opportunity to experience story in a variety of ways, through read-alouds, independent reading, response, and discussion (Galda, Ash, & Cullinan, 2000). Adding to the learning curve is the fact that books offer a safe, eye-opening look at life through vicarious experiences. There are situations that we would not want our children exposed to in reality because they may be unduly frightening, painful emotionally or physically, or even deadly. Viewed from a safe vantage point, however, such experiences can broaden a reader's perspectives about people, places, and events by reading about them and then discussing them with a knowledgeable adult.

While the list could go on, we'll conclude with the fact that wonderful books fuel the imagination. Whether children are reading for enjoyment or hearing a book read aloud, the imagination is getting a gentle nudge. So, fill the classroom library with a wide, rotating collection of books, at least seven titles per child, to enable readers to experience different genres (International Reading Association, 2000).

Linking Literature and Learning: An Overview

Filling many classroom hours with time to read and to hear books read well would be a gift for every reader. You can infuse your teaching with fine books, too, showing your students how to use reading strategies within the context of a good book and how to learn from writers themselves. The following sections—The Reading Connection and The Writing Connection—which are featured in each chapter, will give you a variety of ideas to try.

The Reading Connection

When the lesson of the day calls for teaching the use of a question mark, what better way to do so than by using the big book you are currently reading together? Perhaps you and the children are enjoying *Is Your Mama a Llama?* (Guarino, 1989). After explaining why one uses a question mark, model its use and find examples of sentences that ask a question as you reread the big book of the day. Then let students practice asking their own questions, adding the correct punctuation, and scouting its use in other favorite titles. At other times, you might be teaching rhyming words as you chorally read a poem, pointing out the qualities of a good sentence in a read-aloud title, or underscoring the role that adjectives play in making the writing more vivid in a novel you are reading as a class. You have superb tools at the tips of your fingers as you teach reading and writing skills, the elements of literature, and essential comprehension strategies (Galda et al., 2000).

Another vital argument for linking literature and learning is that well-crafted chapter books and novels, with their layers of meaning, encourage readers to think carefully about what they are reading. Once students move beyond the basic decoding stage, they are more than mere word callers. Now they can begin to "engage with thought-provoking literature in order to nurture the deep thinking that will be equated with literacy in the next millennium" (Martinez & McGee, 2000, p. 167). In short, reading children's literature and immersing students in authentic learning experiences with great titles across the genres are critical steps toward helping students develop a broader understanding of what it means to be literate.

It won't take long to match the skill or strategy to be taught to several examples from the classroom library. You are no doubt doing so already. Teaching reading skills and strategies within the context of exciting children's literature is strongly endorsed by researchers in the field (Farris et al., 2004; Martinez & McGee, 2000; Norton, 2003). To demonstrate this process, ideas and suggestions will be modeled in this section for a

Have You Read These?

A FEW OF OUR FAVORITE BOOKS THAT CELEBRATE READING

Picture Books

+ *Wolf!* (Bloom, 1999)

+ *More Than Anything Else* (Bradby, 1995)

+ *Book! Book! Book!* (Bruss, 2001)

+ *Miss Malarkey Leaves No Reader Behind* (Finchler & O'Malley, 2006)

+ *Miss Smith's Incredible Storybook* (Garland, 2003)

+ *Richard Wright and the Library Card* (Miller, 1997)

+ *A Library for Juana* (Mora, 2002)

+ *The Boy Who Was Raised by Librarians* (Morris, 2007)

+ *Reading Makes You Feel Good* (Parr, 2005)

+ *Wild About Books* (Sierra, 2004)

+ *The Librarian of Basra: A True Story From Iraq* (Winter, 2005)

Share books that celebrate reading!

Chapter Books

+ *The Book Without Words: A Fable of Medieval Magic* (Avi, 2005)

+ *Frindle* (Clements, 1996)

+ *Inkheart* (Funke, 2003)

+ *Inkspell* (Funke, 2005)

+ *The Library Card* (Spinelli, 1997a)

+ *King of the Castle* (Stinson, 2000)

+ *The Shadows of Ghadames* (Stolz, 2004)

primary- and an intermediate-grade lesson. In addition to presenting ways to teach several comprehension strategies, a number of the lessons will teach/review the elements of literature.

The Writing Connection

Lee Galda and Bernice Cullinan (2003), experts in the field of children's literature, underscore the importance of using real writers to teach your students the fundamentals of writing. They explain that, "Literature helps students become better writers. When students read a lot, they notice what writers do. They see that writers choose from a variety of language possibilities in their writing. When readers write, they borrow the structures, patterns, and words from what they read" (p. 50).

And why not do that? They are learning from accomplished writers whose lessons are vivid and memorable, adeptly supporting the skills you are teaching as a part of the curriculum. When you are teaching students to write in a particular genre, give them plenty of opportunities to read authors who do it well. Using picture books across the grade levels is an excellent way to introduce a writing strategy within the context of a short, manageable text. Follow up with several examples from novels or nonfiction, depending on the lesson at hand. Then, have an enticing display of books for the students to immerse themselves in, so that they absorb meaningful examples to try on their own.

Teaching the Traits of Good Writing

You will find sample lessons for primary and intermediate readers in each of the genre chapters. They reflect lessons that tie neatly into the traits of good writing (Culham, 2003, 2005; Spandel, 2004, 2005).

The Traits at a Glance	
Ideas	Ideas are the heart of the piece. A writer's ideas should be focused and include rich detail.
Organization	A writer can organize a piece in various ways depending on the purpose and audience. In a well-organized piece, ideas flow and make sense to the reader.
Word Choice	Accomplished writers choose the perfect words to express their ideas.
Sentence Fluency	Fluent writing is music to the ears. It includes varied sentence types and lengths.
Voice	When you read a piece with strong voice, it sounds like the writer is whispering in your ear. The writing speaks to the reader.
Conventions	Precise spelling, punctuation, and grammar are the hallmarks of a ready-to-publish piece.

Have You Read These?

A FEW OF OUR FAVORITE BOOKS THAT CELEBRATE WRITING

Picture Books

- *The Jolly Postman, or Other People's Letters* (Ahlberg & Ahlberg, 1986)
- *Arthur Writes a Story* (Brown, 1996)
- *Patches Lost and Found* (Kroll, 2001)
- *Author: A True Story* (Lester, 1997)
- *A Sign* (Lyon, 1998)
- *The Journey of Oliver K. Woodman* (Pattison, 2003)
- *Coyote School News* (Sandin, 2003)
- *Stringbean's Trip to the Shining Sea* (Williams, 1988)
- *You Have to Write* (Wong, 2002)

Chapter Books

- *The Burning Questions of Bingo Brown* (Byars, 1988)
- *Clarice Bean Spells Trouble* (Child, 2005)
- *Dear Mr. Henshaw* (Cleary, 1983)
- *The School Story* (Clements, 2001)
- *Love That Dog: A Novel* (Creech, 2001)
- *Fur-Ever Yours, Booker Jones* (Duffey, 2001)
- *By Lizzie* (Eccles, 2001)
- *Harriet the Spy* (Fitzhugh, 2001)
- *Jazmine's Notebook* (Grimes, 1998)
- *The Private Notebooks of Katie Roberts, Age 11* (Hest, 1995)

Share books that celebrate writing!

In concluding this chapter on the values of integrating children's literature into your classroom, we would like to offer helpful Internet support. An important piece of each genre chapter will be Four Fine Web Sites. Carefully selected sites can prove to be invaluable to you and your students as you read, teach, learn, or simply savor wonderful books together. These critically reviewed, stable sites are meant to assist you in your search for new ideas to use as you connect books and children. There will also be a selection of safe sites in each chapter for your students to investigate as they broaden their knowledge and their understanding of technology.

Four Fine Web Sites

Read, Write, Think
www.readwritethink.org
A collaborative project between the International Reading Association, the National Council of Teachers of English, and the MarcoPolo Education Foundation, this site offers extensive lessons that use children's literature to teach a skill or strategy.

The Children's Literature Web Guide
www.acs.ucalgary.ca/~dkbrown/index.html
This site categorizes a number of Internet resources tied to books for children and young adults.

The Internet Public Library
www.ipl.org
The first public library of and for the Internet community, it contains both "Kidspace" and "Teenspace."

Celebrating Cultural Diversity Through Children's Literature
www.multiculturalchildrenslit.com
Find links to annotated bibliographies of children's (K–6) multicultural books. Books are categorized by genre and linked to other resources for elementary teachers.

Summary

After reviewing the ingredients necessary in a good book and sampling relevant outstanding titles, you are now well prepared to select only the best for your students and your lessons. As you continue through this book we are confident that you will find an invaluable collection of quality children's literature and practical teaching ideas. Use it to review a genre, tackle teaching a strategy in a new way, and meet book after wonderful book along the way. Enjoy the journey through the realm of children's literature as much as we enjoyed suggesting possible routes for you to travel.

Chapter 2

Picture Books

THE PERFECT TEACHING PARTNERS

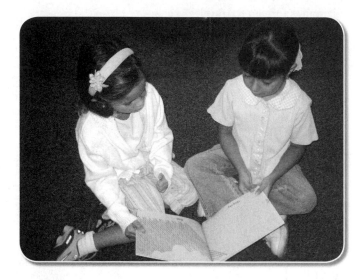

PART 1

BUILDING BACKGROUND FOR
TEACHING WITH PICTURE BOOKS

Picture Book Magic

The end of a hectic teaching week is in sight. Glancing up from the class, you see the clock tick, tick, ticking instructional minutes away. Sometimes you feel as though you are on a treadmill, always racing, trying to complete all that you've planned. Even after your students rush out of the room at the end of the day, "the teacher bag" awaits. It is brimming with papers to check, report cards to complete, and all the other tasks you are sure you will have time to finish tonight. Refocusing your thoughts on the schedule ahead, you breathe a sigh of relief. Ahhhhh! It's time for reading workshop, a time to gather learners at your toes and read. The perfect book awaits on the easel, the one you've been eager to share all week. The kids gather around, and you begin reading. It's like magic. There is a stillness in the room. The anticipation of another great story. A story told with a perfect blend of vivid illustrations and engaging words: a picture book.

What Are Picture Books?

Picture books appeal to readers of all ages. But what is it that sets them apart from other books children read? First, note that the term *picture book* refers to the format rather than the content of the books (Hillman, 1999). That means that these books are typically 32 to 48 pages in length. They appear in a variety of shapes and sizes. The growing collection of picture books covers almost any topic, with a range of complexity from a simple board book to more involved tales designed for older readers. You can locate the perfect picture book for a reader who is just beginning to figure out how words work or a reluctant intermediate student who is interested in the battles of the Civil War. One of the most gratifying classroom experiences is sharing a favorite picture book with your class regardless of their ages. Students will remember these precious moments for years to come.

What makes picture books so unique? An engaging picture book draws the reader into the story as both words and pictures contribute to the meaning. "In a true picture book, the story would be diminished, and in some cases confused without the illustrations..." (Lynch-Brown & Tomlinson, 2005, p. 76). Kiefer (1995) explains that there is an interdependence between the pictures and text that allows a reader to come away with an experience that is more than the sum of the parts. Clearly, the illustrations in a picture book are as important or more important than the text. These books add pizzazz to literacy lessons, illuminate topics of interest, provide models of effective writing techniques, and serve as a springboard for creative writing. Without a doubt, picture books should have a prominent place in your curriculum and classroom.

A Peek at Picture Book Art

After browsing through a collection of excellent picture books, you will quickly recognize that picture books are an art form. From classics to contemporary, there is something that appeals to every child. Our youngest readers are drawn to the bold, colorful illustrations and die-cut pages in Lois Ehlert's (1989) Caldecott Honor book *Color Zoo*. Animal lovers pore over the detailed illustrations created by Steven Kellogg to find his beloved dog Pinkerton. Fantasy fanatics connect with the stunning illustrations of the Budwing brothers' outrageous adventures in Chris Van Allsburg's *Jumanji* (1981) and

A fine example of an illustrator's use of perspective.

the sequel *Zathura* (2002). Older readers who enjoy realism walk in the woods with Grandad in Douglas Wood's (1999) *Grandad's Prayers of the Earth* or bike to Grandma's in *Saturdays and Teacakes* (Laminack, 2004). With so many talented picture book illustrators from which to choose, we are able to fill our classroom libraries with books that will invite all readers to sit down, browse, and enjoy.

As you read and enjoy picture books with your students, teach them about the illustrations. Point out that readers usually take in the illustration all at once, but they should go back to investigate the little details that make up the whole picture. Depending on the artwork, it could take longer to "read" the picture than it does to read the accompanying text (Lukens, 2007). When teaching readers to understand the different ways illustrators approach their work, highlight the artistic elements of line, color, space, perspective, shape, and texture. Provide captivating examples of each element to study. A practical application of their learning is an exploration of artistic elements, a meaningful topic for a writing workshop mini-lesson. You may choose to do this mini-lesson as your students prepare to illustrate their first published piece of writing. Showing students samples of illustrators who use these elements effectively will help your young author/illustrators develop an understanding of how picture book art is created.

The art media of picture books is constantly expanding as technological advances provide unlimited possibilities to illustrators. From the classic watercolor illustrations of Beatrix Potter to the computer-generated art of today as found in *The Mystery of Eatum Hall* (Kelly & Tincknell, 2004), contemporary illustrators have a wide range of options available when choosing the perfect art media to complement and extend a story. Helping students become familiar with picture book media is an invitation to experiment in their illustrations. A humorous book that will introduce them to the art of 14 different illustrators is *Why Did the Chicken Cross the Road?* (Arnold et al., 2006). Students can also get to know how their favorite author/illustrators create images if you share a video of an illustrator at work. For young students, consider *Eric Carle, Picture Writer* (Searchlight Films, 1993), in which Eric invites viewers into his studio to show how he creates his signature collage illustrations. Older students interested in painting can learn from viewing *Get to Know Gerald McDermott* (Soundworks Production, 1996), as McDermott demonstrates his unique painting technique. There are also many picture books that give

The Elements of Picture Book Art

Artistic Elements	Examples to Share
Line: The way an illustrator closes and opens space.	*Harold and the Purple Crayon* (Johnson, 1955) *Yo! Yes?* (Raschka, 1993) (line defines characters and propels plot)
Color: Illustrators choose their color palette to match the theme of the book. Many use color to show a change in mood.	*In My World* (Ehlert, 2002) (bold colors) *Millions of Cats* (Gag, 1956) (black and white) *A Tree Is Nice* (Udry, 1956) (alternating color and black-and-white)
Space: Illustrators use space creatively to show an emotion. Others choose to use borders to enrich their illustrations.	*Honey...Honey...Lion!* (Brett, 2005) (side panels on each page) *Little Red Riding Hood* (retold by Hyman, 1983) (borders) *Miss Rumphius* (Cooney, 1982)
Perspective: Illustrators choose to shape their world from a variety of points of view.	*The Napping House* (Wood, 1984) (point of view moves upward and back down) *Round Trip* (Jonas, 1983) (book is read forward, then backward and upside down) *Two Bad Ants* (Van Allsburg, 1988) (perspective shifts)
Shape: A line that encloses space.	*Arrow to the Sun* (McDermott, 1974) (geometric shapes) *In a Small, Small Pond* (Fleming, 1993) (shapes show movement) *My Name Is Celia: The Life of Celia Cruz* (Brown, 2004) (shapes give a musical feel to book)
Texture: The sensory qualities of illustrations.	*If You Decide to Go to the Moon* (McNulty, 2005) (textured pages) *Make Way for Ducklings* (McCloskey, 1941) (sepia illustrations) *The Wave of the Sea-Wolf* (Wisniewski, 1994) (cut paper)

(Huck et al., 2004; Gangi, 2004; Kiefer, 1995)

readers a glimpse into the world of an illustrator. Eileen Christelow's (1999) *What Do Illustrators Do?* follows two different artists illustrating the same story. Along with discussing layout, scale, and point of view, readers see the same illustration rendered in different media. David McPhail takes a different approach and has a bear explain how he became an artist in *Drawing Lessons From a Bear* (2000). In *The Shape Game* (2003), Anthony Browne writes about how a trip to an art museum changed the course of his life. In this book, readers also learn a drawing game. As you select picture books for literacy lessons throughout the year, try to choose books that are examples of different media.

Share this example of computer-generated art.

Try This! Teaching Students About Picture Book Art: The "Tiger" Medal

A clever way to engage students in an exploration of picture book art is to invite them to be the judges. Each year, first graders at Gwendolyn Brooks Elementary School learn about the history of the Caldecott Medal. They have an opportunity to look through the past winners of this award and learn about the different artistic media used to create picture books. Once they are budding experts, the teachers and librarian gather a collection of five to ten hot-off-the-press picture books, and over a two-week period teachers share and critique these books with their students. Finally, the students vote to award The Tiger Medal (named for school's mascot) to the best picture book. The librarian announces and rereads the winning tale at an end-of-year Reading Celebration. Each Tiger award–winning book gets its own medal to be proudly displayed for years to come. This clever award was originally created by Spring Brook School LMC director, Jenny Giambalvo.

A Sampling of Picture Book Art Media

Media	Examples to Share
Paper Craft: Collage, Paper Making, Cut Paper	*The Snowy Day* (Keats, 1962) *The Very Hungry Caterpillar* (Carle, 1979) *What Do You Do With a Tail Like This?* (Jenkins & Page, 2003)
Pencil/Colored Pencil	*Amelia and Eleanor Go For a Ride* (Ryan, 1999) *Jumanji* (Van Allsburg, 1981) *The Relatives Came* (Rylant, 1985)
Computer-Generated Art	*Henny-Penny* (retold by Wattenburg, 2000) *The Red Racer* (Wood, 1996) *Shibumi and the Kitemaker* (Mayer, 1999)
Acrylic Paint	*Joe Louis: America's Fighter* (Adler, 2005) *Miss Rumphius* (Cooney, 1982) *Saladin* (Stanley, 2002)
Oil Paint	*King Bidgood's in the Bathtub* (Wood, 1985) *Time Flies* (Rohmann, 1994) *Up the Learning Tree* (Vaughan, 2003)
Photography	*Knuffle Bunny: A Cautionary Tale* (Willems, 2004) *The Prairie Builders* (Collard, 2005) *Shapes, Shapes, Shapes* (Hoban, 1986)
Story Quilt/Stitchery	*Memories of Survival* (Krinitz & Steinhardt, 2005) *Tar Beach* (Ringgold, 1991) *The Whispering Cloth* (Shea, 1995)
Watercolor	*Click, Clack, Moo: Cows That Type* (Cronin, 2000) *Grandfather's Journey* (Say, 1993) *The Three Pigs* (Wiesner, 2001)
Woodcut	*Drummer Hoff* (Emberley, 1967) *Snowflake Bentley* (Martin, 1998) *Song of the Water Boatman* (Sidman, 2005)

Picture Books: Types, Titles, and Teaching Ideas

Since the focus of this book is on using children's literature to enhance literacy instruction in elementary school, we chose to categorize picture books according to how they are commonly referred to in the classroom. We recognize that many of the books discussed in one category could easily appear in another category. For each of the categories, we've included suggestions of books and related teaching ideas. When appropriate, we've also provided summaries of book so you can quickly see if they meet your needs. Join us now as we take you on a picture book parade through the following categories: the classics, toy books, concept books—including alphabet books and counting books, wordless/nearly wordless books, predictable books, picture storybooks, easy-to-read books, transitional books, and picture books for older readers.

The Classics

Beatrix Potter's delicate watercolor picture books have delighted young readers for more than 100 years. Her books are one example of what many consider to be classic picture books (Gangi, 2004). Many classic picture books continue to appeal to young readers. In Maria Walther's first-grade classroom, she invites parents to sneak in for a surprise visit as "The Mystery Reader" and read aloud a family favorite. Recently a parent chose *The Little House* (Burton, 1942). As she read, the children were fascinated with both the story and the illustrations. With all the new books available, we sometimes forget to share time-tested favorites with our students.

A parent volunteer shares the classic picture book *The Little House.*

Toy Books

Toy books used in an elementary classroom include pop-up books and other mechanical books. The *ooohs* and *ahhhhs* heard while reading pop-up books make them a must-have for every read-aloud collection. *Goodnight Moon Room: A Pop-Up Book* (1985) brings to life Margaret Wise Brown's classic tale *Goodnight Moon* (1947). Students interested in exploring pop-up book art can access Robert Sabuda's Web site (www.robertsabuda.com), which will lead the curious illustrator to links for making their own pop-up books. Sabuda's books are amazing examples of pop-up artistry. *America the Beautiful* (2004) is a patriotic addition to the study of the United States, and reading *Winter's Tale* (2005) will brighten a gray winter

Classic vs. Contemporary Picture Books

To highlight classic children's books throughout the year, read aloud a classic children's book along with a contemporary picture book on a similar topic. After reading both titles, compare and contrast the two books, focusing on the artistic elements and art media of the illustrations. Display the two books along with your observations in the reading center for continued enjoyment. We've listed a few classic and contemporary book pairings to get you started.

Classic and Contemporary Picture Book Pairings	
The Little Engine That Could (Bragg, 1930; originally published as *The Pony Engine*)	*The Caboose Who Got Loose* (Peet, 1971)
The Noisy Book (Brown, 1939)	*The Listening Walk* (Showers, 1991)
Make Way for Ducklings (McCloskey, 1941)	*Have You Seen My Duckling?* (Tafuri, 1984)
The Little House (Burton, 1942)	*The Napping House* (Wood, 1984)
The Carrot Seed (Krauss, 1945)	*The Tiny Seed* (Carle, 1987)
Millions of Cats (Gag, 1956)	*So Many Cats* (de Regniers, 1985)

day. Looking for a creepy Halloween tale? Share *Haunted House* (2005) by Jan Pienkowski and you will surely hear, "Read it again!"

When it comes to mechanical books, Eric Carle has perfected the art of clever techniques to amaze children. His innovative mechanical elements include, among others, the die-cut pages in *The Very Hungry Caterpillar* (1979), the chirping cricket in *The Very Quiet Cricket* (1990), and the acetate pages in *Mister Seahorse* (2004). He has mastered the art of toy bookmaking for children while creating a collection of books that can be used to enhance many science units. Mechanical books and toy books are appealing tools for sharing stories and information with students.

Concept Books

Concept books convey knowledge and answer curious youngsters' questions about the world. They are essential resources for primary teachers to help illuminate the basic concepts explored in the curriculum. These books are also useful in helping children who are learning a new language identify, label, and understand their environment. This type of book explores or explains an idea or concept, often providing specific examples to clarify the understanding of the concept. While some books are told in story format, most do not follow a story line. Instead, authors may use repeated elements in text and pictures to help the book flow together.

Eric Carle has mastered the art of toy bookmaking.

Concept Picture Books That Explore Color	
Book	**Quick Summary**
Freight Train (Crews, 1978)	Simple text and illustrations depict train cars of various colors.
Little Blue and Little Yellow (Lionni, 1959)	A little blue spot and a little yellow spot are friends. When they hug, they become green.
Mouse Paint (Walsh, 1991)	Three white mice discover what happens when they mix red, yellow, and blue paint.
Planting a Rainbow (Ehlert, 1988)	A child relates in ten simple sentences the yearly cycle of planning, planting, and picking flowers in a garden.
White Is for Blueberry (Shannon, 2005)	Readers look at nature from different perspectives and observe colors in new ways, as shown in this example: "Pink is for crow . . . when it has just hatched from its egg."

Alphabet Books

Alphabet books are a versatile teaching material. First, they are handy tools to help young students develop the alphabetic principle. When looking for alphabet books for this purpose, ask these questions:

- Are the pages uncluttered, with only a few words?
- Are both capital and small letters displayed?
- Is the font simple and easy to read?
- Are the pictures easily recognizable to students?

A pair of books that meet these criteria are *Alligator Alphabet* (Blackstone, 2005) and *ABC: A Child's First Alphabet Book* (Jay, 2003). *Alligator Alphabet* has simple text and colorful illustrations that invite the youngest readers to interact with this book. *ABC: A Child's First Alphabet Book* is an example of a conventional alphabet book in which each page features a scene highlighting one object, corresponding upper- and lowercase letters, and a simple declarative sentence.

While many view alphabet books as a tool for strengthening young readers' knowledge of the alphabet, these books are also valuable in other ways. For example, they can provide students with an introduction or overview of a topic, serve as a stimulus for further research, or be a way to enhance oral or written language development (Chaney, 1993). Begin a study of the solar system with the enticing *Stargazer's Alphabet: Night-Sky Wonders from A to Z* (Farrell, 2007). If you are starting a geography unit, grab *Geography From A to Z: A Picture Glossary* (Knowlton, 1988) to introduce students to 63 geographical terms. To launch a study of the United States, choose Martin Jarrie's (2005) *ABC USA*, an alphabetical tour of the country's geography, culture, and history complemented by folk art illustrations. Students interested in music meet famous musicians through poetic

This alphabet book demonstrates that writers share ideas in many different ways.

introductions in *Jazz A B Z* (Marsalis, 2005). The versatility of alphabet books makes them a pleasing addition to the curriculum.

Alphabet books are also created for children who already recognize letters. When searching for an alphabet book to enhance your literacy lessons, strive to foster students' love of language and sharpen their powers of deduction and observation. Choose books created by authors and illustrators who have "come up with new ways to surprise, engage, and instruct with new twists that expand the original concepts" (Engelfried, 2001, p. 32). If you are teaching the elements of a mystery, add Doug Cushman's (1996) *The ABC Mystery* about stolen Art, a suspicious Butler, and a footprint Clue. For secret agent fans, read *Agent A to Agent Z* (Rash, 2004), an engaging spy adventure. During writing workshop, reach for *Action Alphabet* (Rotner, 1996) to hear a collection of vivid verbs to improve student writing.

Reading and Writing Mini-Lessons Based on Alphabet Books	
Alphabet Book	**Mini-Lesson Idea**
Achoo! Bang! Crash! (MacDonald, 2003)	**Word Choice:** Adding onomatopoeia can give writing added zing. Discuss the uses of onomatopoeic words in writing. Collect these words on a chart or in writers' notebooks.
Carmine: A Little More Red (Sweet, 2005)	**Vocabulary:** After enjoying this innovative version of the Little Red Riding Hood tale, discuss some of the interesting vocabulary words.
SuperHero ABC (McLeod, 2006)	**Organization:** Introduce writers to speech bubbles and the comic book format while reading this hilarious book.
The Turn-Around, Upside-Down Alphabet Book (Ernst, 2004)	**Visualization:** Ernst offers readers many images related to each letter. Use this book to introduce the concept of visualization.
Winter: An Alphabet Acrostic (Schnur, 2002)	**Acrostic Poems:** Share this book with your writers to model simple and graceful acrostic poems. Also available: *Autumn* (1997), *Spring* (1999), and *Summer* (2001).
Written Anything Good Lately? (Allen & Lindaman, 2006)	**Organization:** This book is perfect for sharing all the different options writers have to share their ideas.

Counting Books

Another type of concept book is the counting book. Just as some alphabet books help students strengthen their alphabetic knowledge, counting books are written to help children develop their counting skills. Counting books that are designed for aiding young students in learning to count should have numbers that are clear and easy-to-identify with corresponding objects. It is also helpful if there is no background clutter. This type of counting book helps children develop one-to-one correspondence and to count sequentially from 1 to 10 (Norton, 2003).

For older children, there are counting books that help develop number concepts like addition and subtraction, or invite them to search for groups of objects. One popular author of many books that explore mathematical concepts is Stuart Murphy. His books cover a range of mathematical topics. A book to help you teach the concept of dividing is *Divide and Ride* (1997b), in which children divide themselves into groups to go on carnival rides. In *Elevator Magic* (1997a), Murphy shares a tale of subtraction. Older readers can make the math connection through Greg Tang's inventive series. Two recent titles include *Math Potatoes* (2005) and *Math-terpieces* (2003), both aimed at teaching grouping strategies and problem-solving skills.

Two titles from Greg Tang's inventive series.

10 Books You Can Count On!	
Book	**Quick Summary**
100th Day Worries (Cuyler, 2000)	Jessica is worried she won't find a collection for the 100th day of school. Fortunately, her family pitches in to give her ten mini-collections of ten items. Perfect for counting by 10s to 100.
Click,Clack, Splish, Splash: A Counting Adventure (Cronin, 2006)	A basic introduction to numeric concepts starring the farm friends from *Click, Clack, Moo: Cows That Type* (2000).
Fiesta (Guy, 1996)	Bilingual text provides counting in both English and Spanish.
The First Day of Winter (Fleming, 2005)	Fleming uses "The Twelve Days of Christmas" as her inspiration for this clever counting book about building a snowman.
My Little Sister Ate One Hare (Grossman, 1996)	As the sister eats slimy creatures and ants' underpants, children count along in this hilarious cumulative tale.
Ten Black Dots (Crews, 1986)	After reading this book, give children sticky dots and have them create their own image with a select number of dots.
Ten Little Fish (Wood, 2004)	Wood uses digitally created art to give this book a 3-D appearance. Readers count down from 10 to 1.
10 Little Rubber Ducks (Carle, 2005)	This book is based on a factual incident in which ten rubber ducks fell overboard and were swept off in ten different directions. Ordinal numbers are highlighted in bold type.
Ten, Nine, Eight (Bang, 1983)	Children can practice counting backward in a rhythmic counting lullaby.
The Water Hole (Base, 2001)	Designed for upper grades, this book offers its readers a counting book, an introduction to ten different animals from ten different countries, and a fascinating hidden picture challenge.

Wordless/Nearly Wordless Books

In wordless or nearly wordless picture books, the illustrations tell the story. *Changes, Changes* (Hutchins, 1971) is a wordless book that has delighted readers for decades. It tells the story of two wooden dolls rearranging building blocks to create new objects. Although many wordless books are for the youngest readers, there is a growing collection designed for older readers. Wordless books stimulate creative thinking, enhance visual literacy, and allow children with different backgrounds and reading abilities to share the same book (Norton, 2003). Wordless books are thought-provoking catalysts for writing. For example, Chris Van Allsburg's intriguing illustrations in *The Mysteries of Harris Burdick* (1984) present a series of loosely related drawings, accompanied by titles and

Stretch the imagination of young writers with this wordless story.

captions that invite the reader to create his or her own story. The 14 original drawings are also available in a large portfolio edition of individual posters ready to hang on a bulletin board with students' original stories. *The Red Book* (Lehman, 2004) recounts a story about adventure and friendship, leaving the ending open to interpretation and creative writing. You might also try *Flotsam* (Wiesner, 2006), a story of a curious young beachcomber who finds an ancient underwater camera filled with unusual photos, which will stretch the imagination of young writers.

Choose wordless picture books to support the writing process for all students. These books are especially supportive for struggling writers, too. For example, a first grader with autism who had difficulty creating his own stories used wordless picture books to provide a structured way to write. He wrote stories based on Mercer Mayer's *A Boy, a Dog and a Frog* (1967) and *Good Dog, Carl* (Day, 1985), successfully joining the rest of his classmates as a writer.

As you select wordless books to use in your classroom, Lukens (2007) reminds us that the best wordless books "require focus and unity, created by pictures and the format of presentation. Complexity and detail may accompany continuity, consistency, and a unique personal vision" (p. 69).

10 Wordless or Nearly Wordless Picture Books

Book	Quick Summary
Deep in the Forest (Turkle, 1976)	This is a wordless version of the Goldilocks tale.
The Grey Lady and the Strawberry Snatcher (Bang, 1980)	A strawberry snatcher follows the grey lady through the shops and woods.
The Last Laugh (Aruego, 2006)	A clever duck outwits a bullying snake.
Museum Trip (Lehman, 2006)	A boy on a field trip imagines himself inside the museum exhibits.
Peep! (Luthardt, 2003)	A boy finds an egg that hatches into a duckling.
Sector 7 (Wiesner, 1999)	On a class trip to the Empire State Building, a boy is spirited off to Sector 7 and the Cloud Dispatch Center.
Sidewalk Circus (Fleischman, 2004)	As a young girl watches, the activities across the street from her bus stop become a circus.
Snow Day (Peddle, 2000)	This is the story of a snowman's one glorious day. Pair this with Raymond Briggs' classic, *The Snowman (1978).*
Tuesday (Wiesner, 1991)	Frogs flying on lily pads explore the neighborhood.
Zoom (Banyai, 1995)	This book shows a series of scenes, each one from farther away.

Picture Storybooks

Marching through our picture book parade, we've seen many books that rely heavily on the illustrations to get their message across. Much of the content in concept books and, of course, wordless books is delivered through illustrations. Picture storybooks, the most common type of picture book, are a bit different. The hallmark of this type is that the text and narrative complement each other so that readers cannot figure out the whole story by merely looking at the illustrations or only reading the words. If the balance between text and illustrations is handled skillfully, the illustrations will support the text but not in a completely predictable manner. Readers are more actively engaged if they have to infer part of the meaning of the story from looking at the illustrations (Temple, Martinez, Yokota, & Naylor, 2002).

When you look at your collection of picture books, you should find that there are more picture storybooks than any other kind of picture book. Therefore, you will find a wealth of picture storybook suggestions throughout this text. Take the time to savor them with your students.

What Makes a Perfect Picture Storybook?

Look for the following elements:

- Text contains a well-developed story line.
- Plots are simple, clearly developed, and brief.
- Story involves characters to whom children can relate.
- Setting unfolds through illustrations.
- Themes relate to children's needs and understandings.
- Perfectly selected words create vivid images. Often the style includes rhyme, rhythm, or repetition.
- The text is original and encourages the use of imagination.
- Humor often occurs in both text and pictures.
- Surprising and unexpected events and illustrations often occur.

(Norton, 2003)

Easy-to-Read Books

For decades, youngsters have grown up reading Dr. Seuss' *The Cat in the Hat* (1957). Thankfully, Seuss was up to the challenge when a publisher asked him to write a picture book with fewer than 300 words. In the process, the easy-to-read picture book was born. Easy-to-read picture books are different from picture storybooks described earlier, although they do include a generous amount of illustration to support the beginning reader (Temple et al., 2002). The controlled vocabulary of easy readers makes them a challenge to write without sounding like the basal readers of the past. Many authors have risen to this challenge, creating series of books that hook beginning readers who love to read "chapter books." Cynthia Rylant, an award-winning writer, began her series about Henry and his dedicated, drooling dog, Mudge, with *Henry and Mudge: The First Book of Their Adventures* (1987) and in 2007 wrote *Henry and Mudge and the Big Sleepover: The Twenty-Eighth Book of Their Adventures*. Rylant's simple yet poetic text paired with Sucie Stevenson's illustrations support and amuse readers in book after book. Rylant has continued this tradition of quality easy-to-read books with her other two series about Mr. Putter and Tabby and Poppleton. All three provide readers with brief text, plenty of repetitive phrases, and lots of visual clues. Rylant is joined by other authors, including Arnold Lobel, Edward and James Marshall, and Dav Pilkey, whose books nudge readers along the path to independence.

Characteristics of Easy-to-Read Picture Books

- Limited amount of text on each page
- Large print
- Wide line spacing
- Short sentences
- Controlled language
- Short and familiar words (Lynch-Brown & Tomlinson, 2005)

Easy-to-read books continue to delight readers.

Popular Easy-to-Read Series		
Title of Book or Name of Series	Author	Fountas & Pinnell Guided Reading Level
Amanda and Oliver Pig	Jean Van Leeuwen	L
Arthur books	Lillian Hoban	K
Dragon books	Dav Pilkey	I
Fox books	Edward and James Marshall	J
Frog and Toad	Arnold Lobel	K
Henry and Mudge	Cynthia Rylant	J
Mr. Putter and Tabby	Cynthia Rylant	J
Poppleton	Cynthia Rylant	J

Transitional Books

As children grow as readers, it is our job to provide books that are a perfect fit. For some readers, transitional books provide the support needed to make the jump from easy readers to full-length juvenile fiction and nonfiction. A transitional book is characterized by:

Kate DiCamillo's series of transitional books.

♦ An uncomplicated writing style and vocabulary

♦ Slightly enlarged print and easy-to-read typefaces

♦ A length between about 50 to 100 pages (Lynch-Brown & Tomlinson, 2005)

The Center for Children's Books and the Graduate School of Library and Information Science at the University of Illinois at Urbana-Champaign established the Gryphon Award in 2004 as a way to focus attention on transitional reading. The Gryphon Award winners include *Stinky Stern Forever* (Edwards, 2005), the fourth book in a series that focuses on the serious topic of the death of a classmate. In this book, Pa Lia Vang is not sure how to remember the second-grade bully, Stinky Stern, after he is hit by a van on his way home from school. Edwards handles the topic skillfully and with sensitivity. In *Little Rat Rides* by Monika Bang-Campbell (2004), Little Rat must overcome her fear of getting on a huge horse. She knows she must get back on Pee Wee after falling off. This challenge helps to boost her confidence as she prepares for the horse show. Guiding children toward transitional books will help support readers as they make this leap from easy readers to full-length juvenile fiction and nonfiction.

Transitional Book Series

- Best Enemies series
  by Kathleen Leverich

- Encyclopedia Brown series
  by Donald J. Sobol

- The Magic Tree House series
  by Mary Pope Osborne

- Mercy Watson series
  by Kate DiCamillo

- Nate the Great series
  by Marjorie Weinman Sharmat

Picture Books for Older Readers

A number of the picture books available today contain longer and more complex text than is typical for books written for younger readers. In addition, the topics covered are more appropriate for the interests and conceptual abilities of upper-grade students. A selection of these convey strong content and visually impacting messages that can be somewhat disturbing (Bishop & Hickman, 1992). These thought-provoking titles are definitely not

Use Picture Books for Older Readers to:

- introduce a topic

- provide background for upcoming study

- offer quality reading materials for struggling readers

- provide light and enjoyable reading

- offer an opportunity to study a number of different artistic styles

- provide examples of the craft of writing and use of the literary elements (Bishop & Hickman, 1992; Kiefer, 1995) appropriate for children in the primary grades. However, for a number of reasons, they are perfect for older readers.

One of the values of these books for readers in the intermediate grades is tied to their visual aspect. The artwork in picture books can create gripping stories about weighty topics like war, homelessness, the struggle for human rights, and the loss of family (Huck et al., 2004; Kiefer, 1995). For example, students who are interested in slavery can read *The People Could Fly: The Picture Book* (Hamilton, 2004). This folktale illuminates the plight of African slaves working in the cotton fields of an abusive master. Those interested in civil rights might select *The School Is Not White! A True Story of the Civil Rights Movement* (Rappaport, 2005), about experiencing the fears tied to desegregation. Others who are considering the different faces of war might choose *Boxes for Katje* (Fleming, 2003) or *The Scarlet Stockings Spy* (Noble, 2004).

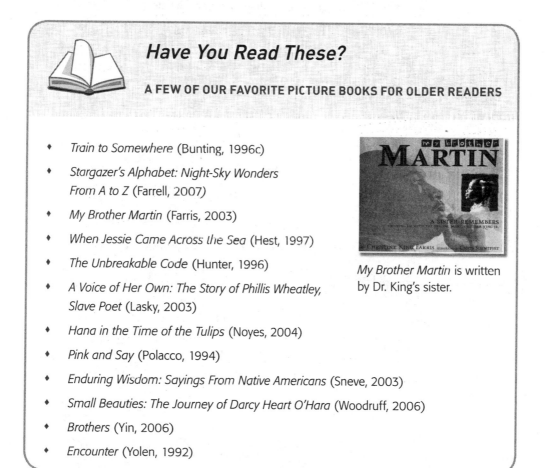

Have You Read These?

A FEW OF OUR FAVORITE PICTURE BOOKS FOR OLDER READERS

- *Train to Somewhere* (Bunting, 1996c)
- *Stargazer's Alphabet: Night-Sky Wonders From A to Z* (Farrell, 2007)
- *My Brother Martin* (Farris, 2003)
- *When Jessie Came Across the Sea* (Hest, 1997)
- *The Unbreakable Code* (Hunter, 1996)
- *A Voice of Her Own: The Story of Phillis Wheatley, Slave Poet* (Lasky, 2003)
- *Hana in the Time of the Tulips* (Noyes, 2004)
- *Pink and Say* (Polacco, 1994)
- *Enduring Wisdom: Sayings From Native Americans* (Sneve, 2003)
- *Small Beauties: The Journey of Darcy Heart O'Hara* (Woodruff, 2006)
- *Brothers* (Yin, 2006)
- *Encounter* (Yolen, 1992)

My Brother Martin is written by Dr. King's sister.

Throughout this book, we have made careful and conscious choices about the picture books we recommend. We have scoured shelves of bookstores, talked to knowledgeable booksellers, listened to authors discuss their works, read reviews, and, most important, talked to teachers and read books to eager listeners. We have tried to include books, both classic and new, that are appealing to children and that have made a contribution to the growing body of children's literature. As you continue to select picture books to share with your students, we offer the guidelines (see box below) that helped us make our decisions.

Searching for a High-Quality Picture Book?

Here's what the experts tell us to look for as we peruse the shelves:

- original ideas presented in an original format

- accurate illustrations that correspond with the content of the story

- illustrations that complement the setting, plot, and mood of the story

- text and illustrations that avoid stereotypes, including race and gender

- language and writing style that are rich and varied but not so complicated a young child couldn't comprehend

- an appealing plot

- a worthwhile theme

(Huck et al., 2004; Norton, 2003; Lynch-Brown & Tomlinson, 2005)

Why Are Picture Books Important for My Students?

As you have discovered throughout this chapter, picture books are the perfect fare for reading aloud, whether you are using the book to teach a skill or concept or simply reading it for pleasure. Daily read-aloud is an essential component of effective literacy instruction. In fact, "Teacher read-aloud has been shown to be one of the major motivators for children to read" (Cunningham, 2005, p. 88). A perfectly selected picture book plays an important role in effective literacy instruction.

Why Reach for a Picture Book?
Research says:

1. To inspire children's visual, mental, and verbal imaginations (Huck et al., 2004)

2. To stimulate imagination for creative writing (Norton, 2003)

3. To give children experience with the wider world (Hillman, 1999)

4. To introduce concepts for cognitive and language development

5. To provide an easily accessible and understandable way to study the elements of literature (Jenks, 1992)

6. To explore and learn about the ways in which illustrations convey meaning (Bishop & Hickman, 1992)

7. To provide personal pleasure and aesthetic satisfaction (Bishop & Hickman, 1992)

8. To actively engage readers in dialogue that includes questioning, hypothesizing, speculating, inferring, and interpreting both pictures and text (Bainbridge & Pantaleo, 2001)

9. To build background and strengthen visualization skills in struggling readers (Hibbing & Rankin-Erickson, 2003)

Endings and Beginnings

As the sounds of the picture book parade fade away, we hope you will march along to your school library or favorite bookstore to gather some of the titles we've highlighted in this chapter. Whether you teach primary or intermediate grades, picture books offer abundant opportunities for reading aloud, illustrating teaching points, supporting thoughtful discussion, and providing quiet enjoyment. Continue with us as we put picture books to work with a few tried-and-true mini-lessons for reading and writing.

The Reading Connection

Primary Lesson Plan: Understanding the Concept of Making Connections

Purpose:

In this reading workshop mini-lesson we want our young readers to begin to understand the concept of making connections.

Materials/Preparation:

- Objects that represent your students' interests, such as a baseball, movie ticket stub, seashell, sailboat, postcard, stuffed animal, etc.

- *Anna's Table* (Bunting, 2003)

- Prewrite on large chart paper the following sentence frame: "When I saw the _____ it made me think about _____. By making this connection I let you know that _____ is important to me."

Mini-Lesson:

1. Read *Anna's Table* to your class. This book tells about a young girl who collects nature objects that remind her of special events.

2. Model and think aloud as you orally fill in the blanks on the chart using an object. For example: When I saw the movie ticket stub, it made me think about going to the movies with my daughter, Katie. By making this connection I let you know that spending time with Katie is important to me.

3. Give students time to select an object and think of how they would fill in the blanks on the chart. Students take turns sharing their selected object and completing the sentence frame on the chart orally.

4. Discuss how good readers make connections to the book from their own experiences while they are reading to help them better understand the story. These connections from their experiences are called text-to-self connections.

Intermediate Lesson Plan: Making Text-to-Self, Text-to-Text, and Text-to-World Connections

Purpose:

Louise Rosenblatt reminds us that there is a reciprocal relationship between a reader and the book. When the connection between the two is strong, it is like a "live current between reader and the text" (1976, p. 25). One way to help older readers build such a connection is to model how it works for you. In this mini-lesson, you will demonstrate how a picture book stimulates your personal thoughts, ties to other reading experiences, and connects to world events. Remind your students how important it is to connect with both text and pictures.

Materials/Preparation:

Pick a favorite picture book with ties to an upcoming lesson. You will be thinking aloud as you read to model text-to-self connections, text-to-text connections, and text-to-world connections.

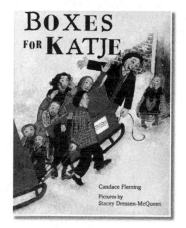

Boxes for Katje is a good book for modeling making connections.

Mini-Lesson:

1. Read the title, author, illustrator, and the dedication page. For demonstration purposes, you might use *Boxes for Katje* by Candace Fleming (2003). The illustrations are by Stacey Dressen-McQueen. Tell the students the story is built around a childhood memory.

2. Look at the cover together. Model a *text-to-self connection*: "It looks like Christmas to me. It is winter and there certainly are lots of boxes coming to Katje's house. I'm curious about the picture of the little girl who seems to be packing a box. Since I love getting presents, I'm looking forward to finding out what is in those boxes."

3. Study the endpapers together. Model a *text-to-self connection*: "This shows part of a small town in the Midwest. I have lived in the Midwest for many years and can relate to the white-spired church, the old brick schoolhouse, and what looks like a community park. These were a part of my childhood."

4. Read the first page aloud. Model *text-to-text* and *text-to-world connections*: "I see articles in the newspaper and reports on the news about families that are without so many things in the Middle East because of the war. I have also heard about classrooms in

town where children are raising money and sending boxes to our servicemen and -women. I can only imagine what it must be like to be without basic things during wartime. I'm hoping there are practical necessities in those boxes."

5. Read through page 5; study the text and illustrations. Model a *text-to-self connection*: "I love chocolate. I can almost taste it as they savor that chocolate. I'm thinking it must be a wonderful treat to receive such a surprise."

6. Read through page 16 and study the picture of people donating things for the boxes. Model a *text-to-world connection*: "I'm remembering the collections of food that are gathered at holiday time and, again, when Hurricane Katrina caused such devastation. After Katrina hit, I saw many people in our town who were helping just like these people are doing."

7. Continue modeling connections as demonstrated for your learners.

8. Ask students to share their connections to this story. Remind them that making these three kinds of connections helps them understand the story much better.

9. Provide students with sticky notes during independent reading. Encourage them to note a few connections they make and share them with the class.

The Writing Connection

Primary Lesson Plan: Writers Get Their Ideas From Memories

Mini-Lesson:

1. Read *Treasures of the Heart* (Miller, 2003).

2. Send a note home asking students to bring in one favorite treasure: a photograph, a gift, a keepsake, or a simple object found on an outing.

3. Invite students to share their treasure in small groups or as a class. Guide the discussion to focus on how each object is connected to a special memory.

4. Share the book *Wilfrid Gordon McDonald Partridge* (Fox, 1984).

5. Discuss how the objects we treasure keep us connected to our thoughts, recollections, hopes, and dreams.

6. Students may choose to write a narrative piece about the memory connected to their treasured object.

My Memory

Written by: Sam
October, 2003

My hat reminds me of me as a baby and my grandma. My grandpa used it. I only saw him when I was born. He died when I lived in Pennsylvania.

A first grader writes about the memory of his grandfather.

Literature Is Back!

Have You Read These?

A FEW OF OUR FAVORITE RECENTLY PUBLISHED PICTURE BOOKS

- *Superdog: The Heart of a Hero* (Buehner, 2004)

- *Leaf Man* (Ehlert, 2005)

- *Actual Size* (Jenkins, 2004)

- *The Hello, Goodbye Window* (Juster, 2005)

- *Once Upon a Time, the End* (Kloske, 2005)

- *The End* (LaRochelle, 2007)

- *17 Things I'm Not Allowed to Do Anymore* (Offill, 2007)

- *Cookies: Bite-Size Life Lessons* (Rosenthal, 2006)

- *The Great Fuzz Frenzy* (Stevens & Crummel, 2005)

- *Probuditi!* (Van Allsburg, 2006)

A father reads his own shortened versions of bedtime stories so that his child will quickly go to sleep.

Intermediate Lesson Plan: How Do Writers Narrow Topics and Add Rich Details?

Purpose:

Vicki Spandel (2004) explains that "ideas are the heart and soul of good writing, the writer's main message or story line" (p. 7). Where do those ideas live? In *When I Was Your Age* (1996), Amy Ehrlich points out that writers are observers with good memories, and they carefully select which memories to use in their stories. Share these thoughts with your students. Remind them that when it comes to selecting topics, writers write about what they know, what they would like to know more about, what speaks clearly to their imaginations, and about topics they fervently believe in. Highlight the fact that each writer is different, selects his or her own collection of words, and deftly paints word pictures that reflect what he or she sees. Then, as readers, we create that live connection between author and ourselves as we draw on our background experiences to connect with text.

Materials/Preparation:

♦ *Thank You, Mr. Falker* (Polacco, 1998), an autobiographical snapshot of Patricia Polacco's struggles when learning to read.

♦ You and your students each need a photo of a memorable event to help you focus and fuel the writing process. If that is not possible, a sketch of the event can be used.

♦ Copies of A Checklist for Writing About a Memory.

Mini-Lesson:

1. Read and discuss *Thank You, Mr. Falker.*

2. Model writing the first paragraph about your memorable event, using the overhead so that students can see you write, rewrite, and struggle to get the words just right.

3. As you write, carefully follow the guidelines in the checklist.

4. Provide students with time to write and share their beginnings.

5. Over the next few days, you and your students continue your memory pieces. Begin each writing session by modeling part of the process, such as adding details, examining vivid verbs, or using the thesaurus to find just the right word.

6. Once the rough drafts are complete, students use the chart to critique their writing. First, students assess their own writing. Next, they work with a peer to review the checklist again.

7. The checklist may also be used as an assessment rubric once the piece has been polished.

8. Publish and display the final writing with the photo and/or illustration.

Name _____ Date _____

A Checklist for Writing About a Memory

☐ Start with a snapshot, or draw a sketch of your memory. Examine the details in the photo or add details to your sketch. Include the same details in your writing.

☐ Keep your ideas small. Focus on one thing and explain it well. If you tackle too much, it is difficult to stay on target.

☐ Add interesting details so that the reader can "see" what you have experienced. Use your five senses to draw a picture in words.

☐ Write with a thesaurus at hand so that you can find the best words to express vivid thoughts filled with rich details.

☐ Find words that are new ways to say everyday things.

☐ Pick words that are descriptive, verbs that show action, adjectives that stay in the reader's mind.

☐ Read your piece aloud to yourself to hear how it sounds. Check that you followed the guidelines above. Revise as needed.

☐ Share your piece with a friend. Revise as needed.

☐ Edit, polish, and publish along with photo and/or an illustration.

(Kiefer, 1995; Spandel, 2004)

Four Fine Web Sites

The American Library Association and the Association for Library Service to Children

www.ala.org/alsc

This site includes lists of literary and related awards, including the Newbery, Caldecott, and Sibert. It also has handy children's notables lists recommending exemplary books, videos, recordings, and computer software for children.

Carol Hurst's Children's Literature Site

www.carolhurst.com

A collection of reviews of great books for kids and ways to use them in the classroom, and of books and activities about particular subjects, curriculum areas, themes, and professional topics.

Children's Literature Assembly

www.childrensliteratureassembly.org

Affiliated with the National Council of Teachers of English, this site includes lists of outstanding trade books in language arts.

Kay E. Vandergrift's Special Interest Page

www.scils.rutgers.edu/~kvander

This scholarly site includes articles and information related to many aspects of children's literature.

Summary

As our picture book parade draws to a close, we hope you've rediscovered an "old favorite" to share with your class and found some new titles that piqued your interest. As you share expertly illustrated titles with your students, take a moment to note the artistic elements and media. Select books that will not only enhance your lessons but will enrich the lives of your students. We know your days are busy, but remember to take the time to gather your students together to enjoy a perfect picture book.

Chapter 3

Traditional Literature

A TREK THROUGH ORAL TRADITION

PART 1

BUILDING BACKGROUND FOR TEACHING
WITH TRADITIONAL LITERATURE

Tales From Long Ago

For many of your students the words "Once upon a time…" or "Long ago and far away…" elicit memories of tales they have read or heard. No doubt, several favorites quickly come to your mind. That experience is an important one. Over the years, these tales become a part of a reader's personal literary history. As such, they serve as valuable links to other readers who can also relate to a familiar, shared literary heritage. In addition, tales from childhood become touchstones for different kinds of literature that will be read in the future. Stories that fall under the umbrella of traditional literature go back farther than one's personal history, however. In truth, they connect mankind across time and across cultures. They are as old as the spoken word and as well traveled as the most intrepid voyager.

If you choose to take your students on an imaginary road trip through the realm of traditional literature, what might you expect to encounter along the way? As with any road trip, would there be places not to be missed? What would make this realm different from others in this book? In answer to those questions, let's begin with a description of what this genre entails.

What Is Traditional Literature?

What separates traditional literature from its closest neighbor, modern fantasy or literary tales, is the fact that these stories are rooted in the oral tradition. They have been passed down from grandparent to parent, from parent to child, through countless generations. The originator is long lost in time. Imagine how the stories have been honed and embellished upon over the years as each teller adds a bit of herself to the tale. As a result, while the stories that we have been gifted with today probably remain true to the original core, they have been flavored with the creativity of one reteller after another. That unique flavoring will continue; there will never be a definitive version of any such tales because of their very nature (Lukens, 2007).

How Was Traditional Literature Collected?

The reason that a variety of traditional literature is available today is that industrious folklorists began collecting and transcribing tales several hundred years ago. Students might be interested in knowing the origins of some of their favorites. They also might be intrigued to learn that although many tales were originally written for an adult audience, children also heard them. Joseph Jacobs is credited with gentling some of the English tales, thus making them worthy fare for even the youngest listener (Huck et al., 2004; Jacobs & Tunnell, 2004).

Others joined the gathering and recording effort. Appealing Jewish folklore has been recorded by Isaac Bashevis Singer, while Peter Christian Asbjørsen and Jorgen E. Moe published most of the Scandinavian tales we read today. An example of the latter can be found in *East o' the Sun and West o' the Moon* (Lewis, 2005). Henry Rowe Schoolcraft began the efforts to capture early Native American tales. Anthropologists and linguists continue that work. Over time, dedicated sleuths have captured numerous oft-told tales in writing before their words disappeared into obscurity. Just what might these tales look like?

Origins of Favorite Tales		
Origin/Time Period	**Collector**	**Tales**
France (late 1600s)	Charles Perrault	Little Red Riding Hood Beauty and the Beast Cinderella Stone Soup
Germany (early 1800s)	Joseph and Wilhelm Grimm	The Elves and the Shoemaker Hansel and Gretel Rumpelstiltskin Snow White
England (late 1800s)	Joseph Jacobs Andrew Lang	Jack and the Beanstalk The Little Red Hen The Three Little Pigs Tam Lin

What Are the Types of Traditional Literature?

When you and your students trek through this territory, you will find that traditional literature offers a variety of imaginative vistas, including folk and fairy tales, fables, myths, epics, and legends. As you explore each one in turn, readers will be treated to stories of the underdog who courageously overcomes the odds, of origins of natural phenomena, of wondrous magic, of heroes whose feats defy belief, and much more. With such a variety, traditional literature appeals to readers in different ways. Stories range from those offering pure entertainment to others that leave readers with a message to ponder long after the tale is told. Should the traveler need directions along the way, it is possible that an articulate pig, a sleepy dwarf, a hovering fairy, or a wicked stepmother might offer guidance. The cast of characters that inhabits the realm of traditional literature is distinctive indeed. We explore specific types of literature in depth later in the chapter.

What Are the Characteristics of Traditional Literature?

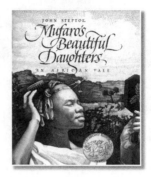

While traditional literature is represented by different kinds of stories, it is recognizable by a number of definite characteristics. Knowing them makes recognizing this genre relatively easy. It also makes patterning one's writing after them a manageable task for budding writers (Fuhler, 2000; Young & Ferguson, 1995; Young, 2004).

One of the many traditional literature titles to earn the Caldecott Medal.

The Caldecotts: Two Decades of Winners and Honor Books

1988   *Mufaro's Beautiful Daughters: An African Tale* (Steptoe)*

1989   *The Boy of the Three-Year Nap* (Snyder; A. Say, Illus.)*
        Goldilocks and the Three Bears (Marshall)*
        Mirandy and Brother Wind (McKissack; J. Pinkney, Illus.) *

1990   *Lon Po Po: A Red-Riding Hood Story From China* (Young)
        Hershel and the Hanukkah Goblins (Kimmel; T. S. Hyman, Illus.) *
        The Talking Eggs (San Souci; J. Pinkney, Illus.) *

1991   *Puss in Boots* (Perrault) *

1993   *The Stinky Cheese Man and Other Fairly Stupid Tales* (Scieszka; L. Smith, Illus.) *
        Seven Blind Mice (Young) *

1994   *Raven: A Trickster Tale From the Pacific Northwest* (McDermott) *

1995   *John Henry* (Lester; J. Pinkney, Illus.) *
        Swamp Angel (Isaacs; P. O. Zelinsky, Illus.) *

1996   *Tops & Bottoms* (Stevens) *

1997   *Golem* (Wisniewski)

1998   *Rapunzel* (Zelinsky)
        There Was an Old Lady Who Swallowed a Fly (Taback) *

2000   *Joseph Had a Little Overcoat* (Taback)

2002   *The Three Pigs* (Wiesner)

2003   *The Spider and the Fly* (Howitt; T. DiTerlizzi, Illus.) *
        Noah's Ark (Pinkney) *

*Caldecott Honor Books

As children read across the genre, they will quickly recognize the characteristics that distinguish it from others.

The Characteristics of Traditional Literature

 ◆ Heroes and heroines display traits like cleverness, bravery, or outright silliness.

 ◆ Plotlines are straightforward.

 ◆ Stories are to the point: good is supremely good; evil is clearly evil.

 ◆ The conflict is quickly evident, with the resolution wrapping the tale up conclusively.

 ◆ Characters are flat or one-dimensional rather than being fleshed out.

 ◆ Themes express the values and beliefs of the people who created the stories.

 ◆ Language is direct and reflective of its cultural origins.

 ◆ Setting is without much detail; time is not pinpointed.
 (Galda & Cullinan, 2006; Lukens, 2007)

Why Is Traditional Literature Important for My Students?

While preparing for your travels through this chapter, you may have been wondering how reading a fairy tale could be of much importance. What might seem like just a little light reading actually has substantial value. Consider the following learning opportunities.

Deepens Cultural Understanding

One of the primary values of traditional literature is that it offers its readers a unique look at humanity from an engaging perspective. Folktales, in particular, lend themselves to teaching cultural insights. For example, keen readers can glimpse cultural beliefs, spiritual qualities, and psychological aspects of the people represented depending upon the tale they select (Huck et al., 2004; Norton, 2005). In order to highlight and strengthen cultural understanding, however, it is important that such reading is coupled with conversation. Social interaction is a proven strategy to deepen comprehension after reading both fiction and nonfiction selections (Gambrell, 1996; Pearson & Fielding, 1996; Pressley, 2000). It is a natural partner to the offerings in this chapter.

Sparks the Imagination

Another value is that each story can fire up your students' imaginations. Margaret Meeker (2003) suggests that imagination has no limits. "It cannot be fully accounted for in words. Instead it creates and renews all experiences, hopes, wishes, feelings, and thoughts" (p. 106). Lively characters invite young readers to pretend or to retell the story as they act it out alone or with classmates, building early literacy skills in the process. Older readers can imaginatively interpret the actions of characters through Readers Theater or pen their own variants inspired by a favorite tale. We see imagination in action in each case.

This reminder about the potency of one's imagination is timely. In our present era of instant gratification dispensed through television, movies, and intensity-driven video or Internet games, the topic of refueling the imagination of today's children is a vital one to discuss. Balance the exposure to ever-ready visual stimulation with inviting opportunities to engage with the well-crafted words and stunning art proffered by traditional literature. Imagination-healthy changes are bound to occur.

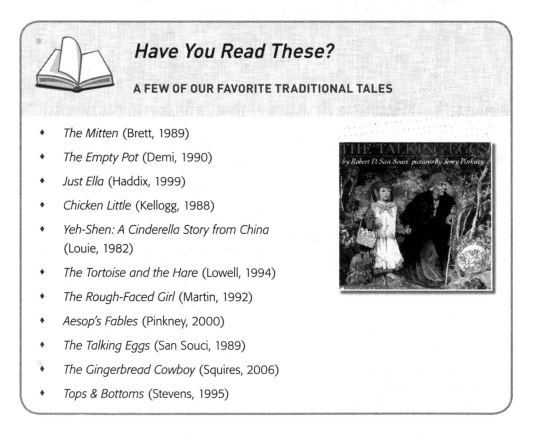

Have You Read These?

A FEW OF OUR FAVORITE TRADITIONAL TALES

- *The Mitten* (Brett, 1989)
- *The Empty Pot* (Demi, 1990)
- *Just Ella* (Haddix, 1999)
- *Chicken Little* (Kellogg, 1988)
- *Yeh-Shen: A Cinderella Story from China* (Louie, 1982)
- *The Tortoise and the Hare* (Lowell, 1994)
- *The Rough-Faced Girl* (Martin, 1992)
- *Aesop's Fables* (Pinkney, 2000)
- *The Talking Eggs* (San Souci, 1989)
- *The Gingerbread Cowboy* (Squires, 2006)
- *Tops & Bottoms* (Stevens, 1995)

Provides Reading Enjoyment

A third value to underscore is that these stories are enjoyable to read. The characters quickly become recognizable, the plots move rapidly, and many elicit a smile or two. And much to the young listener's delight and sense of justice, the wicked are deservedly punished (Bettelheim, 1976). Another positive factor is that in these tales wishes do come true. However, this good fortune is not simply due to wishful thinking; readers learn that there are tasks to be completed to achieve one's reward. Children are also encouraged when they see how the underdog—the youngest, the weakest, or the smallest—overcomes adversity. Finally, many a tale ends happily ever after, leaving no loose strings to worry the sensitive reader.

Builds a Rich Literary Background

How many times have you come across a phrase, a word, a character, or a theme that reminded you of a folktale you read as a child? As mentioned earlier in the chapter, another value to point out is that traditional literature is the foundation of your readers' literary backgrounds. Experiences with this genre form an invaluable thread that connects past stories to other readings, music, or plays to be experienced in years to come. Bits and pieces of folktales have a propensity to pop up in novels, nonfiction, and the popular press from time to time. Readers who have been raised on these stories quickly recognize the connections.

Consider, for example, the commonly used words from Greek and Roman myths like *cereal, labyrinth, siren, nymph, Saturday, Cupid, Venus,* and *Mars* that flavor our speaking and reading. Do you remember saying, "Open Sesame!" when playing an imaginative game as a child? These magical words were spoken by Aladdin in the tale "The Thousand and One Nights." Then, think about references to other stories that appear in novels. In Katherine Paterson's (2002) *The Same Stuff as Stars*, young Angel is worried about being abandoned by her Mama. She thinks, "It was one thing to leave your kids in an all-night diner by mistake. It was something else to leave them in the country on purpose. That would be too much like Hansel and Gretel" (p. 66).

In addition, cautionary advice from Aesop's fables surfaces from time to time. Have you heard the following bits of wisdom (Pinkney, 2000)?

"You are judged by the company you keep," from "The Stork and the Cranes"

"Look before you leap," from "The Fox and the Goat"

"One good turn deserves another," from "The Ant and the Dove"

It appears that remnants from traditional literature follow a reader throughout life.

Traditional Literature: Types, Titles, and Teaching Ideas

As you begin to select tales to link literature and learning, we offer a closer look at some of the types of traditional literature. From light-hearted to serious, from magic to legends with a whiff of truth, the journey promises to be memorable.

Folktales

It is not always an easy task to decide the particular category in which to place some of the traditional tales. As you read about them, you will see that they could easily cross into another category or maybe even two. Let's begin with the largest category in traditional literature, folktales. See the Glance Chart on pages 76–78 for an overview of the different types of folktales. Every culture has examples to sample. For each type of folktale, you will find a brief description of the representative tales, enticing titles to try, and catalyst activities for using them in your classroom. No doubt many of these will be familiar to you.

Using Folktales to Build a Positive Understanding of Different Cultures

With regard to all of these tales, readers can study them to learn a little more about the culture in which they originated. Trickster tales lend themselves particularly well to such study. Far more than mere entertainment, they bring to light pertinent cultural values. Because of this, they are an excellent way to help students begin to build a positive understanding of different cultures (Norton, 2005; Young, 2004). A closer look at titles from other cultures will reveal insights into the people and the beliefs behind the tales.

One could easily travel around the world by sampling trickster tales through engaging lessons. As students compare and contrast variants and different tales in general, have them highlight the cultural values or lessons being taught (Farris, Fuhler, & Walther, 2004). Again, classroom conversations are a must to share the learning and to be certain no misconceptions about a culture are formed. Not only will readers better understand these stories as a result, but their comprehension will be heightened through discussion, an invaluable way to spend classroom time (Alvermann, 2000; Pearson & Fielding, 1996).

Other Types of Traditional Literature

There are still more tales to read and celebrate. You will find an overview of the categories of tall tales, fables, myths, epics, ballads, legends, and religious stories in the chart that follows. Each area has books to be read aloud, to be savored silently, and to serve as the focus of a relevant literacy lesson. Note that some of these retellings do not fit simply and neatly into the box into which they have been thrust. Talk about the characteristics of the tales with your class and decide together where you think they best belong.

Sharing Myths With Students

Compared to other types of tales, myths seem to receive less exposure in and out of school, perhaps because their content is more complex. When you scan the library shelves, however, you are sure to find titles to whet the appetites of readers of varying ages. For example, two of the titles written several decades ago for younger readers are the familiar *D'Aulaires' Book of Greek Myths* (D'Aulaire & D'Aulaire, 1962) and *D'Aulaires' Norse Gods and Giants* (D'Aulaire & D'Aulaire, 1986). Traditionally, though, it is in the upper grades that myths are introduced.

An Overview of Folktales in Traditional Literature

Type of Folktale/ Description	A Literature Sampling	Research-Supported Literacy Activities
Cumulative Stories progress with a line or two added at a time; repetition is the essential ingredient.	*The Gingerbread Baby* (Brett, 1999) *One Fine Day* (Hogrogian, 1971) *There Was an Old Lady Who Swallowed a Fly* (Taback, 1997) *The House That Jack Built* (Winter, 2000)	Strengthen verbal expression and fluency skills by performing a tale as a choral reading or Readers Theater production.
Pourquoi Tales explain to the curious reader why things in the world are the way they are; have also been called "origin" or "how and why" stories.	*Beautiful Blackbird* (Bryan, 2003) *Bluebonnet Girl* (Lind, 2003) *How the Stars Fell Into the Sky* (Oughton, 1992) *Nacho and Lolita* (Ryan, 2005)	Pick a natural phenomenon. Work in triads to write and illustrate an original pourquoi tale following the pattern of a favorite tale.
Beast As main characters, anthropomorphized animals display recognizable human behaviors, both good and bad.	*The Three Little Pigs* (Galdone, 1970) *Anansi and the Magic Stick* (Kimmel, 2001) *Jabuti, the Tortoise* (McDermott, 2001) *The Musicians of Bremen* (Puttapipat, 2005)	In a whole-class activity, compare and contrast different versions of a favorite tale like "The Three Bears" or "The Three Little Pigs."
Noodlehead The often good-hearted character behaves in silly or foolish ways in these amusing tales.	*Chanukah in Chelm* (Adler, 1997) *The Three Sillies* (Kellogg, 1981) *Epossumondas* (Salley, 2002) *Six Foolish Fishermen* (San Souci, 2000)	Read a selection of tales from different countries and discuss the characteristics of the main characters. What is it that makes them all noodleheads?

An Overview of Folktales in Traditional Literature

Type of Folktale/ Description	A Literature Sampling	Research-Supported Literacy Activities
Trickster Tales feature a main character who survives using wit, wisdom, pranks, cunning, deceit, lies, or mischief.	*Borreguita and the Coyote* (Aardema, 1991) *Coyote and the Fire Stick* (Goldin, 1996) *The Tales of Uncle Remus* (Lester, 1987) *Raven* (McDermott, 1993)	Focus on one trickster, reading tales from several cultures. Chart the cultural values depicted. Research to see if identified values are accurate.
Fairy Tales/Wonder Tales These tales about wonder and magic may involve magical objects (some good, like Cinderella's coach, and some bad, like a poisoned apple); the oppressed outwit wicked adversaries to live happily ever after.	*The Crane Wife* (Bodkin, 1998) *Sleeping Beauty* (Craft, 2002) *Jack and the Beanstalk* (Nesbit, 2006) *Lon Po Po* (Young, 1989)	Examine a number of tales that involve transformations, such as "Beauty and the Beast." Work in groups to read tales and chart the transformations, a motif or pattern found in many folktales.
Realistic Tales A small number of tales are woven around a real person, like Dick Whittington, a major in London, or Johnny Appleseed.	*Dick Whittington and His Cat* (Brown, 1950) *Johnny Appleseed* (Lindberg, 1990)	Research the person behind the tale. Discuss why the tales might have been created about this particular individual.

An Overview of Other Types of Traditional Literature

Type of Folktale/ Description	A Literature Sampling	Research-Supported Literacy Activities
Tall Tales Similar to legends, but these tales include a unique flavoring from the region of origin. They contain two distinct characteristics: exaggeration and humor.	*Pecos Bill* (Kellogg, 1986b) *John Henry* (Lester, 1994) *Dona Flor* (Mora, 2005) *Not One Damsel in Distress* (Yolen, 2002)	Read several captivating tales aloud to the class. Work in pairs or triads to read several more. Then, write a short tall tale. Present polished tales.
Fables These are typically short, didactic tales with a clean, crisp style that have a moral to the story. Characters are often animals.	*Doctor Coyote: A Native American Aesop's Fables* (Bierhorst, 1987) *Aesop's Fables* (Pinkney, 2000) *Seven Blind Mice* (Young, 1992)	Enjoy a selection of tales, then write a fable that teaches a contemporary lesson. Read a collection of tales to another class.
Myths Stories from primitive cultures featuring supernatural forces, gods, or goddesses. They look at the moral, spiritual, and worldly order of things.	*Greek Myths* (Coolidge, 2001) *King Midas and the Golden Touch* (Craft, 1999) *In the Beginning* (Hamilton, 1988) *Pegasus* (Mayer, 1998)	Read a collection of myths; categorize each as creation, nature, or hero myths on a large class poster. Discuss the decisions.
Epics, Ballads & Legends Epics are formal retellings of hero journeys; ballads are similar, but they were sung; legends have an element of truth at their core.	*The One-Eyed Giant: Tales from the Odyssey* (Osborne, 2002) *Beowolf: A Tale of Blood, Heat, and Ashes* (Raven, 2007) *Sundiata, Lion King of Mali* (Wisniewski, 1992) *Sword of the Rightful King* (Yolen, 2003)	Make a class list of the characteristics of heroes. Apply that list to today's heroes. Is there a match?
Religious Stories These stories try to answer such basic questions as what happens after death; they originate in the sacred writings of Buddhism, Christianity, Hinduism, Islam, and other world religions	*Hanukkah, Shmanukkah!* (Codell, 2005) *Buddha Stories* (Demi, 1997) *Wonders and Miracles* (Kimmel, 2004) *Creation* (McDermott, 2003)	Use these as companion tales to trickster tales and multicultural folktales, looking for values that are underscored in both.

Literature Is Back!

In middle school and high school, readers meet Apollo, Zeus, and other Roman and Greek gods and goddesses. Some myths show how the gods periodically stretched out of their realm to interact with humans. In those instances, they usually had a memorable lesson to teach. As with folktales, every culture has its own myths. To expand one's understanding of the range of myths, readers might sample *Gods and Goddesses of the Ancient Norse* (Fisher, 2001), *Moon Tales* (Singh, 1999), or *One-Hundred-and-One Asian Read-Aloud Myths and Legends* (Verniero, 2001), in addition to those titles highlighted in the Glance Chart. Just from this brief overview of books, it is apparent that these oldest of tales are well worth a closer examination than is typically afforded them. For exciting reading-writing connections, log onto the Scholastic Web site at the following address: http://www.teacher.scholastic.com/writewit/mff/folktalewshop_index.htm. Once you are there, you and your students can work together with Alma Flor Ada and Rafe Martin in their motivating folktale writing workshop. Students can publish their polished efforts online.

Endings and Beginnings

So ends this brief road trip through the hills and dales and across the realm of traditional literature. As with any memorable journey, there are places that no doubt touched you and your students in a special way. It is often true that you can scarcely wait to go back to such locations and tarry awhile, exploring a little further. How fortunate you are that this particular sojourn is relatively inexpensive and easily repeated. To do so, just reach for a book of your choice and travel freely amid its pages. Do not stop with one, however, and please don't come alone. Friends of all ages are welcome to journey with you.

Our investigation of the various types of traditional literature begins in a different way in the pages ahead. Specific ideas for integrating traditional literature into the literacy curriculum across primary- and intermediate-grade levels will be demonstrated. After working with these ideas and reading through a selection of titles, if you still have concerns about picking the best books for your learners, you will find the Guidelines for Selecting Quality Traditional Literature on page 80 helpful. It is based upon the advice of experts in the field and is meant to be helpful as you pick books that are certain to inspire readers and writers in your class. Adjust them and adapt them to meet the needs of your unique learners. Then, read further to learn how traditional literature enhances the learning in the classroom in myriad ways.

Guidelines for Selecting Quality Traditional Literature

	Yes	No	Somewhat
Evaluating the role of language:			
Reflects the origins of the tale using symbols, imagery, and vocabulary			
Maintains its cultural origin and richness			
Sounds like spoken language, moving rhythmically through the tale			
Pulls the reader quickly into a straightforward plot			
Comments:			
Evaluating the role of the illustrations:			
Corresponds to and enrich the story line			
Presents cultural details accurately			
Exposes readers to exemplary artwork			
Comments:			
Evaluating the role of the theme, message, or moral:			
The theme, message, or moral seems to be a natural extension of the tale			
Comments:			
Evaluating the role of background information:			
Includes author's note with information about the source of the tale			
Provides evidence that the adaptation was carefully and skillfully done			
Comments:			

Adapted from Galda, L., & Cullinan, B. E. (2006). *Literature and the child* (6th ed.). Belmont, CA: Wadsworth; and Huck, C. S., Kiefer, B. Z., Hepler, S., & Hickman, J. (2004). *Children's literature in the elementary school* (8th ed.). Boston: McGraw-Hill.

Literature Is Back!

PART 2

LINKING LITERATURE AND LEARNING

The Reading Connection

As you've seen in previous chapters, the research reminds us that one of the best ways to improve reading abilities is simply to read (Allington, 1977, 2002). The variety of tales within traditional literature can make that practice a pleasure, and at the same time offer opportunities to apply skills that will enhance reading comprehension. For example, once the predictable framework of a story or its story grammar is mastered, one possible roadblock to children's comprehension is eliminated. Now, readers recognize that there is a beginning, middle, and end to a story. Armed with that knowledge, they are able to anticipate how the tale will unfold. They predict what might come next, read to confirm or adjust those predictions, and conclude the well-read tale with a sigh of satisfaction. Then, if there are few clues to help them, making those predictions encourages creative thinking (Beck, 1989). As they practice predicting, they draw on another important reading skill: their ability to understand sequential relationships. In addition, readers are able to see how helpful text information can be used when making inferences, an essential comprehension strategy. With its relatively uncomplicated plot lines, traditional literature can easily support the teaching, modeling, and practice of a number of important comprehension strategies.

Primary Lesson Plan: Comparing Story Elements

Purpose:

The purpose of this lesson is to introduce and explore the elements of a narrative. Students will identify and compare these elements in variations of a traditional tale.

Materials/Preparation:

♦ Collect different versions of the same folktale, fairy tale, or other familiar story. For this example, we are using the following titles:

The Enormous Watermelon (Parkes & Smith, 1997)

The Enormous Turnip (Tolstoy, 2003)

The Enormous Carrot (Vagin, 1998)

♦ Create a chart (see sample, p. 82) on a large piece of paper to record students' responses.

Comparing Story Elements	Characters	Location (Setting)	Action	Problem (Goal)	Solution
The Gigantic Turnip by: Aleksei Tolstoy	old man old woman mouse	in a garden	trying to pull the turnip out	it was stuck because it was GIGANTIC	they asked for help.
The Enormous Watermelon by: Brenda Parkes	Old Mother Hubbard Nursery Rhyme Friends Wee Willy Winky	in a garden	trying to pull the watemelon out	it was stuck because it was ENORMOUS	she asked for help.
The Giant Carrot by: Jan Peck	Papa Joe Mama Bess Brother Abel Little Isabelle	in a garden	taking care of seed and trying to pull the carrot out	it was stuck because it was GIANT	they helped each other
The Giant Cabbage by: Cherie B. Stihler	Moose Vole	in a garden	trying to put the cabbage in Moose's truck	it was stuck because it was giant	they used tools and helped each other
Big Pumpkin by: Erica Silverman	Witch Mummy Vampire Ghost Bat	in a garden near a graveyard	trying to pull the pumpkin off the vine	it was stuck because it was BIG	bat told them to help each other
The Enormous Potato by: Aubrey Davis	Farmer Mouse	in a garden	trying to pull the potato out	it was stuck because it was ENORMOUS	farmer asked for help

A chart comparing story elements using C.L.A.P.S.

Mini-Lesson:

1. Introduce the elements of a narrative. You will notice as you look at the sample chart that we used the acronym C.L.A.P.S. (Characters, Location, Action, Problem, Solution). This creative idea comes from children's author Candace Fleming, who shares this "secret formula" when she works with children on their own writing. Young readers can also use this acronym to help identify the elements in their favorite stories.

2. Read a variety of familiar tales and discuss the elements of each tale. Pose the following questions to help guide your discussion: *Who are the main characters in this book? Where did this story take place? What are the characters doing? What is the problem they encounter or goal they are trying to achieve? Did they solve the problem or reach their goal? How would this story change if it had different characters or a different setting?*

3. Once students understand and can identify the story elements, choose a few different versions of the same story. For this example we used different versions of the traditional Russian folktale "The Enormous Turnip."

4. Read one story each day and record the elements on a large classroom chart.

5. As you add to the chart, discuss how understanding the elements of one story can help readers to read the next. Also point out how a writer can change the story by

simply changing one or two elements. Discuss the possibilities this opens for your young writers. Beginning writers love to write different versions of familiar books. For example, a student might choose to write *The Enormous Sunflower*. What characters would they create to help pull the plant out? Who would be the last little character who finally gets the job done?

6. To extend this lesson, provide students with books at their level and a small copy of the chart. They can work with a partner or small group to complete their own comparison of story elements.

Intermediate Lesson Plan: Enhancing Comprehension Using the S.C.A.M.P.E.R.S. Approach

Purpose:

Researchers remind us that students improve their comprehension of books they read when they revisit the material through carefully planned extension opportunities. While we wouldn't suggest using extension activities for every book that is read, it is beneficial to delve deeper into some books periodically and to do so in a variety of motivating, comprehension-enhancing ways. By completing the following activity, students are encouraged to look at the events in a traditional story in a new light, and in following the steps outlined in S.C.A.M.P.E.R.S., to think creatively and at a higher level. This adapted version of S.C.A.M.P.E.R. (original source unknown) includes a final *S* for *Scrutinize*. This "scrutinizing" step draws on visual literacy skills as students study the accompanying illustrations and draw inferences about what they add to the story line.

Materials/Preparation:

♦ A collection of folktales, including *Hansel and Gretel* (Ray, 1997), to model the lesson

♦ Copies of the S.C.A.M.P.E.R.S. planning sheets

Mini-Lesson:

1. Begin by reading an appropriate folktale or fairy tale aloud to the class.

2. To teach students how to use the S.C.A.M.P.E.R.S. planning sheet, model the steps in a whole-class demonstration using an overhead transparency, chart paper, or the computer projected on a large screen.

3. As you work through each letter on the planning sheet, give students a few minutes to create a response, and then take several suggestions. In this way, students will quickly realize that there are no right answers and that careful, higher-level thinking results in the most creative suggestions. The sample below illustrates one way that *Hansel and Gretel* might be done.

4. After careful thought about the resulting responses to the steps and organization of their written reactions, explain to students that they will rewrite or retell their folk- or fairy tale based upon their revised thinking about the original story.

5. For the application of S.C.A.M.P.E.R.S., provide the class with a collection of wonderful tales. Students work individually or in pairs to read a book of their choice, complete the prescribed steps, and rewrite the original tale. Polished versions can be illustrated by hand or by using computer-generated art. To address visual literacy and apply the "Scrutinize" process, challenge students to include additional information in the artwork to enrich or expand the story.

6. Finally, to celebrate and publish selected tales, a storytelling troupe might be formed to go from classroom to classroom sharing this higher-level, creatively written extension of a popular folk- or fairy tale.

A Completed S.C.A.M.P.E.R.S. Sample for *Hansel and Gretel* (Ray, 1997)

S	<u>Substitute</u>:	What might have happened if the father had married a different woman?
C	<u>Combine</u>:	In what ways are the witch and the stepmother alike?
A	<u>Adapt</u>:	If the forest animals had helped Hansel and Gretel, how would the story have changed?
M	<u>Modify</u>:	What would the children have done if the house they discovered was owned by a friendly fairy godmother?
P	<u>Put to Use</u>:	How many ways could Gretel have tried to outwit the witch?
E	<u>Eliminate</u>:	How could father have kept his family together without abandoning his children?
R	<u>Rewrite</u>:	Rewrite the story as it might have been if the children had decided to stay in the witch's house.
S	<u>Scrutinize</u>:	According to the illustrations, it appears that the animals throughout the story are ever watchful of the children. Could they have forewarned them of the trouble ahead or were they bewitched?

Name _____ Date _____

S.C.A.M.P.E.R.S. Planning Sheet

S   <u>Substitute</u>   What might have happened if…

C   <u>Combine</u>   In what ways are _____ and
_____ alike?

A   <u>Adapt</u>   If _____ , how would the
story have changed?

M   <u>Modify</u>   What would _____ have done
if _____ ?

P   <u>Put to Use</u>   How many ways could _____
have _____ ?

E   <u>Eliminate</u>   How could _____
have _____ without
_____ ?

R   <u>Rewrite</u>   Rewrite the story as it might have been if
_____ .

S   <u>Scrutinize</u>   According to the illustrations, it appears that
_____ because
_____ .

The Writing Connection

Sylvia McElveen and Connie Dierking (2001) are strong advocates of using children's literature as writing models in their classrooms. They discovered that carefully selected picture books could be used to focus on a particular writing skill they wanted to teach their students. For example, tall tales could be used to model the use of exaggeration or humor, the books serving as models for the students to follow in their own attempts at applying these skills. Another writing idea is to examine the basic parts of a plot: the beginning, the middle, and the end. With primary-grade learners, you might begin that study with nursery rhymes. With short snippets of text, it is relatively easy to illustrate these three basic parts. Later, expand the students' understanding to include the elements of literature as you read and discuss folk- and fairy tale offerings.

A first grader dramatizes Humpty Dumpty.

For students in middle-grade classrooms, you can extend that skill to an examination of the plot line in traditional literature. One critical writing skill for students to master is being able to develop a simple plot in order to follow the tale through from beginning to end. Traditional literature, with its emphasis on fast-moving plots, provides excellent examples for students to follow. See the following sample lesson for creative writing ideas that evolve from exceptional examples of traditional literature.

To help budding writers learn various organizational techniques, creative teachers share models of effective story structure (Culham, 2005). For our youngest writers, traditional literature provides a wealth of writing models as they compose stories with a clear beginning, middle, and end. For this lesson, we will explore the organization in the folk rhymes of Mother Goose. These simple rhymes not only engage students in choral reading and improve their phonemic awareness, but they possess a clear narrative structure with easily identified characters, setting, and a beginning, middle, and end.

Primary Lesson Plan: Teaching Organization Using Mother Goose Rhymes

Purpose:

Familiarizing children with Mother Goose rhymes and basic story elements: character, setting, plot.

Mini-Lesson:

1. As surprising as it may seem, many young children are not familiar with nursery rhymes. Before beginning this lesson, spend a week or so sharing favorite nursery rhymes with your class. Once they become familiar, you may choose to have students dramatize their favorite rhymes and present them to the class.

2. When students are familiar with nursery rhymes, model how to identify the elements of the rhyme using a story chart.

3. Divide students into pairs.

4. Provide each pair with a favorite nursery rhyme and a large copy of a story chart.

5. Students work with their partners to identify and record the elements of their nursery rhyme on the chart.

6. After the story charts are completed (see below), each pair shares its chart with the class.

7. Encourage students to try writing their own story using the elements they discovered.

Sample Story Chart for Humpty Dumpty		
Name: Humpty Dumpty	**Characters** Humpty Dumpty King's horses King's men	**Setting** The Wall
Beginning Humpty sat on the wall.	**Middle** Humpty fell off the wall.	**End** They couldn't put Humpty together again.

Intermediate Lesson Plan: Organization—Looking at the Plot Line

Purpose:

In order for creative writers to develop their own original folktales or to pen a variant of their favorites, they must be aware of plot and how it works in this genre. Remind writers that the plot is the sequence of events that moves a story along. In this genre, the plot is typically related in chronological order, with one event following quickly on the heels of another. When examining the plot line in the majority of traditional literature, readers will find that these stories are characterized by fast-paced plots. The setting is sketched briefly. The characters are interesting but they lack depth typically found in novels. Thus, it is the plot line that keeps the reader engrossed from beginning to end.

Materials/Preparation:

- A collection of folk- and fairy tales
- Plot diagram tool available at www.readwritethink.org/materials/plot-diagram

Mini-Lesson:

In this activity, students are to read a sampling of folk- and fairy tales, paying particular attention to the plot. They should study the tales to note the pattern of action used by the author. Thus, the retellers of each tale will be providing models for their own writing. For ease of practice, writers can try using the pattern of action below (Lukens, 2007). For instance, based upon their reading research, student writers may write a tale in which one event follows another at a pleasant pace but there is little tension and no high action. The problem or situation in the story is naturally resolved. This is an example of a horizontal pattern of action. Eric Kimmel's (1988) *Anansi and the Moss-Covered Rock* reflects this pattern.

If there is increased action or tension in the story, a more familiar plot line is used. In this case, there is rising action as one event builds upon the other to a climax, and then the problem or situation is resolved. Such a pattern would resemble the model below.

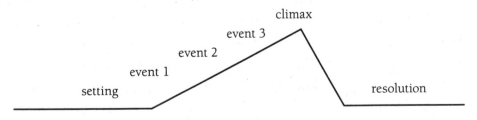

Literature Is Back!

A fairy tale with more tension in its plot is Paul O. Zelinsky's (1986) *Rumpelstiltskin*. A humorous variant of this tale is *Rumpelstiltskin's Daughter* (Stanley, 1997). Both tales are fine examples to use as writing models.

The last piece to consider when coming up with the plot is how to create the conflict. Students will remember the four types of conflict from previous studies: person-against-self, person-against-person, person-against-society, and person-against-nature. As readers sample the writing of various authors, they will see that conflicts in the majority of folk- and fairy tales typically involve person-against-person.

After careful reading and teacher modeling of each plot example, students may work in pairs to write. If they keep the basics of plot in mind, along with the characteristics of traditional literature as described earlier in the chapter, they will have the tools at hand for an enjoyable writing experience. Be sure to publish the polished creations, reading them to classmates, to children in lower grades, and, later, displaying them in the library or learning center.

 Four Fine Web Sites

Web-Travelers Toolkit: Essential KidLit Web Sites

www.acs.ucalgary.ca/~dkbrown/general.html
This site contains a wealth of helpful Web sites related to children's literature.

Native American Children's Literature

www.oyate.com
You will find this to be an invaluable site for learning about quality Native American literature.

Minneapolis Institute of the Arts: World Myths and Legends in Art

www.artsmia.orn/world-myths
Here is a student-friendly, teacher-informative site to expand knowledge about myths.

Folklinks: Folk- and Fairy-Tale Sites

www.pitt.edu/~dash/folklinks.html#generalfairytale
Use this site to research or just read numerous tales from around the world.

Summary

Traditional literature offers a variety of imaginative vista, including folktales, fables, fairy tales, myths, epics, and legends. With its myriad characters, its fast-paced plots, and its invitation to imaginative adventures, it is a welcome addition to the classroom. In addition to the pure reading enjoyment it provides, traditional literature is rich with the promise of improving reading comprehension, inspiring creative writing, and strengthening visual literacy. It is a genre that you and your students will delight in exploring as you build a literacy heritage and fuel life skills at the same time.

Chapter 4

Modern Fantasy

EXPERIENCING THE PAST, PRESENT, AND FUTURE

> ### MY Favorite Place
>
> My favorite place is inside a book. One reason that I like the world of books is that I can get lost in them. In a fiction book like "Harry Potter" I can feel like I am the main character. I can feel what he feels and do what he does. I can imagine that I'm learning spells, playing Quiddich, competing in the Tri-Wizard Tournament, and flying on my broom.

The beginning of Michael's essay.

PART 1

BUILDING BACKGROUND FOR TEACHING WITH MODERN FANTASY

Tales From Then and Now

Imagine, for a moment, that there are ambassadors for each genre much like there are ambassadors for many nations of the world. During their appointed terms these particular ambassadors would heighten interest in their respective genres, promote their values, herald new offerings, and gather eager readers for periodic genre celebrations. If

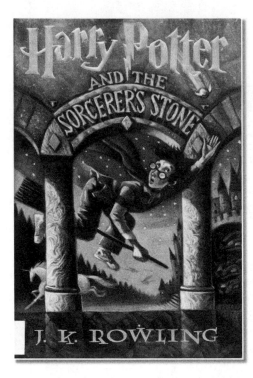

Harry Potter is the Ambassador for Modern Fantasy.

we were in charge of appointing the current Ambassador for Modern Fantasy, our choice would be Harry Potter. Thanks to the writing genius of J. K. Rowling, Harry has propelled fantasy to the forefront of the literary landscape. Harry's quest to best Lord Voldemort is a hallmark battle between good and evil. This young wizard's positive impact is far-reaching, since Harry's efforts are followed by so many avid readers from middle grades through adult. But it is more than a numbers phenomenon.

We are excited to hear about students who admit they were reluctant readers but now read enthusiastically. Harry is to be highly commended for that. Then, many who once shunned fantasy are now quite comfortable with it. Harry Potter has inspired a celebration of fantasy to the point where enticing new titles are filling bookstore shelves across the nation. As is frequently the case with leadership, however, Harry is not without his vehement critics. Voices have been raised in concern about wizardry and magic having a negative impact upon readers. No doubt the actions of Harry and some of his counterparts will energize classroom discussions.

In order to introduce fantasy into the curriculum, we'll need to consider the following: *What is fantasy? What are its values for today's readers? Can it enrich the lives of readers and writers in your classroom?* We will investigate those questions and more in the upcoming pages. Be prepared to believe what you know is not possible, to meet some ingenious characters, and to travel to unique worlds tucked creatively into the genre of modern fantasy.

What Is Modern Fantasy?

Modern fantasy is a genre that requires its readers to move beyond what is rational and realistic. They must practice disbelief as they enter worlds layered in magic, metaphor, and imagination. Science fiction, the second arm of this two-pronged genre, takes readers to worlds set somewhere in the future. It typically examines technology

Literature Is Back!

applied in unusual or extreme ways. Whether it is modern fantasy or science fiction, readers will find books in which the events, settings, and/or characters are outside of the realm of possibility. These stories explore alternate realities and scientific possibilities and grapple with "age-old questions about life, goodness, and balance" (Galda & Cullinan, 2006, p. 163). Even though these tales may be set in nonexistent realms or explore future worlds, they are crafted with such care that they are surprisingly believable. Works of fantasy and science fiction ask the reader to wonder "what if." They present a meticulously set stage and let readers take it from there. As they experience the people and places in their minds and hearts, readers may return from a book journey not quite the same as when they left.

Have You Read These?

A FEW OF OUR FANTASY SERIES FOR INTERMEDIATE-GRADE READERS

- Prydain Chronicles by Lloyd Alexander
  The Book of Three (1964)

- Tales of Dimwood Forest by Avi
  Ragweed (1999)

- The Merlin Series by T. A. Barron
  The Lost Years of Merlin (1996)

- The Spiderwick Chronicles by Tony DiTerlizzi and Holly Black
  The Field Guide (2003)

- The Catwings Series by Ursula LeGuin
  Catwings (1988)

- The Time Fantasy Series by Madeleine L'Engle
  A Wrinkle in Time (1962)

- Chronicles of Narnia by C. S. Lewis
  The Lion, the Witch, and the Wardrobe (1950)

- The Borrowers Series by Mary Norton
  The Borrowers (1953)

- The Harry Potter Series by J. K. Rowling
  Harry Potter and the Sorcerer's Stone (1998)

What Are the Characteristics of Modern Fantasy?

Readers of fantasy quickly note its kinship with traditional literature in many a tale. Sometimes there is magic afoot. At other times stories are interwoven with the threads of ancient myths and legends (Huck, Kiefer, Hepler, & Hickman, 2004; Jacobs & Tunnell, 2004). Modern folktales, known as literary tales, resemble the traditional fairy tale in that they are written according to the familiar parameters of little character description, strong conflict, fast-paced plots, and rapidly resolved problems. These tales contain familiar motifs, including magic, heroism, and unique characters, and they typically emphasize that good is rewarded and evil is punished.

> "Tolkien calls ancient myths 'the cauldron of story.' Everyone is free to dip into this marvelous cauldron, which is one of our great cultural heritages, and use whatever material they want. The difference is that each of us filters it through our own individual personalities, and that is what makes each work different."
>
> Lloyd Alexander quoted in Tunnell, 1989, p. 87

One particular characteristic that distinguishes modern fantasy from traditional literature is that the authors are known. For instance, Hans Christian Andersen is credited with writing the first fairy tale for children (Norton, 2003). Creator of such favorites as "The Ugly Duckling" and "The Little Match Girl," he has been designated the father of modern folktales.

To sum up its origins, then, fantasy is deeply rooted in the world of traditional literature, but it blossoms into tales that are fresh, previously untold or cleverly retold, and masterfully penned from a known author's ingenuity.

The Characters

While some of the characters in fantasy are realistic, like the friend across the street, readers are certain to meet some fanciful characters (Farris, Fuhler, & Walther, 2004). Young children delight in the talking animals so popular in fantasy, such as Winnie-the-Pooh and the Velveteen Rabbit. Children of varying ages are intrigued with the hobbits, dwarves, elves, dragons, and other magical beings. As if that were not enough, characters also come in all sizes, from immense giants to thumb-sized heroes. You will notice that in longer tales, especially, these characters change in some way during the course of the story. For instance, in high fantasy, the multidimensional heroes or heroines are on a quest that may take them through one, three, or even seven books, and leave them considerably matured as a result of their experiences (Cruz & Pollock, 2004; Galda & Cullinan, 2006).

Finally, more often than not, there are heroes to be emulated.

The Setting

Readers of the modern fantasy are treated to some most unusual locales. There are stories that begin in the primary world, or the world as we know it. Then, readers are transported to a secondary world, an imaginary domain so carefully crafted that you scarcely question its actual existence. Think of Alice, who began a leisurely afternoon in the English countryside only to be interrupted by a harried, waist-coated rabbit who worried, "Oh, dear! Oh dear! I shall be too late!" (Carroll/Oxenbury, 1999, p. 11). Alice pops down the rabbit hole after him into Wonderland, a world that has delighted readers since they, too, found it in 1865. And remember the seemingly ordinary wardrobe that

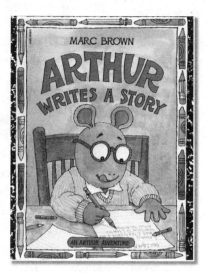

Arthur and his friends are popular talking animals.

the Pevensie children walked through to enter Narnia? Other tales are deliberately set in secondary worlds like Lloyd Alexander's Prydain, where Taran courageously battles evil, or Neverland, where Peter and the Starcatchers (Barry & Pearson, 2004) battle Captain Hook. These characters and their book companions wage heroic battles in distant lands drawn from myth and legend.

When crafting these unique settings, the author is challenged to create a logically related set of physical laws for each new world and stick to them unerringly so that the story remains credible throughout. As a result, Jacobs and Tunnell (2004) explain that fantasy is probably the most demanding genre to write. Norton (2003) suggests that the writer must develop the setting so completely that every reader can see it, hear it, and feel it. Readers come to wish that world were real and, wrapped up in the pleasure of reading, willingly believe it is so for the duration of the book (Lukens, 2007).

The Themes

When immersed in the worlds of fantasy and science fiction, readers will discover that there are valuable lessons to learn, themes to think about, and truths to digest. While trekking through alternate worlds with memorable characters, readers may find truths that could help them more clearly understand the world in which they live. Sharon Black (2003) explains the phenomenon this way:

Then, paradoxically, just as we think we have escaped from the world, they [book characters] help us find the power to live in it. The places and characters we imagine sustain us as we struggle with places and people who trouble us—including ourselves (pp. 540–541).

Writers take this aspect of the genre seriously; consequently, the underlying themes are worth careful consideration. They are proffered with care, often cloaked in metaphor. Because of this, they seem less like a didactic lesson and more like a personally discovered "aha!" In fact, Lukens (2007) cautions against a didactic approach, which she suggests is better left to the textbooks. She reminds us that literature does not directly teach as much as it helps us to understand. She worries that "The preached-at child may come to reject all reading and thus close off the vast discoveries about human beings and society available in literature" (p. 138) if we are not careful. Note, then, that fantasy not only offers pleasurable escapes but also affords the reader reflective moments during and after reading.

The Role of Metaphor

Because of its power to create vivid images in readers' minds, metaphor plays a key role in fantasy. These implied comparisons can connect something the writer is trying to say with a concrete example from the reader's life. As you remember, this form of figurative language compares one thing to another without using the words *like* or *as*. The writer presents an idea or an object as if it were another thing, such as "seeing the light at the end of the tunnel" when the end of a demanding project is in sight. Size comparisons might include "he was a mountain of a man," while the use of the season of winter could symbolize old age or impending death. In *Tuck Everlasting* (1975), when Tuck alludes to the cycle of life, author Natalie Babbitt writes:

Natalie Babbitt's writing includes the use of metaphor.

> It's a wheel, Winnie. Everything's a wheel, turning and turning, never stopping. The frogs is part of it, and the bugs, and the fish, and the wood thrush, too. And people. But never the same ones. Always coming in new, always growing and changing, and always moving on. That's the way it's supposed to be. That's the way it *is* (p. 62).

The use of metaphors encourages readers to dig a little more deeply for meaning as they read, and to look for possible ties between what the characters are experiencing and their own experiences. Metaphors also aid readers in seeing something in a fresh way, touching their minds and their hearts in the process (Jacobs & Tunnell, 2004).

Why Is Modern Fantasy Important for My Students?

Develops the Imagination

The benefits of reading and writing modern fantasy are similar to those of traditional literature. Both genres envelop readers in the realm of imagination, offering opportunities to see the world through different eyes. Perhaps it is better said that fantasy releases our students from day-to-day affairs as they slip into other worlds, watching, learning, laughing, crying, worrying, and troubleshooting side by side with characters they enjoy. It's difficult to return from such a sojourn unchanged. In the process of having their imagination liberated, readers may have expanded their problem-solving abilities, broadened their way of thinking about diversity, or lingered thoughtfully in a unique time and place long after the book has been tucked back onto the shelf. In that case, we are helping our students deepen their response to reading as they continue to think about what they have experienced. In brief, fantasy affords readers an opportunity for some divergent thinking and invites them to look at life a little differently and more creatively (Black, 2003; Hillman, 2002).

Have You Read These?

A FEW OF OUR FAVORITE MODERN FANTASY READ-ALOUDS FOR THE PRIMARY GRADES

- *The Chocolate Touch* (Catling, 1979)*
- *The Mouse and the Motorcycle* (Cleary, 1965)*
- *The Magician's Boy* (Cooper, 2005)*
- *Corduroy* (Freeman, 1968)
- *My Father's Dragon* (Gannett, 1948)*
- *Miss Smith Reads Again* (Garland, 2006)
- *The Mysterious Tadpole* (Kellogg, 1977)
- *Up* (LaMarche, 2006)
- *The Whingdingdilly* (Peet, 1970)
- *Alice the Fairy* (Shannon, 2005)
- *Boing!* (Taylor, 2004)

*chapter book

Encourages Critical Thinking

Another value of reading fantasy is that it encourages readers to be critical thinkers (Galda & Cullinan, 2006). During a genre study, students might be asked to examine the following broad, important issues:

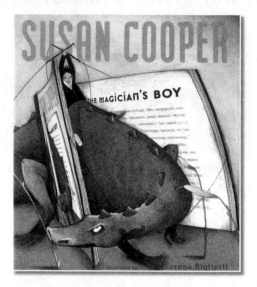

- relativity of size, time, and space

- interdependence of all things in the universe

- many guises of good versus evil

- importance of personal integrity (p. 164)

So, reading and eventually digesting fantasy can stretch and strengthen critical thinking as weighty issues such as these are discussed comfortably in small groups with classmates. While quiet reflection within the pages of a journal is a valuable activity, conversation facilitates understanding (Pressley, 2000). In the process of sharing personal reactions, students might even think about how book issues reflect current events, making a text-to-world connection. Modern fantasy is rich fare in which to explore the preceding topics and others that emerge from serious conversations.

Enables Readers to Experience Life Vicariously

An additional value to highlight is that readers are able to explore real or potential problems from a safe and comfortable vantage point as they read. Fantasy writers can tackle issues that could be painful or disturbing if presented more realistically. Readers may vicariously experience the impact of such things as loss, betrayal, prejudice, anger, death, war, and jealousy while avoiding personal or emotional harm (Cruz & Pollock, 2004). Jacobs & Tunnell (2004) state that while it may be uncomfortable for some, "…good fantasy actually tells the truth about life. It clarifies the human condition and captures the essence of our deepest emotions, dreams, hopes, and fears. If fantasy doesn't do these things, it fails" (p. 93).

Therefore, fantasy teaches its perceptive readers about life in general and themselves personally while taking them out of this world and allowing them to travel much farther afield. It offers a place for the dreamer to dream and the thinker to think inside and outside of its borders. Fantasy can enrich and illuminate the lives of its readers because it, too, mirrors the complexities of our lives (Norton, 2003; Kurkjian, Livingston, Young, & Avi, 2006). In brief, this genre is entertaining, imaginative, and worthy of serious, ongoing reflection.

Modern Fantasy: Types, Titles, and Teaching Ideas

Although we will divide fantasy into general categories or types for ease of discussion, books are not bound by the category into which they are placed. As you read about them, you will see that many titles easily fit into several different types. Sample the fascinating titles found in the Glance Chart on pages 100–101.

A tale of good versus evil

Readers of literary tales will find quite a variety of stories, from modern versions of folktales to novels that are rooted in tales from traditional literature, as noted below. You will find that one appealing title after another begs to be read aloud or savored silently.

Novels That Emerged From Traditional Literature	
Beauty (McKinley, 1978)	A retelling of the tale "Beauty and the Beast"
Rose Daughter (McKinley, 1997)	A fresh retelling of her novel *Beauty*
Ugly (Napoli, 2006)	A novel version of "The Ugly Duckling"
East (Pattou, 2003)	An absorbing retelling of "East of the Sun and West of the Moon"
Briar Rose (Yolen, 1992)	Intertwines "Briar Rose" with events of the Holocaust

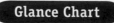

Glance Chart

An Overview of Types of Fantasy		
Type of Fantasy Tale/ Description	**A Literature Sampling**	**Research-Supported Literacy Activities**
Modern Folktales/ Literary Tales Folk- and fairy tales use the same motifs, mirroring traditional literature. The exception is that these stories are written by a known author.	*The Nightingale* (Andersen/ Mitchell, 2002) *Into the Forest* (Browne, 2004) *Muti's Necklace* (Hawes, 2006) *The Snow Princess* (Sanderson, 2004)	Working in pairs, students use the familiar motifs and themes from traditional literature to pen a literary tale. Once completed, authors read their polished tales to children in a lower grade.
Animal Fantasy Animal characters display human capabilities and characteristics, showing man's potential and his pitfalls.	*The Miraculous Journey of Edward Tulane* (DiCamillo, 2006) *Once Upon a Marigold* (Ferris, 2002) *The Jungle Book* (Kipling/Bayley, 2005) *The Mistmantle Chronicles* (McAllister, 2005)	Strengthen fluency skills through Readers Theater. Teacher and/or students write scripts from a favorite tale, practice their parts, and present to classmates and other classes.
Personified Toys/ Objects Using personification, inanimate objects are given human traits or characteristics.	*The Tub People* (Conrad, 1989) *Little Oh* (Melmed, 1997) *Winnie-the-Pooh* (Milne, 1966) *The Mennyms* (Waugh, 1994)	Teach the figurative language technique of personification. Then, have students pick an object from a basket, personify it, and write an engaging paragraph about it. Share.
Unusual Characters/ Situations Unique characters stretch the imagination as they behave in truly unusual ways.	*Peter Pan* (Barrie, 1911) *James and the Giant Peach* (Dahl, 1961) *Mary Poppins* (Travers, 1934) *Ignis* (Wilson, 2001)	Work on characterization by developing a personable character complete with sketch or illustration. Display on a "Bulletin Board of Possibilities." Ask your budding writers to consider where they might go with these characters in a story.
Supernatural Events/ Mystery Tales include ghostly characters and supernatural happenings; mysteries involve events to be solved. Suspense moves the plot along quickly.	*Wait Till Helen Comes* (Hahn, 1986). *The Ghost Sitter* (Griffin, 2001) *Sweet Whispers, Brother Rush* (Hamilton, 1982) *The Ghost Belonged to Me* (Peck, 1997)	Students will read a varied selection of ghost stories and/ or mysteries and jot down in writing journals tricks of the trade that authors use deftly to write this type of story. Make a classroom chart of these writing tips. Invite willing writers to pen a short mystery.

An Overview of Types of Fantasy

Type of Fantasy Tale/ Description	A Literature Sampling	Research-Supported Literacy Activities
Time Warps Stories involve time travel, typically going back in time to solve a problem. Travelers bring insights back to the present time.	*Riddle in the Mountain* (Burkard, 2005) *Tom's Midnight Garden* (Pearce, 1959) *Summer Reading Is Killing Me* (Scieszka, 1998) *Marco's Millions* (Sleator, 2001)	Guide students as they examine the importance of setting in time-warp tales. Use the Internet to research authors who write these stories and learn about the kind of research they must do to create an authentic setting. Share the findings in a whole-class discussion, creating an information sheet for students' writers' notebooks.
Quest Story Stories involve a hero/heroine who must follow a quest pattern while facing various challenges in order to defeat evil and restore order.	*The Book of Three* (Alexander, 1964) *Eldest* (Paolini, 2005) *Fire Arrow* (Pattou, 1998) *Harry Potter and the Half-Blood Prince* (Rowling, 2005)	Study the effects of using metaphors in writing. Teach the meaning of the term, model its use, and encourage students to integrate metaphors into their writing. Ask them to collect examples from their reading in their writers' notebooks to be shared periodically in class.
Science Fiction This "futuristic fiction" is based upon scientific fact. Readers consider how physical laws and/or scientific principles might be used to alter lives in future worlds.	*A Wrinkle in Time* (L'Engle, 1962) *Mrs. Frisby and the Rats of NIMH* (O'Brien, 1971) *The Wreck of the Zephyr* (Van Allsburg, 1983) *Sector 7* (Wiesner, 1999)	Students work in teams to take an effective use of technology or a successful scientific application and demonstrate how it could be misused in a future society. Each team presents a basic story line graphically, as in the popular graphic novels now available.

Let's Chat About Dragons

Dragons, fierce or friendly, and their irresistible tales are an integral part of the genre of modern fantasy. As you examine the Glance Chart (pages 100–101), you will see that it would be logical to place these tales in the category of Unusual Creatures/Situations, but these fascinating characters deserve some attention in their own right. To raise students' interest in dragons, begin by reading a few poems from *The Dragons Are Singing Tonight* (Prelutsky, 1993). Colorfully illustrated by Peter Sis, the book features artwork as enjoyable as the poems about a variety of dragons. Take time to review the suggested titles on page 103, for there are wondrous dragons breathing their fiery breaths into many a fantasy title. Then extend the reading experience for your students through the following activities.

1. Describe a dragon. After reading one of the suggested books, work with students to write a description of that dragon. Emphasize using words that paint a picture. Students can then create their own dragons, displaying them through a drawing or a model. Each one could be accompanied by a written description.

2. Compare dragons. Use a Venn diagram to compare dragons from two different books. Help students focus on each dragon's character traits, actions, and physical characteristics.

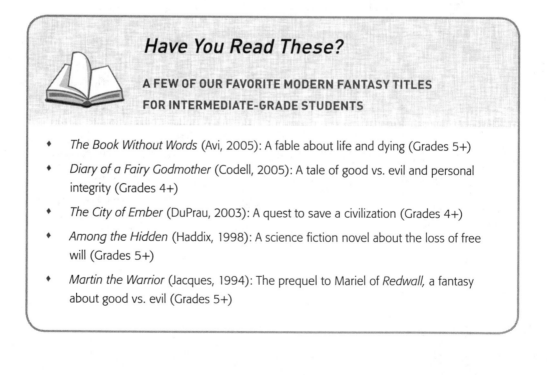

Have You Read These?

A FEW OF OUR FAVORITE MODERN FANTASY TITLES FOR INTERMEDIATE-GRADE STUDENTS

- *The Book Without Words* (Avi, 2005): A fable about life and dying (Grades 5+)

- *Diary of a Fairy Godmother* (Codell, 2005): A tale of good vs. evil and personal integrity (Grades 4+)

- *The City of Ember* (DuPrau, 2003): A quest to save a civilization (Grades 4+)

- *Among the Hidden* (Haddix, 1998): A science fiction novel about the loss of free will (Grades 5+)

- *Martin the Warrior* (Jacques, 1994): The prequel to Mariel of *Redwall,* a fantasy about good vs. evil (Grades 5+)

If It's Dragons You're After . . . A Collection of Books

Picture Books for Primary Grades:

+ *Matthew's Dragon* (Cooper, 1991)

+ *The Paper Dragon* (Davol, 1997)

+ *The Library Dragon* (Deedy, 1994)

+ *The Knight and the Dragon* (dePaola, 1980)

+ *Dragon Tooth* (Falwell, 1996)

+ *The Reluctant Dragon* (Graham, 2004)

+ *The Best Pet of All* (LaRochelle, 2004)

+ *The Paper Bag Princess* (Munsch, 1980)

+ *The Dragon Snatcher* (Robertson, 2005)

+ *The Popcorn Dragon* (Thayer, 1953/1989)

+ *Happy Birthday, Good Knight* (Thomas, 2006)

Robert Munsch's popular dragon tale.

Novels and Collections for Intermediate Grades:

+ *Fire and Wings: Dragon Tales From East and West* (Carus, 2002) (Grades 3–6)

+ *The Runaway Princess* (Coombs, 2006) (Grades 5+)

+ *The Dragonslayers* (Coville, 1994) (Grades 4–6)

+ *Jeremy Thatcher, Dragon Hatcher* (Coville, 1991) (Grades 5+)

+ *Dragon Rider* (Funke, 2004) (Grades 4–6)

+ *The Book of Dragons* (Hague, 1955) (Grades 3–6)

+ *Eragon* (Paolini, 2002) (Grades 5+)

+ *The Return of the Dragon* (Rupp, 2005), sequel to *The Dragon of Lonely Island* (Grades 3–6)

The Second Arm of Fantasy: Science Fiction

Science fiction, a relative newcomer on the children's literature scene, involves fantasy with a forward focal point. It is sometimes called "futuristic fiction" (Jacobs & Tunnell, 2004, p. 92). Readers travel to future worlds, invited to ponder the possibilities of technological advances that could change the lives of people in worlds to come. Rather than being rooted in mythology as high fantasy is, this subgenre is based in scientific fact. Authors consider existing physical laws and scientific principles when writing their stories, and then extend them into possible outcomes in the years ahead. Hillman (2002) explains what quality science fiction looks like: "The best science fiction not only balances science and fiction, but also provides a vision of the future. It can cause us to rethink gender roles, to plan for a just society, and to reshape institutions—and it can warn us what might happen if we do not change our habits" (p. 150).

When enjoying these stories, readers are invited to consider the emotional, psychological, and mental effects of scientific advances. They should be encouraged to keep an open mind to the possibilities science offers and consider the outcomes if they are abused or get the upper hand. Science fiction provides readers with an imaginative glimpse into the future, affording an opportunity to speculate upon the look of life in decades to come. This arm of fantasy has its devoted followers, although others simply cannot bring themselves to read it.

Endings and Beginnings

Fantasy is a masterful blend of realism and impossibility. The elements of fantasy are related to natural occurrences closely enough to be believable in some cases, but they are also truly unique. This genre kindles the imagination and invites readers to be thinkers in creative ways. These stories lend themselves to appealing options for building literacy skills in both primary and intermediate grades.

When looking for the best books for the readers in your classroom, use the guidelines found on pages 106 and 107. After assessing a few books against these guidelines, you will soon be able to select just the right titles for the unique readers in this year's class.

Themes of Science Fiction

- mind control
- genetic engineering
- space technologies and travel
- visitors from outer space
- future political and social systems
- life in the future
- survival

(Galda & Cullinan, 2006; Tomlinson & Lynch-Brown, 2002)

Guidelines for Selecting Quality Modern Fantasy

Characters	Yes	No
Are recognizable, believable, and not stereotypical		
Are well rounded, multidimensional		
Display consistent and logical behavior		
Develop and change over the course of the story		
Comments:		

Plot	Yes	No
Is well constructed		
Enables the reader to suspend disbelief		
Unfolds in a logical manner		
Is inventive and imaginative		
Comments:		

Setting	Yes	No
Is rich in details so that the reader can visualize the story		
Is fresh or unique and believable		
Remains internally consistent throughout the story		
If set in the historical past, is authentic		
Comments:		

Theme(s)	Yes	No
Are meaningful		
Help readers find philosophical or universal truths to understand today's world better		
Are discovered rather than taught		
Comments:		

Guidelines for Selecting Quality Modern Fantasy (continued)		
Style	**Yes**	**No**
Features insightful use of figurative language		
Uses authentic dialogue		
Is appropriate to the story		
Comments:		
Point of View	**Yes**	**No**
Suspends readers' disbelief by developing a consistent point of view in every detail possible		
Comments:		
Elements of Fantasy	**Yes**	**No**
Literary tale		
Primary or secondary worlds		
Magic		
Personified toys or objects		
Anthropomorphized animals		
Supernatural events or mystery		
Type of Fantasy Literature		
Is the book time travel, quest, or science fiction?		
Comments:		
How does this book compare with others by the same author or those in this genre?		
Comments:		

(Adapted from Galda & Cullinan, 2006; Hillman, 2002; Huck, Kiefer, Hepler, & Hickman, 2004; Tomlinson & Lynch-Brown, 2002)

The Reading Connection

From wordless picture books to weighty novels, fantasy lends itself to motivational ways of teaching and learning a variety of literacy skills. The suggestions that follow will give you specific ideas for helping primary readers tell the difference between what is make-believe and what is real in the stories they enjoy. Then, because it plays a significant role in quest stories read by students in the intermediate grades, the topic of theme will be the focus of the lesson for these learners.

Primary Lesson Plan: Distinguishing Between "Real" and "Make-Believe" Stories

Purpose:

To begin the study of modern fantasy with young students by helping them identify the characteristics of stories that are "real" compared to those that are "make-believe." This mini-lesson can be repeated throughout the year with different stories to strengthen students' understanding.

Materials/Preparation:

◆ A large piece of paper to make a chart with the headings "Real Stories" and "Make-Believe Stories" (see following page)

◆ One "real" and one "make-believe" story

Mini-Lesson:

1. Post the chart near your meeting place and ask students to share their prior knowledge about the differences between real and make-believe stories.

2. Read aloud and discuss a "real" story, focusing on the "real" elements.

3. List the "real" elements that you and your students identified in the book.

4. Read aloud and discuss a "make-believe" story, focusing on the "make-believe" elements.

5. List the "make-believe" elements that you and your students discovered in the book.

6. Before independent reading, give each student a sticky note. Ask them to label the book they are reading as either "real" or "make-believe." During sharing time, invite students to share their books, the label, and the characteristics they used to identify the type of book.

REAL books have...
- people acting like people
- animals acting like animals
- real places
- events that can happen in real life

REALISTIC FICTION

MAKE BELIEVE books have...
- talking animals
- animals wearing clothes
- animals doing people things
- magic events

FANTASY

A chart created to explore the differences between real and make-believe stories.

"Real" Stories	"Make-Believe" Stories
Henry and Mudge in Puddle Trouble (Rylant, 1987)	Franklin and the Thunderstorm (Bourgeois, 1998)
I Love You the Purplest (Joosse, 1996)	Koala Lou (Fox, 1988)
First Day Jitters (Danneberg, 2000)	Never Spit on Your Shoes (Cazet, 1990)
Ira Sleeps Over (Waber, 1972)	Owen (Henkes, 1993)
We Are Best Friends (Aliki, 1982)	George and Martha (Marshall, 1972)
Peter's Chair (Keats, 1967)	Julius, the Baby of the World (Henkes, 1990)

Intermediate Lesson Plan: Thinking About Themes— The Theme Teams

Purpose:

To review the role of the theme in a story and help students discover that it is an essential ingredient in any story worth reading. Begin by reviewing the meaning of theme as explained in Chapter 1. Remind students of these key aspects of theme:

♦ The theme is not to be confused with the moral of a story.

♦ To discover the theme of a story we ask the question, "What does it all mean?" (Lukens, 2007).

♦ Readers can detect the theme if they look for the main idea or the underlying significance below the surface of the story.

♦ Themes deal with big ideas, rather than details.

♦ We all take different messages away from what we read. There is not just one "right" theme per story.

As students work in small groups or "theme teams," they will hone their knowledge of themes and strengthen their discussion skills. When discussions revolve around themes, readers must think critically and be prepared to defend their choices.

Materials/Preparation:

♦ Prepare a chart of "Types of Themes" to have as a handy resource. (See page 112.)

♦ Prepare a copy of "Thinking About Themes" (page 111) for each theme team and one for the overhead projector.

♦ Select a literary folktale picture book.

♦ Provide sets of modern fantasy books for small groups.

Mini-Lesson:

1. To model what you would like your students to do in their theme team, read aloud a literary folktale picture book. Themes in this format of fantasy are relatively easy to pinpoint since they reflect the genre of traditional literature. Commonly occurring themes include these:
   • good can usually conquer evil
   • hate, greed, or fear can be overcome with love and generosity
   • happiness can be achieved through tenacity, courage, and sacrifice
   • the small can overcome the domineering with wit and patience

Theme Team Members _____ Book Title _____

Thinking About Themes
What do I think the author's purpose was in writing this story? Why?
What are the big ideas behind this story? Give examples.
Does this book emphasize a universal truth? Explain.
Did this book take a reflective look at society, human nature, or the human condition? Give examples.
Have I gained any insight into people and how they think and feel? Explain.
Is there a topic covered here that I found to be worthy of my attention? Could that be considered a theme? Give examples.
Are there symbols or metaphors used throughout the story that will help me identify the theme?

2. After reading, work with your students to complete "Thinking About Themes" on the overhead.

3. Students will now work together in their theme teams to read a modern fantasy book, discuss it, complete the "Thinking About Themes" activity, and share their learning with the class. Once they have discovered the theme, suggest that students express it in a complete sentence rather than just a word or two. For example, after reading *Charlotte's Web* (White, 1952), a reader might explain that friendship adds richness to everyone's life versus just saying the theme is friendship. Friendship is a topic that is discussed in the book, but by expanding upon it, you turn it into a theme.

Types of Themes	
Explicit Theme	Author states the theme in the text; is easy to locate and to find supporting sentences.
Primary Theme	Theme is strongly suggested. Readers "discover" the theme as they fit pieces of the story together.
Secondary Themes	These themes are more personal, depending on the backgrounds and experiences of the different readers.

The Writing Connection

Powerful lessons occur when hardworking teachers connect their reading and writing instruction. As we collected lessons for this book, we strived to make these connections as often as possible. For example, the lesson in The Reading Connection section for primary students was designed to help young readers distinguish between "real" and "make-believe" books. Once students understand the elements of "make-believe" books, it just makes sense to guide them in writing a make-believe story.

Primary Lesson Plan: Writing a "Make-Believe" Story

Purpose:

At the Midwest Literary Festival in Aurora, Illinois (September 2004), children's author Candace Fleming shared her "secret formula," C.L.A.P.S., for writing a make-believe

Literature Is Back!

narrative. This lesson guides young writers as they learn about writing a narrative.

Materials/Preparation:

♦ A chart listing the acronym C.L.A.P.S. down the left edge

Mini-Lesson:

1. Begin, as Candace does, by brainstorming character names on 3" x 5" index cards. Some might include Myron the Alligator, Chelsea the Detective, Katie the Astronaut, etc. Write the names on cards in the pocket chart or make a chart to hang for easy reference.

C.L.A.P.S. chart created during writing workshop.

2. Next, share Candace's secret formula, which she calls "C.L.A.P.S.":
Character
Location
Action
Problem
Solution
You'll remember we used this acronym to compare different versions of the same folktale in Chapter 3.

3. Choose a character name from your collection. Print that character's name on the chart. A group of first graders chose Bubbles the Fish for the chart above. Invite your students to share two words to describe that character's physical features and two other words to describe the character's personality. Then, tell the beginning of the story.

4. Query the students about locations for their story. Candace shared that a key to making a story interesting is choosing a location where the reader would never expect to find the character. So we cannot put Bubbles in a fish bowl, ocean, lake, or stream. The students agreed upon a bowl of soup. Stop once again to orally tell the story. As you continue identifying the different elements of the story, you will tell the story to your students. This oral modeling is so important because it supports students' efforts later as they scribe their own pieces.

5. Decide what your character is doing (the action). In this case, Bubbles was swimming in the soup.

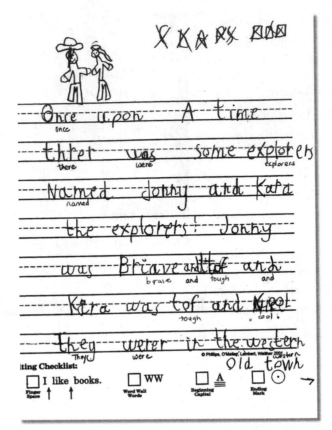

Keith's C.L.A.P.S. story: A first grader creates his own graphic organizer.

6. It is time to move on to the most important element of a narrative, the problem. To select a problem, invite students to share all of their ideas for different problems or goals the character could overcome or achieve. List their ideas on the chalkboard, overhead, or a separate piece of chart paper. Once you have a collection of problems, ask students to vote for the one they want you to use. This part of the lesson is excellent because it gives students many ideas for their own stories.

7. Decide how your character will solve the problem or reach his goal. When Candace explained this portion of her formula, she emphasized that the character should use his traits to solve the problem. Also, the first two attempts at a solution must fail, and the final attempt will work. This idea is helpful for students who have difficulty adding events or details to their narrative writing. Young students have had much success using Candace Fleming's "secret formula." It provides an organizational framework for creating a narrative that is easily understood by budding authors.

Intermediate Lesson Plan: Searching for Superb Leads

Purpose:

Share the following thoughts with students: "One effective way that authors reach out to potential readers is through the first words, sentences, or paragraphs of the story. It is the story's lead that is written to catch your attention, leaving you wanting more. A strong lead raises questions in your mind. It does this so skillfully that you can't resist reading further. The author has thrown out the bait, set the hook, and is deftly reeling you in."

Materials/Preparation:

To show rather than tell students how important a lead is in a story, select four or five novels that begin in an especially inviting manner. If possible, use an ELMO™ to project them on a large screen or make overhead transparencies. Consider the following examples:

Sample 1: Dialogue Lead: *Charlotte's Web* (White, 1952)
"Where's Papa going with that ax?" said Fern to her mother as they were setting the table for breakfast. "Out to the hoghouse," replied Mrs. Arable. "Some pigs were born last night." (p. 1)

Sample 2: "What's Next" Lead: *Riddle in the Mountain* (Burkhard, 2005)
It wasn't the wind that woke Kathy Henley in the middle of the night or the scratching of twigs at the window. With eyes wide and alert, she huddled against the headboard of her bed and pulled the covers close to her chin. She could swear she had heard a voice in the dark. Just a whisper. Calling. (p. 1)

Sample 3: Setting Lead: *Dragon Rider* (Funke, 2004)
All was still in the valley of the dragons. Mist had drifted in from the sea nearby and was clinging to the mountains. Birds twittered uncertainly in the foggy damp, and clouds hid the sun. (p. 1)

Sample 4: Character Lead: *Molly Moon's Incredible Book of Hypnotism* (Byng, 2002)
Molly Moon looked down at her pink, blotchy legs. It wasn't the bathwater that was making them mottled like Spam; they were always that color. And so skinny. Maybe one day, like an ugly duckling turning into a swan, her knock-kneed legs might grow into the most beautiful legs in the world. Some hope. (p. 1)

Mini-Lesson:

1. Closely examine sample leads. Ask the students to make a list of what these leads accomplish. Once they have done so, discuss their observations and make a class chart of their findings. We discovered that superb leads...
   - briefly set the scene
   - convey the tone or mood at the beginning of the book (dreary, worried, angry, excited)
   - raise questions in your mind about what is going to happen next, who this person is, and why he/she is in this situation

2. Instruct students to hunt for leads that they think are exceptionally well done. Have them record the title, author, and effective lead in a specified section of their writer's notebook.

3. Encourage each student to find three or four samples to share with the class. Remind the class that nonfiction leads are as critical as leads in fiction materials, so urge students who spend most of their reading lives in nonfiction materials to bring in selections that work well. Reinforce the fact that as they read, they are using authors as their teachers in the writing process.

4. Spend the first part of writing workshop listening to the sample leads collected by classmates. Ask students to read a favorite example from the book itself rather than from notes. This is a nice way to highlight the book and its author. Leads should be practiced ahead of time so that they are delivered smoothly. After listening carefully, ask students to react to the opening paragraphs they have heard. How do they compare to the leads previously shared in class? Talk together about the impact of each one. Are there pointers to add to the class chart?

5. Now, urge students to practice what they have learned from the authors they have been reading. Return to a piece of writing that is in progress and focus on the opening lines. Conference briefly with individual students as they work on rough drafts of stories or research they are writing, reinforcing or redirecting their efforts to develop a strong lead.

6. Together, students can begin developing a classroom resource for compelling leads. Once they have had an effective example approved by the teacher, leads could be posted in a designated folder on the desktop of the classroom computer or added to a bulletin board in the writing center.

Four Fine Web Sites

Tales of Wonder

www.darsie.net/talesofwonder

You'll find this a useful archive of folk- and fairy tales from around the world.

Harry Potter

www.scholastic.com/harrypotter

This engaging site offers a wealth of information about Harry and his world.

The Brian Jacques Home Page

www.redwall.org/dave/jacques.html

The official Web site of Brian Jacques is filled with information, games, and more.

Aesop's Fables

http://AesopFables.com

Click on Fairy Tales to read 127 literary tales by Hans Christian Andersen.

Summary

Modern fantasy has its origins in traditional literature, from folk- and fairy tales to ancient mythology. It is distinguished from that genre because authors of modern fantasy are known. There are a number of different categories of fantasy, including a branch of science fiction with a focus on life and possibilities in future worlds. Using books from this genre invites students to be imaginative, to be creative thinkers, and to come away from some of these stories able to look at life through new eyes. It also has the potential to help its readers focus on previously unimagined possibilities. From animal adventures to thought-provoking quests, modern fantasy can provide utterly enjoyable time to read.

Chapter 5

Contemporary Realistic Fiction

GLANCE IN THE MIRROR, PEEK THROUGH A WINDOW

PART 1 BUILDING BACKGROUND FOR

TEACHING WITH REALISTIC FICTION

Mirrors and Windows

Why is contemporary realistic fiction one of the most popular genres of children's literature? Think back for a moment to your treasured childhood tales. Many of us recall, with a smile, spending time with our favorite characters. Was Margaret in Judy Blume's *Are You There God? It's Me, Margaret* (1970) one of your friends when you were growing up? Did you sympathize with poor Alexander in *Alexander and the Terrible, Horrible, No Good, Very Bad Day* (Viorst, 1972) when you were having a bad day? Over the years, realistic fiction readers have rooted for Little Willy and his sled dog Searchlight in *Stone Fox* (Gardiner, 1980) or joined Ramona Quimby for a chuckle as she grew from a 4-year-old in *Beezus and Ramona* (Cleary, 1955) to a fourth grader in *Ramona's World* (1999). It is easy to see why the lifelike experiences shared between readers and "book friends" draw them back for more of the same, time and time again.

For some children, realistic fiction titles are sought after because the stories act as a mirror that reflects their own life happenings. For others, the books become windows allowing readers to experience ideas, emotions, places, and lives that are new to them. Literature has a way of helping us make sense of our experiences and even lends a hand as we try to figure out the world around us (Eeds & Hudelson, 1995). Realistic fiction is, perhaps, the perfect vehicle for doing just that. Teachers who are diligent "kid watchers," like Miss Malarkey in *Miss Malarkey Leaves No Reader Behind* (Finchler & O'Malley, 2006), continually search to find that "just right" book for their most reluctant reader. For many children this may be a realistic fiction title. To help you in locating appealing selections for your students, we will share important background information about this genre. Join us as we glance into mirrors and open inviting windows to meet the interesting characters and engaging stories that inhabit the realm of realistic fiction.

What Is Realistic Fiction?

The roots of realistic fiction are traced back to great escapades like those found in *The Adventures of Tom Sawyer*, penned by Mark Twain in 1876, and *Treasure Island* (Stevenson, 1883). Memorable characters such as the title characters in *Heidi* (Spyri, 1884), and *Anne of Green Gables* (Montgomery, 1908), and Mary Lennox in *The Secret Garden* (Burnett, 1911) were introduced to readers long ago and are still enjoyed today. Another perennial favorite, Louisa May Alcott's (1868) classic family tale *Little Women*, continues to warm many a heart. Moving from those memorable roots, you might wonder just what are the characteristics of contemporary realistic fiction. Here is a

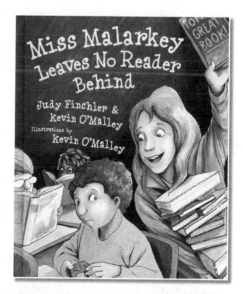

Miss Malarkey strives to find books for her reluctant readers.

quick overview of the characteristics that distinguish contemporary realistic fiction from the other genres we've explored thus far:

- ◆ Characters are multidimensional, realistic people.

- ◆ Contemporary settings are real or believable locations.

- ◆ Plots reflect real-life situations that are important to the reader.

- ◆ Tales are frequently narrated in first person by the main character.

- ◆ Themes reflect important issues in today's society.
  (Anderson, 2006; Galda & Cullinan, 2006)

Realistic Characters

The memorable friends we meet in this genre are real in our imaginations because we are familiar with the events in their lives, including their problems, family situations, and the communities in which they live (Hillman, 1999). The characters in realistic fiction are well-defined people with believable needs, wants, and emotions. That is one of the reasons children, especially intermediate-grade readers, savor these books. They can relate to strong characters such as Brian, as he struggles to survive in the adventure tale *Hatchet* (Paulsen, 1987), or Hollis, as she yearns for a real family to call her own in *Pictures of Hollis Woods* (Giff, 2002). See The Reading Connection section for two lessons exploring characterization.

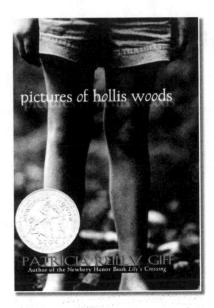

Hollis is a strong, realistic character.

Contemporary Settings

As we highlight realistic fiction titles throughout this chapter, you will quickly see that they are set in contemporary times. In addition, the locations of these stories are places we recognize or those that could possibly exist. For example, Caldecott winner *Smoky Night* (Bunting, 1994) takes place in the midst of the Los Angeles riots, while readers of the novel *Ida B.* (Hannigan, 2004) join this unforgettable character in rural Wisconsin. Talented writers develop realistic settings through the use of sensory images and rich description. They provide their audience with just enough detail about the time and place to connect with the story but avoid lengthy descriptions. This strategy encourages readers to activate their imaginations to fill in the rest (Kasten, Kristo, & McClure, 2005).

> "Contemporary realistic fiction tells a story that never happened but that *could* have happened. The events and characters in contemporary realistic fiction flow from the author's imagination, just as they do in fantasy. Unlike fantasy, however, which includes at least one element not found in this world, everything in contemporary realistic fiction is possible on the planet Earth" (Darigan, Tunnell, & Jacobs, 2002, p. 236).

Plots Contain Real-Life Situations

The scenarios in realistic fiction are as varied as the situations people encounter throughout their lives. Two examples of the real-life situations in this genre that you might find useful in your classroom are stories about characters dealing with death and children who face special challenges. We would like to draw your attention to some noteworthy books on each topic.

Death and Dying

Students often experience the death of a pet. As a result, they can relate to the little boy in *The Tenth Good Thing About Barney* (Viorst, 1995) as he tries to think of the ten best things to remember about his cat. Older readers who are faced with a family member who dies will empathize with 10-year-old Spoon. In *Sun & Spoon* by Kevin Henkes (1997), Spoon observes the changes in his grandfather after his grandmother passes away. The death of a sibling is the topic of Barbara Park's (1995) heart-wrenching novel *Mick Harte Was Here*. Phoebe, Mick's eighth-grade sister, is the narrator of this tale about her family's reaction to her 12-year-old brother's accidental death. The emotions surrounding the death of a friend are explored in *A Taste of Blackberries* (Smith, 1973), a long-popular story. In this book, Jamie's best friend grieves after he dies from an allergic reaction to a bee sting. A welcome addition to the collection of books about death and dying is Pat

Katherine Hannigan set this book in rural Wisconsin.

Brisson's (2006) *I Remember Miss Perry*. This picture book tells the story of Stevie and his classmates, who take turns sharing memories of their teacher after her unexpected death in a car accident. As you can see, there is a wealth of sensitively written titles on this topic, should you need one for a particular student in your classroom.

Special Challenges

Sharing a picture book like *Thank You, Mr. Falker* (Polacco, 1998) can help set the stage for a discussion of different learning styles. Well-written children's books that contain honest stories of individuals with special challenges can help students gain understanding and empathize with their peers who have special needs and challenges (Lynch-Brown & Tomlinson, 2005). In *Be Good to Eddie Lee* (Fleming, 1993), Christy and JimBud learn to see the world in a new way through the eyes of Eddie Lee. He is a young neighbor with Down syndrome who has an eye for beauty.

Books About Children With Special Challenges

Title	Special Challenges Addressed
Joey Pigza Swallowed the Key (Gantos, 1998) (Gr. 5+)	Joey suffers from severe ADHD. This book is part of a series and is written in first-person narrative.
Bluish (Hamilton, 1999) (Gr. 5+)	Natalie Windburn is a new arrival to Dreenie's fifth-grade class. In a wheelchair, a knitted cap covering her head, she both intrigues and frightens her classmates.
Ian's Walk: A Story About Autism (Lears, 1998) (Gr. 1–2)	Julie realizes how much she loves her seemingly troublesome brother when he becomes lost on a trip to the park.
Rules (Lord, 2006) (Gr. 4+)	Twelve-year-old Catherine's younger brother is a child with autism, and she befriends Jason, a nonverbal paraplegic who uses pictures to communicate.
Stranded (Mikaelsen, 1995) (Gr. 4+)	Koby has learned to live with her "leggy" that replaces her right leg from the knee down. She refuses to consider her handicap as she fights to save two stranded whales.
Trout and Me (Shreve, 2002) (Gr. 5+)	Ben's first-person narrative focuses on his fifth-grade year, when he meets Trout. Both Ben and Trout are diagnosed with ADD.

First-Person Narration

In many cases the narrator of a realistic fiction book is the main character. The author uses first-person voice to tell the tale. Books written in first person are helpful teaching tools when modeling how to include voice in a piece of writing. See The Writing Connection for writing workshop mini-lessons on this topic. Many realistic fiction narrators have unique voices. Certainly, Junie B. Jones is an example of a main character written with a distinctive voice. For example, on her first day of school Junie tells her readers, "First grade is not what it's cracked up to be. My room is named Room One. I was nervous when I came here yesterday. That's how come daddy had to carry me all the way to the room. Cause my legs felt like squishy Jell-o" (*Junie B., First Grader (at Last!)* Park, 2001, pp. 5–6). Undoubtedly, many of her faithful fans may have also experienced "squishy Jell-o legs" on their first day. Other characters written with inimitable voices include Amber Brown by Paula Danziger, Joey Pigza by Jack Gantos, and Katie in *The Private Notebooks of Katie Roberts* (Hest, 2005), who updates readers about her life through her journal entries, sketches, and letters to a pen pal.

Not all realistic fiction books are written this way, however. For example, Ann Cameron's (1998) *The Secret Life of Amanda K. Woods* is told in third person as we become familiar with the lives of all the characters through the eyes of the author. In *The Tiger Rising* (DiCamillo, 2002) we learn how two children with their own personal problems form a friendship that helps them face the taunts of classmates and a tiger in the woods. Again, we see inside each child's head and heart because of what the author tells us rather than through a first-person viewpoint.

Let's take a look at some of the memorable characters and thought-provoking stories in this genre. As you browse through the next several pages, think about your students' personalities, interests, and learning needs. We hope you discover a title or two that might touch a child or help you teach an essential literacy understanding. In addition, we know you will find a host of books to add to your read-aloud collection.

Realistic Fiction: Types, Titles, and Teaching Ideas

Gifted writers of realistic fiction are able to weave any number of topics into a book. For example, in Katherine Hannigan's *Ida B.* (2004), the protagonist is a fourth grader who enjoys her days on a rural apple orchard in Wisconsin. With her beloved trees for friends, Ida lives life to the fullest. But her situation changes dramatically when her mother develops cancer and she has to go to school instead of being homeschooled. This is a story of family, growing up, nature, and school. *Ida B.* is just one example of why it is difficult to place books into neat, clear-cut categories. To assist you in choosing books to enhance your literacy instruction, we have divided realistic fiction books into the categories we find are the most requested in elementary classrooms.

Stories of Friendship and Growing Up

Topics such as making friends, getting along with others, and resolving conflicts are always relevant to the lives of young readers. Selecting an appropriate book can help set the stage for a meaningful class discussion. Many of us choose to begin our school year by reading books about friendship. This helps create a caring classroom environment where *all* children feel valued and accepted.

As is evident in the sampling of books below, friendship is a multifaceted topic. Next, we will take a moment to discuss some books that deal with the dynamics of peer relationships and investigate books that highlight intergenerational friendships.

Crossing Jordan is sure to spark conversation.

Dynamics of Peer Relationships

Understanding the dynamics of peer relationships is a challenging aspect of growing up. Throughout life children must learn how to react to peer pressure, deal with bullies, accept others who are different, and part with friends at one time or another. A well-crafted piece of fiction allows children to do what they are unable to do in real life: experience relationships from the perspective of more than one character (T. M. & Yokota, 2002). Authors of realistic fiction address these topics at various levels.

There are, of course, some classic friendship tales too good to be missed. One of the best known is Katherine Paterson's (1977) *Bridge to Terabithia*. Paterson is at her best when she tells this story about two 10-year-olds, Jess and Leslie, who are from different backgrounds but share a sense of isolation from their families. Jess and Leslie find solace and friendship in their secret place named Terabithia. You'll want to have your tissues ready when you read this one! Then, Wanda Petronski overcomes the cruelty of peer prejudice in *The Hundred Dresses* (Estes, 1944). She is teased by Maddie and Peggy for wearing the same faded blue dress every day, even though she claims to have 100 dresses at home. After Wanda's family moves away because of the prejudices they face, Wanda mails the girls a drawing of each of them in one of the hundred dresses she has designed. For younger readers, the picture book *Rosie and Michael* (Viorst, 1974) hits home when two friends tell what they like about each other—even the bad things.

If peer pressure is an issue that your intermediate-grade students are facing, consider sharing a novel such as *Wringer* by Jerry Spinelli (1997b). This book tells the tale of Palmer LaRue, who is dreading his upcoming tenth birthday. When he turns 10 he will have to be a wringer in his Pennsylvania town's pigeon shoot. The wringers are the young boys who either retrieve the dead birds or snap the neck of those still alive. Palmer only shares

Stories of Friendship and Growing Up

Book Title	Summary and Discussion Ideas
Beany and the Meany (Wojciechowski, 2005) (Gr. 2–4)	When Beany's best friend decides to work on the upcoming science project with the new girl in class, Beany is teamed up with Kevin, the class bully. **Discussion topics:** bullying, cooperation
A Box of Friends (Ryan, 2003) (Gr. K–2)	Annie moves to a new town and misses her old pals. Her grandmother helps her create a "box of friends" filled with objects that remind her of her former playmates. **Discussion topic:** favorite memories of times spent with friends **Teaching idea:** If a student is moving away, invite each child to contribute one item to a "box of friends" for their classmate.
Crossing Jordan (Fogelin, 2000) (Gr. 5+)	Twelve-year-old Cass befriends her new neighbor Jemmie, who is African American. The girls love to run and become instant pals, but Cass has to hide her friendship from her racist father. **Discussion topics:** racism, civil rights
Each Little Bird That Sings (Wiles, 2005) (Gr. 4+)	Learning to handle what life throws your way and not giving up are 10-year-old Comfort's tasks. **Discussion topics:** death of family members, loss of a friendship, coping with troublesome peers
Pinky and Rex and the Bully (Howe, 1996) (Gr. 1–2)	A bully picks on Pinky because he thinks his nickname and favorite color are "girlish." **Discussion topics:** respecting one another, resolving conflicts in a nonviolent manner
The Recess Queen (O'Neill, 2002) (Gr. K–1)	Mean Jean is the biggest bully on the playground until tiny Katie Sue challenges her status and invites Mean Jean to play with her. **Discussion topic:** dealing with bullies
Safe at Home (Robinson, 2006) (Gr. 3–5)	After the death of his father, Elijah Breeze (aka, Jumper), a 10-year-old African American boy, moves back to Harlem with his mother, attends a baseball camp, and tries to make new friends and adapt to urban ways. **Discussion topic:** welcoming a new friend

his true feelings with his secret friend, Dorothy, who is unpopular and the butt of his gang's cruel jokes. Another fourth-grade character dealing with peer pressure is Keely, whose bossy friend Stef is cruel to Anya because she is wearing a wig. What Keely, Stef, and her classmates don't understand is that Anya has alopecia areata, a disease that causes people to lose their hair. Margaret Peterson Haddix's *Because of Anya* (2002) is a heart-tugging story of overcoming peer pressure and accepting others.

Because of Anya is a story about overcoming peer pressure and accepting others.

Often during the school year, classmates come and go. It is sometimes difficult for children to say good-bye to a friend who is leaving or moving away. Children handle this separation in many different ways. In Bernard Waber's (1988) picture book *Ira Says Goodbye,* after hearing that Reggie is moving, Ira recalls all the fun times they've had together. Later, when Reggie shares his excitement at moving to the city, Ira thinks about all the things Reggie does to bug him. A similar scenario occurs in *Best Friends* (Kellogg, 1986a), when Kathy feels lonely and betrayed because her best friend is going off to summer camp.

For second or third graders in this situation, try *Mallory on the Move* (Friedman, 2004b), in which 8-year-old Mallory moves three hours away from her best friend, Mary Ann. Mallory makes a pinky promise that she will not play with the new boy next door. Even though she resists, Mallory finds a friend in Andrew and has to learn how to balance the relationships with her new friend and her old friend. Another title to sample is *Amber Brown Is Not a Crayon* (Danziger, 1994). In third grade, Amber's best friend, Justin Daniels, is moving away. This transitional chapter book is written in Amber's spunky voice. We learn that she and Justin have been a "great team" since preschool. But, when he decides to throw out the chewing gum ball they've collected together, she resolves never to speak to him again. Amber's mother helps her to see that Justin is protecting himself from the sadness he feels, and Amber works to repair their friendship. Helping children develop positive peer relationships is one of our many roles as a classroom teacher. Adding stories to your read-aloud fare that are peopled with characters who are also honing these skills leads to meaningful discussions and possible teaching opportunities.

Intergenerational Friendships

Not only are children learning how to get along with their peers, but it is also important that they learn how to interact with older adults. There are many tales that show strong intergenerational relationships. Wilfrid Gordon McDonald Partridge, the main character in Mem Fox's (1984) picture book of the same name, befriends Miss Nancy, who is losing her memory. After searching for the answer to the question "What is a memory?" Wilfrid decides to collect of basket of things to help Miss Nancy remember. *Julio's Magic* by Arthur Dorros (2005) is another tale of intergenerational friendship, this time set in a Mexican village before a wood-carving contest. In *The Goat Lady* (Bregoli, 2004), two children befriend an elderly neighbor and are able to look beyond her rundown house, unruly pets, odd clothes, and eccentric ways to see her humble and charitable nature. For second-through fourth-grade readers, consider *The Stray* (King-Smith, 1996), about Henrietta Hickathrift, who, on her 75th birthday, runs away from the old-age home. She finds herself lonely and nearly penniless on the beach until a family of children rescues her. The relationships that are found in books such as these provide students with memorable examples of friendships across the ages. We know from life experience that the dynamics of friendship are ever changing. As a result, each new friend we meet adds another dimension to our lives. Realistic fiction offers students the opportunity to step back and observe as relationships develop, conflicts occur, and characters work through the real-life challenges of being a good friend.

School Stories

Children spend hours and hours together at school. They make friends and learn how to deal with bullies. They experience different teachers, homework, field trips, and tests. The ideas for school stories go on and on. Realistic fiction writers have capitalized on this wealth of story material and have written school tales for readers of all ages. Young children will giggle at David's antics in *David Goes to School* (Shannon, 1999) and relate to Annabelle's fears and feelings in *Annabelle Swift, Kindergartener* (Schwartz, 1988). Older readers will enjoy school stories by Andrew Clements. Consider *The Landry News* (1999), about fifth grader Clara Landry, who exercises her freedom of speech when she writes an editorial about a formerly creative teacher who has burned out to the point of merely passing out worksheets to students. Another Clements favorite is *Frindle* (1996), in which fifth grader Nicholas Allen, prompted by his teacher's love for the dictionary, invents a new word for a pencil—a "frindle." The first stories you read aloud to your class help set the stage for a year of learning together. As you gather your students around you for the first time, you may choose to read a book about the first day of school.

Along with reading stories set in classrooms, encourage students to write about their school experiences. There are numerous topics to suggest, such as describing a first-day

Have You Read These?

A FEW OF OUR FAVORITE REALISTIC FICTION BOOKS FOR THE FIRST DAYS OF SCHOOL

- *First Day Jitters* (Danneberg, 2000). (Available in Spanish, translated by Teresa Mlawer.) Throughout this clever picture book, the reader is led to believe that the main character is a nervous child on the first day of school, but it turns out to be the teacher.

- *Get Ready for Second Grade, Amber Brown* (Danziger, 2002). Amber is nervous about starting second grade with a new teacher and about being in the same class as mean Hannah Burton.

- *Back to School, Mallory* (Friedman, 2004a). In this transitional chapter book, third grader Mallory struggles to adjust to her new school. This is the sequel to *Mallory on the Move*.

- *Mr. Ouchy's First Day* (Hennessy, 2006). Mr. Ouchy is nervous, excited, and worried about his first day of school with primary-grade children.

- *The Upside Down Boy* (Herrera, 2000). Based on the author's experiences in third grade, this book is an upbeat look at a Hispanic boy's adjustment to an Anglo school.

- *The Color of Home* (Hoffman, 2002). Hassan, a recent immigrant from Somalia, is homesick on his first day of school. He communicates this by painting pictures that tell the story of his old life and his hope for a bright future.

- *Herbie Jones* (Kline, 1985). Herbie Jones and his friend Raymond are up for third-grade challenges, meeting them with their own amusing brand of problem solving. For readers who like Herbie, there are additional titles to enjoy.

- *First Day in Grapes* (Perez, 2002). (Also available in Spanish, translated by Jesse A. Perez.) Chico and his family are migrant workers in California, which makes starting third grade in another new school a challenge.

- *My Name Is Yoon* (Recorvits, 2003). This moving picture book depicts a Korean girl's adjustment to her new school and new country.

- *First Grade Stinks* (Rodman, 2006). Haley has fond memories of kindergarten and discovers the routines of first grade are not quite as fun. Luckily, Ms. Gray helps her see that first grade is great!

- *Elizabeti's School* (Stuve-Bodeen, 2002). Set in a Tanzanian village, this picture book shares a girl's mixed feelings about her first day of school.

memory or school moment, complete with sensory details. Because children spend so much time in classrooms, reading and writing about school simply makes sense.

Family Stories

The students in your classroom come from different family backgrounds. It is important that we read books that reflect their family situations and living contexts. We are fortunate to have an abundant collection of titles from which to choose. Students who are living in a broken family may be interested in the chapter book *Lucy Rose, Here's the Thing About Me,* written by Katy Kelly (2004). Kelly uses a diary format to tell Lucy's story as she adjusts to her parents' separating, moving away from her dad and her friends, and living with her mother and maternal grandparents in Washington, D.C. Some children in your classroom may have experienced homelessness or encountered homeless people at one time or another. For younger students, Eve Bunting's (1991) *Fly Away Home* tells the story of a homeless boy and his father living in an airport. The brief text is told from the boy's point of view.

Yoon is one of our favorite books for the beginning of the year.

Students who are the middle child will relate to Daisy, who strives for attention in a boisterous African American family in *Squashed in the Middle* (Winthrop, 2005). A unique novel about fifth-grade twins is *Trading Places* by Claudia Mills (2006). Mills uses lively, easy-to-read dialogue to tell Amy and Todd's story from each sibling's perspective. These very different twins must work together on a school project while dealing with the fact that their father has lost his job and things at home are not the same.

Along with stories about parents and siblings, the library shelves are brimming with realistic fiction books that tell intergenerational family stories. Many of your students may be living with older family members, visiting them often, or helping their parents care for their grandparents or other elderly relatives. Situations such as these change the dynamics of a family and, in turn, impact the students in our classroom. It is helpful to have a title or two on hand to offer to a student or share with your class.

It is important that we choose the right books to reach our readers and plan our instruction. We think about what Jeff Wilhelm and Michael Smith (2005) share in their article "Asking the Right Questions: Literate Lives of Boys." Their study reveals that the reason boys choose to read has as much to do with our instruction as it does with our

Must-Read Intergenerational Family Stories	
Title	**Plot Summary**
A Day's Work (Bunting, 1994) (Gr. K–3)	Francisco helps his grandfather get a day job when he first arrives in this country. A lie and his *abuelo's* poor English skills create a problem the twosome must remedy.
The Wednesday Surprise (Bunting, 1996a) (Gr. K–3)	Much to her family's surprise, Anna teaches her grandmother how to read.
Now One Foot, Now the Other (dePaola, 1991) (Gr. 1–3)	When his grandfather has a stroke, Bobby teaches him to walk again.
The Patchwork Quilt (Flournoy, 1985) (Gr. 1–3)	Tayna, her mother, and her grandmother use scraps from the family's old clothing to make a beautiful quilt that tells the story of their family's lives.
Falling Into Place (Greene, 2002) (Gr. 3–6)	Eleven-year-old Margaret struggles to cope with the hassles of a new stepfamily. While visiting her grandmother, she discovers that her Gran is facing similar concerns after moving into a retirement community.
The Hundred Penny Box (Mathis, 1975) (Gr. 1–3)	Michael makes friends with his Great-Great-Aunt Dew and learns about the box in which she keeps one penny for each year of her life.
Annie and the Old One (Miles, 1971) (Gr. 1–3)	This is the story of a Navajo girl and her grandmother. Annie does not want to help her grandmother complete the rug she is weaving until she realizes that aging and death are a part of life.
Henry and Mudge and the Great Grandpas (Rylant, 2005) (Gr. 1–2)	Henry and Mudge visit great-grandpa Bill and his pals at the "great-grandpa house."
Papi's Gift (Stanton, 2007) (Gr. K–2)	Set in Mexico, this picture book highlights the importance of family relationships when a young girl eagerly awaits a birthday gift from her Papi, hoping for his return from California where he is harvesting crops.

choice of books. Boys are more apt to engage in reading when they feel competent and are provided with books that are just right for them. They want to understand the purpose for reading and receive immediate feedback. In addition, boys read for enjoyment from texts that matter in their lives today. They want opportunities to share with others what they've learned or discovered from their reading. To sum it up, "they call for us to laugh and cry with our students, to teach in a way that recognizes both the heart and the mind, and to cast reading as a fundamentally social activity" (p. 788). The realistic fiction titles that follow in the form of adventure and survival tales and mystery stories are among the many tales that appeal to all readers, and specifically to boys.

Tales of Adventure and Survival

In tales of adventure and survival, determined characters endure and often overcome incredible challenges. Whether in real life or in a work of realistic fiction, people who encounter and confront dangers in nature or society need to develop and deepen strength of character (Norton, 2003). Tales such as these are especially appealing to children in the intermediate grades and beyond. When you think of adventure stories, a few titles quickly come to mind. One of the most popular survival stories is *Hatchet* by Gary Paulsen (1987). In this page-turning novel, young readers join 13-year-old Brian, who survives in the wilderness with a hatchet and his keen problem-solving skills. As we've found with all the titles in this chapter, *Hatchet* is not only a survival story, but also a story of a young boy dealing with his parents' divorce. Students who enjoy *Hatchet* will reach for the other books about Brian, including *The River* (1991),

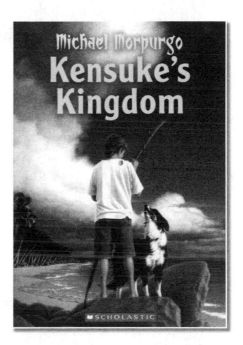

A modern-day Robinson Crusoe.

Brian's Winter (1996), *Brian's Return* (1999), and *Brian's Hunt* (2003). If your students enjoy Paulsen's books, you may want to suggest *Kensuke's Kingdom* (Morpurgo, 1999), about an 11-year-old who is stranded on a hostile jungle island inhabited by an old Japanese soldier named Kensuke. Adventurers may enjoy spending *A Week in the Woods* (Clements, 2002) with Mark. Mark runs away from his teacher, Mr. Maxwell, during an annual weeklong outing in the state park and has to survive alone in the woods.

Fourth graders discuss an adventure tale.

Two adventure tales for second and third graders are *Roxie and the Hooligans* (Naylor, 2006) and *The Several Lives of Orphan Jack* (Ellis, 2003). The main character in *Roxie and the Hooligans*, a beginning chapter book, is Roxie Warbler, who is stranded on an island with four bullies and a couple of nasty thieves. Fortunately, she remembers the survival tips her Uncle Dangerfoot shared and is able to lead the gang to safety. In *The Several Lives of Orphan Jack*, Otherjack, the orphan, runs away from his harsh life in the orphanage and carries a battered dictionary on his many adventures. This story highlights the power of words and ideas. As children peek through windows to experience a thrilling tale of adventure and survival, they witness how writers of this genre effectively employ the literary elements to create suspenseful plots, character-against-nature conflicts, and harsh settings that most of us would rather observe from afar.

Mysteries

A puzzling occurrence sparks a search for clues. The reader quickly turns the pages as suspects are queried and the suspense builds. Fitting the clues together, the inquisitive detective questions, makes inferences, and predicts the outcome page after page. Finally, the mystery is solved and the curious child grabs for another and another. Mystery stories have long tickled the fancy of people of all ages. Many of us enjoyed solving strange incidents with Nancy Drew and the Hardy Boys. Readers today still enjoy spending time with these dedicated young detectives.

The Elements of a Mystery
Puzzling Happening:
The Detective:
The Clues:
The Solution:

Help students solve a mystery with the Elements of a Mystery story chart.

In *Room One: A Mystery or Two,* Andrew Clements (2006) invites children to join 12-year-old Ted, an avid mystery reader, to solve his own mystery when he sees a face in the window of a deserted Nebraska farmhouse. As always, Clements masterfully weaves real issues and real emotions into an inviting read for intermediate students. A mystery of a different sort occurs in *Princess for a Week* (Wright, 2006). Roddy Hall is not happy to find out that his visitor is not a dog named Princess, but a girl named Princess. To make matters worse, Princess is spunky, bossy, and determined to investigate a supposedly haunted house. One of Maria's favorite mysteries to read aloud to her first graders is *Key to the Treasure* by Peggy Parish (1966). This book is part of a series about Liza, Jed, and Bill, three siblings who visit their grandparents every summer and work together to solve a mystery. Much to the delight of Maria and her students, the titles in this series, which were out of print for a while, were reissued in 2005. Kids who love mysteries might get hooked on the series that appear in the following chart. We've included the guided reading level (Fountas & Pinnell, 1999, 2001) and a brief summary for each to help you match your young detectives to appropriate, sure-to-be-favorite mysteries.

Mystery Book Series		
Mystery Series	**Brief Summary**	**Guided Reading Level**
Nate the Great by Marjorie Weinman Sharmat	Nate the Great and his dog Sludge solve mysteries in more than 20 books.	K
Cam Jansen by David Adler	Cam uses her photographic memory to detect clues that help her solve many mysteries. (Also available, Young Cam Jansen)	L
Jigsaw Jones by James Preller	With the help of his Top Secret Detective Journal, an eye for detail, and his partner, Mila, Jigsaw cracks cases in book after book.	M
Meg MacKintosh by Lucinda Landon	Readers are encouraged to join Meg in detecting as they work through the clue-filled black-and-white sketches and a series of questions.	O
Encyclopedia Brown by Donald and Rose Sobol	Ten-year-old Leroy Brown helps his father, the police chief of Idaville, solve crimes. Each book contains several short mysteries with the solution in the back.	P
Sammy Keyes by Wendelin Van Draanen	Samantha "Sammy" Keyes is a feisty 13-year-old who solves crimes while living with her grandma in a senior citizens' complex.	T

To help students understand the characteristics of a mystery story, work together to chart each element. Use the sample chart on page 133 to get started.

In addition to the titles we've already explored, the Glance Chart on page 135 highlights additional categories of realistic fiction, including family stories, animal and nature stories, and humorous tales. Use this information as a starting place when looking for titles in these realistic fiction categories.

Literature Is Back!

Additional Realistic Fiction Titles at a Glance

Types of Stories	A Literature Sampling	Research-Supported Literacy Activities
Family Stories	*The Keeper of the Doves* (Byars, 2002) *Anastasia Krupnik* (Lowry, 1979) *Fancy Nancy* (O'Connor, 2006) and *Fancy Nancy and the Posh Puppy* (2007)	To help students understand how authors create memorable characters, work together to compare two diverse characters using an H-chart (see Chapter 1).
Animal and Nature Stories	*The Incredible Journey* (Burnford, 1961) *Stone Fox* (Gardiner, 1980) *A Blue for Beware* (Haas, 1995) *Owls in the Family* (Mowat, 1962) *Shiloh* (Naylor, 1991) *Rascal* (North, 1963)	In animal stories, a human character typically grows or changes as a result of the interaction with the animal (Kasten et al., 2005). After reading aloud an animal tale, discuss the changes in the main character.
Humorous Stories	*Everything on a Waffle* (Horvath, 2001) *Stink and the Incredible Super-Galactic Jawbreaker* (McDonald, 2006) *Soup* (Peck, 1974) *How to Eat Fried Worms* (Rockwell, 1973)	Invite students to retell and write about a humorous life experience. Begin by having students tell their experience orally to a partner. Next, ask them to write their retelling using the same details and excitement they used when sharing it aloud.

Why Is Realistic Fiction Important to My Students?

Realistic fiction offers readers a place to meet characters their own age with similar interests and challenges. Enjoying books such as these extends a child's range of life experiences. Through reading, students can safely explore human relationships and different parts of the world (Hillman, 1999). As they explore they may...

♦ come to feel that they are not alone, that their problems and desires are not unique

♦ broaden their interests and experience new adventures

♦ discover different ways to deal with conflict in their own lives

♦ learn to reflect on their life choices

♦ develop empathy for others

♦ take a humorous, enjoyable look at life
(Norton, 2003; Temple et al., 2006)

We know that the key to enticing many readers is finding a book that matches their interests and provides enough challenge to nudge them along as they broaden their literacy understandings. In addition, we want to select the best books to help teach our students the content of our literacy curriculum. To assist you in choosing titles that match your students' interests and your curriculum, we've included an evaluation checklist on page 137. Consider getting together with some colleagues and dividing up the task of reviewing books. Or better yet, suggest to your administrator that each faculty meeting begin with a short book talk by a teacher. The world of children's literature is too huge to try to explore on your own!

Censorship Issues

We know that in order to help our students develop critical thinking skills, we must expose them to a broad range of reading materials from different perspectives. Because realistic fiction titles mirror real-life situations, issues of censorship often center around this genre. The first step to educating yourself about censorship issues is to ask your school librarian if your school has a selection policy. Also, inquire about how you are expected to deal with a demand for censorship. We've included guidelines (page 138) to help you in carefully choosing books for classroom use and resources to explore further if you are faced with a censorship issue.

Guidelines for Selecting Quality Realistic Fiction

Evaluating the content	Yes	No	Somewhat
Is the topic age-appropriate for your students?			
Does the story satisfy children's basic needs and provide them with insights into their own problems and relationships?			
Is the content presented honestly?			
Comments:			

Evaluating the plot	Yes	No	Somewhat
Does the book tell a good story that students will enjoy?			
Is the plot credible?			
Comments:			

Evaluating the characters	Yes	No	Somewhat
Are the characters convincing?			
Does the author avoid stereotyping?			
Comments:			

Evaluating the theme	Yes	No	Somewhat
Does the theme emerge naturally from the story, rather than being stated too obviously?			
Is the theme worth imparting to children?			
Comments:			

Evaluating the tone	Yes	No	Somewhat
Does the author write in a hopeful tone? Does the story communicate in an honest way that there is hope in this world?			
Does the author avoid didacticism? Does the story encourage readers to draw their own conclusions from the evidence? Does the author respect the reader's intelligence?			
Comments:			

(Anderson, 2006, p. 204; Norton, 2003)

Guidelines for Carefully Selecting Books

♦ *Read the book.* Don't rely on a colleague's opinion or the reviews of the book to determine whether it is appropriate for your students.

♦ *Know your school's material selection policies.* Ensure that the book meets normal literary selection criteria for your school or district.

♦ *Determine the author's viewpoint.* Carefully weigh the positive influences against exposing students to a theme that some people may perceive negatively.

♦ *Know and be able to explain your rationale for using the particular book.* What is the contribution this book will make to the education of your readers?

♦ *Review and be able to discuss both sides of the selection vs. censorship issue.* The following online resources are available to assist you in understanding this issue.

www.ala.org
The American Library Association Web site includes a section on intellectual freedom in its professional tools where you will find a host of resources regarding censorship issues.

www.ncte.org/about/issues/censorship
The National Council of Teachers of English site has an anti-censorship center, including guidelines for selection of materials in English language arts programs and Rationales for Teaching Challenged Books.

Endings and Beginnings

A window is opened, inviting us to reconnect with some favorite book friends and meet a group of new characters. As you read the titles in the realm of realistic fiction, you may have seen a glimpse of yourself or one of your students in a character or two. The universal appeal of realistic fiction makes it a popular genre with children and adults alike. Capitalize on students' interest during your reading and writing lessons. Choose titles such as the selections featured in the following mini-lessons to boost your students' literacy learning.

The Reading Connection

Realistic fiction provides perfect fare for examining characters. Good readers are able to focus on the protagonist and notice how his or her personality traits often direct the action of the story. This is precisely the type of reader we want to develop. The following lessons focus on character in both primary and intermediate grades.

Primary Lesson Plan: Mapping Character Traits

Purpose:

Using realistic fiction to examine characters and personality traits

Materials/Preparation:

- A large piece of chart paper to make a character map
- A collection of books featuring characters with distinct, observable traits; here are some suggested titles:

  Picture books:
  Pinky and Rex (Howe, 1990) (first book in series)
  Insects Are My Life (McDonald, 1995)
  No, David! (Shannon, 1998)

  Chapter books:
  Ruby Lu, Brave and True (Look, 2004)
  Judy Moody (McDonald, 2000) (first book in series)

Mini-Lesson:

1. Read a portion of the text to or with your students.

2. Invite them to tell you things they have learned about the main character. (Note: Students may begin to tell you about things the character "does." Try to focus their attention on what the character *always* does to understand her character traits.)

3. Add their thoughts to the character map (see example, page 140).

4. Continue reading and adding ideas to the map.

5. Discuss how students can use what they know about that character to help them read other books with the same character or connect that character to a different character in another book.

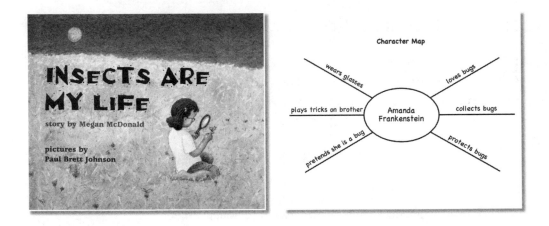

Intermediate Lesson Plan: Character Perspective Charts

Purpose:

Once a reader is absorbed in a story, it doesn't take long to understand how a main character thinks and what his or her perspective on problems to be solved might be. An excellent way to delve more deeply into character development, however, is to look at the events in a story from another character's perspective. Studying the events from diverse points of view is an excellent exercise in creative thinking, as well. As readers compare and contrast two points of view, they are also remembering pertinent details, developing vocabulary, drawing inferences and conclusions, and analyzing goals and actions (Farris, Fuhler, & Walther, 2004). The reading experience is richer because of this deepened thinking.

A tool to use to facilitate the investigation of point of view is A Character Perspective Chart (Shanahan & Shanahan, 1997). We've included a blank chart (page 142) to use with your students. It originated from the popular story map, a graphic organizer that is often used to provide an overview of a recently read story. In its new form, the CPC focuses the reader's attention on two characters in a story and the ways in which the two may perceive the events and outcomes of their book experiences. The surprise for the reader is that the characters don't always see things the same way.

Materials/Preparation:

♦ Blank A Character Perspective Charts

♦ Exceptional titles for charting character perspective:

The Penderwicks (Birdsall, 2005) (Gr. 4–7)
A Week in the Woods (Clements, 2002) (Gr. 4–6)
Ruby Holler (Creech, 2002) (Gr. 4–6)
From the Mixed-up Files of Mrs. Basil E. Frankweiler (Konigsburg, 1967) (Gr. 4–6)
Drita, My Homegirl (Lombard, 2006) (Gr. 4–5)
Moon Runner (Marsden, 2005) (Gr. 3–5)
Holes (Sachar, 1998) (Gr. 4–6)
Amber Was Brave, Essie Was Smart (Williams, 2001) (Gr. 2–5)
Ribbons (Yep, 1996) (Gr. 4–8)

Mini-Lesson:

1. Using a sample on an overhead or the classroom ELMO™, model the thinking that goes into examining perspective using A Character Perspective Chart. Demonstrate with a picture book, a short story, or a novel that you have read aloud to the class. In this way, students will be familiar enough with the characters to participate in the completion of the second column with you. The following demonstration lesson (page 143) is based on the novel *The Same Stuff as Stars* by Katherine Paterson (2002).

2. Pick two characters to discuss. One must be the main character. In this case, it will be Angel Morgan, the main character, and Great-Grandma.

3. Work through the first column of the chart with the class, modeling your thinking. To keep your students actively involved, ask for their input as you frame your thoughts.

4. Next, work through the second column, this time filling in the sections from the perspective of the second character. Once done, examine the results together. Discuss why responses may differ depending on the character in question.

5. Wrap up the activity by discussing the importance of looking at a story from different perspectives. Invite students to complete A Character Perspective Chart for the next story or novel they finish. Set aside a few minutes during an appropriate class period to have students share their completed charts and make their critical thinking visible. See the completed chart for Paterson's *The Same Stuff as Stars* (page 143).

A Character Perspective Chart

Directions: Select two characters from your novel. Complete the chart below. Think carefully about the way a character's perspective can affect the events in the story.

Main character: Who is the main character?	Main character: Select a different important character.
Setting: Where and when does the story take place?	Setting: Where and when does the story take place?
Problem: What is the character's problem?	Problem: What is this character's problem?
Goal: What is the character's goal? What does this character want?	Goal: What is this character's goal? What does this character want?
Attempt: What does the character do to solve the problem or to get the goal?	Attempt: What does this character do to solve the problem or to get the goal?
Outcome: What happened as a result of the attempt?	Outcome: What happened as a result of the attempt?
Reaction: How does the character feel about the outcome?	Reaction: How does this character feel about the outcome?
Theme: What point did the author want to make?	Theme: What point did the author want to make?

Adapted from: Shanahan, T., & Shanahan, S. (1997). Character Perspective Charting: Helping Children to Develop a More Complete Conception of Story. *The Reading Teacher, 50*(8), 668–677.

Literature Is Back! © Copyright © 2007 by Carol J. Fuhler and Maria P. Walther, Scholastic Teaching Resources

A Character Perspective Chart

Main character: Who is the main character? *Eleven-year-old Angel Morgan*	Main character: Select a different important character. *Great-Grandma; Angel's father is her grandson*
Setting: Where and when does the story take place? *The time is present day.*	Setting: Where and when does the story take place? *The time is present day.*
Problem: What is the character's problem? *A father who is in jail for robbery and murder, a 7-year-old brother to care for, and a mother who is both self-centered, irresponsible, and an alcoholic. Angel and Bernie have been abandoned at their great-grandmother's ramshackle home.*	Problem: What is this character's problem? *She is reminded of her two sons' criminal pasts, her trouble raising Wayne when he was left with her, and now has the overwhelming task of caring for two children on her meager funds.*
Goal: What is the character's goal? What does this character want? *She does not want to be placed in foster care again. Angel wants her parents to come home and to have as normal a family as possible. She would like to relinquish her role as head of this dysfunctional family.*	Goal: What is this character's goal? What does this character want? *She wants to mend her broken heart because she feels she was a terrible mother, already ruining two generations of Morgans. She'd like to try again with the children whom she comes to love.*
Attempt: What does the character do to solve the problem or to get the goal? *Takes care of Bernie, signs them up for school, makes friends with a mysterious Star Man (actually her Uncle Ray), helps Grandma as much as she can, and tries to get her father to help them. She also wants to learn more about the stars.*	Attempt: What does this character do to solve the problem or to get the goal? *Shares some of her fears with Angel, lets her know she's special, settles some of her differences with an old friend in order to keep Angel, and hopes to see the family reunited.*
Outcome: What happened as a result of the attempt? *Bernie goes to school until Mama takes only him away with her, Uncle Ray dies of cancer, her father escapes from jail but is caught again, and the social worker comes to try to take her away. She fights to stay with Grandma.*	Outcome: What happened as a result of the attempt? *She works through her guilt, sheds tears, acknowledges her love for her son Ray, and lets the children know they can stay with her. Even though she's failed before, she wants to help them.*
Reaction: How does the character feel about the outcome? *Happy to be a family, including her new friends Miss Izzy and Eric. Hopeful that maybe her parents will assume their roles and make their lives work. Glad to be living with Grandma.*	Reaction: How does this character feel about the outcome? *Happy to have family around her again and hopeful that her bad luck has run its course.*
Theme: What point did the author want to make? *Katherine Paterson wanted us to consider what a family is, what it takes to maintain it, and how it can be more than one's nuclear family.*	Theme: What point did the author want to make? *Each person has value despite his/her history and deserves a chance to try again for happiness.*

Adapted from: Shanahan, T., & Shanahan, S. (1997). Character Perspective Charting: Helping Children to Develop a More Complete Conception of Story. *The Reading Teacher, 50*(8), 668–677.

The Writing Connection

In their idea-filled book *Craft Lessons* (1998), Ralph Fletcher and Joanne Portalupi share a mini-lesson for helping young students find their voice in writing. Maria has successfully adapted this lesson to use with her first graders to show them the connection between spoken and written language.

Primary Lesson Plan: Use Your Talking Voice Today!

Purpose:
Young writers need practice finding their voice.

Materials/Preparation:

- Realistic fiction books (first-person perspective)
- Picture books:
  Fly Away Home (Bunting, 1991)
  I'll Fix Anthony (Viorst, 1988)

- Chapter books:
  Amber Brown Is Not a Crayon (Danziger, 1994)
  Junie B. Jones books by Barbara Park
- Chart paper or overhead projector

Mini-Lesson:

1. Begin by saying, "Imagine you are out at recess chatting with your friend. Well, that's what writing is. Writing is talking to your friend on paper. You use your voice but instead of saying the words out loud you let your voice speak on paper. You talk to the reader when you write down words."

2. Say "Let's look to see how authors do this." Read aloud or display an excerpt from one of the books listed above. Encourage students to listen carefully to notice how the author uses the character's talking voice to share the story.

3. Note: "If you listen very carefully you'll notice how it sounds as though the author is talking to us. You can hear her speaking."

4. Continue reading and discussing the author's use of first-person narrative.

5. Model writing down your own conversation. Something like: "Last night I saw a spider crawling across the kitchen floor. I jumped up on the chair and yelled, 'Somebody come and kill this big ugly spider!' And can you believe that by the time someone finally came to my rescue, the big, ugly, hairy spider disappeared?"

6. Before students begin writing workshop, remind them to try to use their talking voice when they are writing words. Encourage them to whisper the words as they are writing them down.

Intermediate Lesson Plan: Voice in Personal Narratives

Purpose:

To teach students to identify first-person point of view in the reading and use it in their writing.

Materials/Preparation:

♦ Novels written using first-person point of view such as the following: *Joey Pigza Swallowed the Key* (Gantos, 1998), *Shiloh* (Naylor, 1991), *Mick Harte Was Here* (Park, 1995), or *Night of the Twisters* (Ruckman, 1986)

Mini-Lesson:

To begin the lesson, remind students that a first-person point of view occurs when the story is told by the main character, using "I." Thus, "I" does the relating of his or her experiences, thoughts, and feelings and of all other occurrences in the story. We get a sense of how that character thinks because everything is related through his or her eyes.

1. Demonstrate the impact voice has on one's writing by asking students to listen while you read excerpts aloud from several of your favorite first-person selections. You might try a paragraph or two from the above sample titles. Then, reach for an encyclopedia and read a short excerpt on a topic of your choice from that. Ask the students to comment on the difference in voice between the examples.

2. Vicki Spandel (2001) suggests that we ask our students to describe the voices they hear in these excerpts. Can they describe the character based upon what he or she is saying? What did the author do to help us hear these different book people?

3. Put a piece of your own writing on an overhead transparency or the classroom ELMO™. Share an amusing or exciting incident that you experienced, writing in the first person. If you are brave, you might generate it right in front of the class. Otherwise, prepare your words ahead of time. Ask students if they can hear your voice clearly.

4. Next, ask the students to look through their writing or response journals, if you use them. Those are prime examples of first-person narratives. They might also think of text messages they zip to friends. Again, this is authentic first-person voice.

5. Now, it's time for them to write. To avoid the "I don't know what to write" dilemma, brainstorm a list of ideas and topics on the overhead, ELMO™, or whiteboard that will motivate them to write a first-person narrative. Students are to choose one and get started on a rough draft.

6. Follow the Writers Workshop format of drafting, peer editing, revising, and publishing, if that is common practice in your classroom. Finally, consider how you will highlight this celebration of voices.

Four Fine Web Sites

Avi

www.avi-writer.com

This site consists of a brief description of each of Avi's books. In the Info for Teachers section, you will find Avi's Five Secrets to Good Writing!

The World of Beverly Cleary

www.beverlycleary.com

Beverly's colorful site contains a neighborhood map, characters page, book summaries, trivia quizzes, and an author biography.

Megan McDonald

www.meganmcdonald.net

You and your students will meet Megan McDonald, learn the ten things you didn't know about her, and tour her studio. Of course, a synopsis of all of Megan's books is also posted.

Sharon Creech

www.sharoncreech.com

The Web site includes a summary of each of Sharon's books, the inspiration behind the story, and interesting "tidbits" about the tale.

Summary

Realistic fiction titles are a favorite among young readers because they can easily make connections with the characters' lives, problems, and adventures. This genre contains a wealth of material for sparking interesting class discussions and encouraging meaningful written response to reading. Coupled with this is the fact that the books included in this chapter make engaging read-aloud selections. As you prepare for your next literacy lesson, consider one of these titles. For some of your students it may be a much-needed mirror to see aspects of their own lives reflected in literature. Others may find a window to an adventure they may never experience otherwise, or a view of life from different perspectives. It's up to you to take them on this amazing journey.

Literature Is Back!

Chapter 6

Historical Fiction

PASSPORTS TO ANOTHER TIME AND PLACE

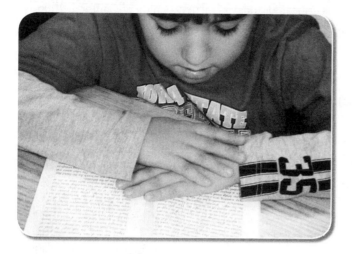

PART 1

BUILDING BACKGROUND FOR
TEACHING WITH HISTORICAL FICTION

Learning About Who We Are by Understanding Where We Have Been

Congratulations! You have received a passport permitting you to do some imaginative travelling. You are entitled to select three different historical periods, pinpoint a specific location within each time frame, and plan a five-day stay. Given the choice, where would you go? Would you sample life in Boston as sentiments whirl toward the Revolutionary War? What about fueling your spirit of adventure as you trundle westward in a covered wagon, hopes fixed on a new life in the Oregon Territory? Perhaps you'll visit the New York docks yearning to meet an Irish ancestor who is determined to begin anew in this land of opportunity. If you're wondering just where to acquire such passports, it's as easy as pulling a book from the shelf. The authorities who thoughtfully grant you the opportunity to travel back in time are the authors of well-written historical fiction. Through their carefully researched, engrossing stories, they open windows into worlds long past. Caught up in them, readers have the opportunity to grasp a sense of what once *was*, doing so from the vantage point of what currently *is*. Because we are who we are based upon past historical events, understanding the implications of those events through a combination of fact and fiction is critical for today's learners (Galda & Cullinan, 2006; Hillman, 2002). When you want to show your students why understanding history is truly vital, historical fiction in the form of picture books and novels can lead the way.

What Is Historical Fiction?

Historical fiction includes stories about people, places, and events set in a world that exists in the past. It is actually realistic fiction, but it occurs in a time distanced enough from today's world so as to be considered history. Just how much distance do you need to make a book historical? Tomlinson and Lynch-Brown (2002) suggest that at least a generation should separate current times from the setting in a reading selection. One appealing example is *Coming on Home Soon* (Woodson, 2004). Set during World War II, it recounts a young girl's anticipation as she waits for her mother to return after leaving home in search of a job. The realistic illustrations bring that particular time period to life.

Stories in this genre span the ages, however. Some are set in a medieval world, like the second book in Avi's Crispin trilogy (2006), *Crispin: At the Edge of the World.* Moving forward in time, another title spotlights disastrous interactions like those between

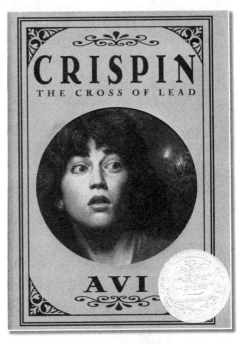

Avi's Crispin trilogy is set in the medieval world.

Have You Read These?

A FEW OF OUR FAVORITE HISTORICAL FICTION TITLES

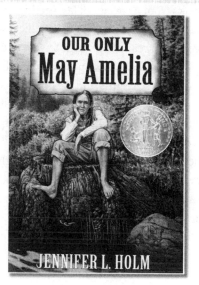

- *Across the Blue Pacific: A World War II Story* (Borden, 2006) (Gr. 2–5) Molly offers a first-person viewpoint of her life during the war.

- *The Watsons Go to Birmingham—1963* (Curtis, 1995). (Gr. 5–8) The Watsons of Flint, Michigan, travel to Birmingham, Alabama, and experience one of the bleakest periods in American history.

- *The Boy Who Saved Cleveland: Based on a True Story* (Giblin, 2006) (Gr. 3–6) Seth lives in a cabin in Cleveland in 1798.

- *Willow Run* (Giff, 2005b) (Gr. 4–7) Eleven-year-old Meggie, who was introduced in *Lily's Crossing* (1997), shares her point of view of the impact World War II had on the people here at home.

- *Our Only May Amelia* (Holm, 1999) (Gr. 5–7) In Washington State in 1899, May Amelia tells her story in first-person narrative.

- *A Family Apart* (Nixon, 1987) (Gr. 5–8) Thirteen-year-old Frances Mary disguises herself as a boy in order to be adopted with her brother from the Orphan Train.

- *The Kite Fighters* (Park, 2000) (Gr. 4–7) In 15th century Korea, two brothers help the king prepare for the kite-fighting competition.

- *The Invention of Hugo Cabret* (Selznick, 2007) (Gr. 3–6) Orphaned Hugo offers a look at a slice of life in Paris in 1931.

- *Mailing May* (Tunnell, 1997) (Gr. K–2) In 1914, May's parents send her as a package to visit her grandparents.

- *The Printer* (Uhlberg, 2003) (Gr. 2–4) This story about the printing industry in the 1940s is related by a boy as he tells about his deaf father who worked for a major newspaper.

Columbus and the Taino Indians in 1492 as depicted in *Encounter* (Yolen, 1992). Years spin by and readers can stop to learn about pioneer life on the prairie in *Sarah, Plain and Tall* (MacLachlan, 1985) or move ahead to experience the 1893 World's Columbian Exposition in Chicago when reading *Fair Weather* (Peck, 2001). Armed with the knowledge of what constitutes quality historical fiction, you can direct an inquisitive reader to fine books from a variety of fascinating historical periods.

As is the case with realistic fiction, these stories are not true, yet the people and events are realistic enough to seem possible. Writers want readers to view characters from long ago as believable people with whom they can relate. They meet children and adults who have strengths and weaknesses just as they do. Galda and Cullinan (2006) remind us that historical fiction brings our past to life through stories grounded in fact but infused with vitality through our imaginations. As readers slip back into Colonial America or the Great Depression, they experience life there vicariously. Then, returning to the present, they can contemplate life today in light of what they are beginning to understand about the past. Augmented by reflection and classroom conversations, readers better understand contemporary times and the promise tomorrow brings based upon valuable insights that are rooted in history (Levstick, 1993; Tunnell, 1993). A necessary genre, historical fiction builds background, illuminates past events, and poses possibilities for future problem solving.

How Is Historical Fiction Presented?

There are two basic types of historical fiction and a third that is an inviting blend. In the first type, a purely imaginary character dominates the action while historical facts are cleverly interwoven into the plot. For example, in *The Ballad of Lucy Whipple* (Cushman, 1996), California Morning (Lucy) Whipple's mother moves the family from Massachusetts to the rugged mining camp Lucky Diggins. From the detailed text, readers learn about how people struggled to survive the rough conditions of a typical mining camp during the California Gold Rush. While the story and characters are fictitious, the time and place have been meticulously researched to enable readers to experience this historical period alongside homesick Lucy. The carefully crafted, integral setting informs readers about a colorful era in our country's growth.

In the second type, the story may include actual historical events, mention real people from the time, and unfold in authentic settings. Think of *Johnny Tremain* (Forbes, 1943). Johnny is a fictional apprentice to a silversmith, but the book is peopled with recognizable historical figures like Paul Revere, John Hancock, and Samuel Adams. Readers come to understand why Johnny would decide to fight for the Patriots' cause based upon his

Historical Fiction in a Series Format

Royal Diaries

- *Cleopatra VII: Daughter of the Nile, Egypt, 57 B.C.* (Gregory, 1999) (Ages 9–14)

- *Elizabeth I: Red Rose of the House of Tudor* (Lasky, 2004) (Ages 9–12)

- *Kazunomiya: Prisoner of Heaven, Japan 1858* (Lasky, 1999) (Ages 9–12)

- *Anastasia: The Last Grand Duchess, Russia, 1914* (Meyer, 2000) (Ages 9–14)

Dear America/My America

- *I Thought My Soul Would Rise and Fly* (Hansen, 1997) (Ages 9–12)

- *Joshua's Diary, the Oregon Trail, 1848* (Hermes, 2001) (Ages 7–10)

- *The Diary of Zipporah Feldman, a Jewish Immigrant Girl, New York City, 1903* (Lasky, 1998) (Ages 9–12)

- *All the Stars in the Sky: The Santa Fe Trail Diary of Florrie Mack Ryder* (McDonald, 2003) (Ages 9–12)

- *My Brother's Keeper: Virginia's Civil War Diary (Book 1)* (Osborne, 2000) (Ages 7–10)

interactions with the Committee of Public Safety and the beliefs of the men he has chosen to help. Here, real people and actual events set the stage for a time-tested novel for upper-grade readers.

Finally, the third type of book is a blend of historical fiction and fantasy. Since these titles include time warps that take the main characters back in time, they are most accurately referred to as "historical fantasy." One popular title is Jane Yolen's (1988) *The Devil's Arithmetic*. Another is *A Girl Called Boy* (Hurmence, 1982), about an 11-year-old girl who goes back to 1853 and experiences slavery. As a result, she understands a future conflict that will impact her family. More light-hearted, Jon Sciezka's titles in the Time Warp Trio series include *The Knights of the Kitchen Table* (1991) and *Marco? Polo!* (2006). Willing readers zip to a number of historical periods to problem-solve alongside the amusing main characters. If time travel holds appeal for you and your readers, this slice of historical fiction offers some memorable reading experiences.

More Historical Fiction in a Series Format

The American Girl Books/Girls of Many Lands

- *Saba: Under the Hyena's Foot* (Kurtz, 2003) Set in Ethiopia. (Ages 9–12.)

- *Kathleen: The Celtic Knot, 1937* (Parkinson, 2003) Set in Ireland. (Ages 9–12.)

- *Meet Kaya: An American Girl* (Shaw, 2002) Set in the United States. (Ages 9–12.)

- *Spring Pearl: The Last Flower* (Yep, 2002) Set in China. (Ages 9–12.)

American Adventures

- *Thomas: 1778—Patriots on the Run* (Pryor, 2000b) (Ages 9–12.)

- *Joseph's Choice: 1861* (Pryor, 2000a) (Ages 7–10.)

- *Joseph: 1861—A Rumble of War* (Pryor, 1999) (Ages 7–10.)

A relatively new way to present historical fiction is in a series. A sampling of these options includes Scholastic's Royal Diaries and Dear America series. Titles present eyewitness accounts of numerous events in history through realistic characters. Many readers will recognize the popular American Girl books, which offer six different series that depict the life of a particular girl in a specific period of history. Be aware that quality may vary from title to title in some of the series. Review helpful guidelines using the checklist provided later in the chapter (page 160) to find the strongest offerings.

With the variety that is available in this genre, you will enjoy the quest for appropriate titles for the readers in your classroom. Offerings are plentiful. The best books meet the criteria of well-written historical fiction. As a result, they are crafted with care to provide readers with an understanding of what life might have been like before DVDs, laptops, iPods, skateboards, or jet travel.

Why Is Historical Fiction Important to My Students?

It is easy to support the use of picture books and novels in historical fiction because there are a number of compelling arguments for their inclusion as common reading fare. Historical fiction helps readers:

> "Regardless of the time period, human beings have always shared common needs. The need to stay alive, the need for good health, for sustenance, for security, for approval . . . there is not a reader today who cannot identify with such needs. For any fiction to work, it needs to have at least a toehold in the familiar."
> —Karen Hesse
> (Beck, Nelson-Faulkner, & Pierce, 2000, p. 548)

- ◆ Experience history in such a way that they learn how people in the past suffered, expressed anger and joy, and faced seemingly insurmountable hurdles just as people do today (Huck et al., 2004; Jacobs & Tunnell, 2004).

- ◆ Think as well as feel what it was like to confront difficulties long ago. This happens more frequently when readers are aesthetically involved in a story (Beck et al., 2000; Rosenblatt, 1978).

- ◆ Build critical thinking through conversations during and after reading, when discussing observations, asking questions, and emerging understanding along the way (Harvey & Goudvis, 2000; Lehr, 1995).

- ◆ Extend their learning. Consider the curiosity factor for a minute. If the writer leaves readers wondering just how much of the story is true, he has fired the reader's curiosity and perhaps sent her off to look for more (Lukens, 2007). If she reaches for informational text to quench that curiosity, she is getting a more complete picture of the past in the process (Soalt, 2005).

- ◆ Understand conflicting points of view about a historical event (Huck et al., 2004). For instance, a social studies textbook will only present one viewpoint, while a novel might present an entirely different perspective. Sharing an informational picture book among other materials will add facts to broaden your students' understanding (Soalt, 2005). As readers search and weigh varying opinions, they will be learning to consider different options before drawing their own conclusions.

- ◆ View the human side of history by fleshing out textbook facts through appealing characters that live in historically accurate settings.

Researcher and writer Susan Lehr (1995, page 115) reflects:

"I'd like to think that real encounters with characters in literature help one define oneself and one's relation to others. I know that knowing Anna Karenina as a teenager shaped my thoughts regarding choices. Reading Ayn Rand freed my thinking with regard to systems and institutions. Knowing the Little Engine That Could challenged me to reach for the stars. Johnny Tremain freed me from thinking that girls couldn't be spies or catalysts for revolution, because I *was* Johnny Tremain."

A fifth grader enjoys a historical fiction novel.

Regarding the last point, Mike Tunnell (1993) cites a number of authorities in the fields of reading, literature, and social studies who promote the use of children's literature rather than textbooks to teach history. That text "is better written, provides clearer historical context, offers varying perspectives, and puts 'real people' back into the study of history" (p. 88). Additional research reports that fifth graders recalled more historical facts and reported that they liked social studies better when textbook materials were tied with historical fiction (Smith, Monson, & Dobson, 1992). Doesn't that make sense?

To conclude this strong endorsement of the value of historical fiction, remember that these books are simply good reading. Don't hesitate to offer a stellar title even if for no other reason than that it is engrossing and pleasurable reading.

Historical Fiction: Types, Titles, and Teaching Ideas

Historical fiction is typically divided into relevant eras of history. While they vary a little from authority to authority, the following eras and book titles that reflect them are representative of those you might teach in your elementary classroom. Some time periods will not be directly applicable to your grade level, but they have been included to give a broad overview of the genre and its possibilities. If you like, select those that are tied to social studies content in your classroom. As always, adapt the book suggestions and alter the related reading and writing activities to best meet the needs of the readers in your classroom.

Author Katherine Paterson (1987, p. 227) explains the role of setting in historical fiction, saying that it is vital that the location in which a story occurs is a true one.

"Because place will shape a story, just as place shapes lives in the actual world. The world of the book must be as accurate as the writer can make it, not only because the writer owes this much to history, but also because she owes this much to fiction . . . and to the reader most of all."

Glance Chart

An Overview of Quality Historical Fiction by Historical Era		
Historical Era	**A Literature Sampling**	**Research-Supported Literacy Activities**
Ancient Times Through the Middle Ages	*A Medieval Feast* (Aliki, 1983) *Malu's Wolf* (Craig, 1995) *Illuminations* (Hunt, 1989) *Nzingha: Warrior Queen of Matamba* (McKissack, 2000) *Place in the Sun* (Rubalcaba, 1998)	Build critical thinking skills through comparison and contrast. Using a Venn diagram, compare the life of a main character to lives of children today. Consider what things: • remain constant over time • have made life easier • are not for the better Write a summary paragraph or poem based upon chart information.

An Overview of Quality Historical Fiction by Historical Era

Historical Era	A Literature Sampling	Research-Supported Literacy Activities
Colonial and Revolutionary War Periods	*Sleds on Boston Common* (Bordon, 2000) *By the Sword* (Castrovilla, 2007) *The Courage of Sarah Noble* (Dalgliesh, 1954) *Guests* (Dorris, 1994) *Sarah Bishop* (O'Dell, 1980)	Examine the setting. Take notes, looking at what can be learned about this time and place based upon clues in the illustrations, text, and author's note. Review findings together. Is there more you want to know? Develop individual research projects based upon interest and curiosity.
Westward Expansion	*Pioneer Cat* (Hooks, 2004) *Nothing Here but Stones* (Oswald, 2004) *I Have Heard of a Land* (Thomas, 1998) *Bound for Oregon* (Van Leeuwen, 1994) *Little House in the Big Woods* (Wilder, 1953)	Connect reading and writing by journaling with a classmate. Assume the role of the main character in the book. Discuss time, place, events, and feelings, comparing and contrasting experiences based upon characters' lives. Then, make personal connections by thinking about personal feelings or similar experiences shared with the main character.
Civil War Era	*Charley Skedaddle* (Beatty, 1988) *A Light in the Storm* (Hesse, 2002) *True North* (Lasky, 1996) *A Good Night for Freedom* (Morrow, 2003) *Pink & Say* (Polacco, 1994)	Partner a picture book or novel with a nonfiction title. Work in small groups. Assess what was represented realistically in the novel or picture book and what might have been added to enhance the story based upon information from the nonfiction title. Then, have each child share: "What I once thought" "What I learned" Share as a whole class.

An Overview of Quality Historical Fiction by Historical Era

Historical Era	A Literature Sampling	Research-Supported Literacy Activities
Immigration and Industrialization	*January, 1905* (Boling, 2004) *Miss Bridie Chose a Shovel* (Connor, 2004) *Nory Ryan's Song* (Giff, 2000) *The Potato Man* (McDonald, 1991) *Coolies* (Yin, 2001)	Ask students to bring the past to life through Readers Theater. Work in small groups to prepare original scripts from a favorite title. Strengthen oral fluency through practice and make a polished presentation to the class or in another classroom.
The Great Depression	*Bud, Not Buddy* (Curtis, 1999) *A Letter to Mrs. Roosevelt* (De Young, 1999) *The Truth About Sparrows* (Hale, 2004) *Sky Boys: How They Built the Empire State Building* (Hopkinson, 2006) *Dust for Dinner* (Turner, 1997)	Strengthen response to literature and writing skills. Invite students to write a letter, poem, or another episode based upon one of the books listed or one they have personally chosen. Use the book's author for writing tips. Polish the piece through the workshop process and publish in a class book focused on learning about the Great Depression.
World War II	*Boxes for Katje* (Fleming, 2003) *Lily's Crossing* (Giff, 1997) *I Am David* (Holm, 1963) *The Harmonica* (Johnston, 2004) *Baseball Saved Us* (Mochizuki, 1993)	Teach and model the strategy of inference or reading between the lines to better comprehend a story. Model how you use the skill with a picture book or snippet from a novel read aloud. Work in pairs with picture books to practice the skill. Follow up later in the week by asking students to journal about how they use inference as they read their current novels.

An Overview of Quality Historical Fiction by Historical Era		
Historical Era	**A Literature Sampling**	**Research-Supported Literacy Activities**
Fifties and Sixties	*Brooklyn, Bugsy, and Me* (Bowdish, 2000) *The Wall* (Bunting, 1990) *The Hero of Ticonderoga* (Gauthier, 2001) *Goin' Someplace Special* (McKissack, 2002) *Freedom Summer* (Wiles, 2001)	Reinforce the value of predicting by following the Directed Listening Thinking Activity (Morrow, 1984). Use a picture book to model the cycle: • Introduce the story, looking at the book's cover, title, and several illustrations. Invite predictions. • Listen to confirm or adjust the prediction. • Predict what will happen next. • Listen to confirm or adjust the prediction. Support predictions with evidence. Ask students how this cycle helps them better connect with and comprehend what they read.

Getting the Best of the Books: Evaluating Historical Fiction

When reading historical fiction, pay close attention to the setting. It is typically an *integral setting*. The action, characters, and theme are clearly influenced by the time and place in which the story is set (Huck et al., 2004; Lukens, 2007). If setting is done well, readers can learn a good deal about a time and place, gathering information about such things as transportation, clothing, household items, colloquial speech, children's responsibilities, and so forth.

Use the guidelines on page 160 to locate exceptional titles in historical fiction. Upper-grade students can use an adapted version of this chart to evaluate books they have read. Their completed critiques could be kept in a folder in the reading center for classmates to review when searching for a new book to read.

Using Historical Fiction Picture Books to Provide a Glimpse of the Past

Revolutionary War
The Midnight Ride of Paul Revere (Longfellow, 2001)
The Scarlet Stockings Spy (Noble, 2004)
They Called Her Molly Pitcher (Rockwell, 2002)
Katie's Trunk (Turner, 1992)

Slavery
Under the Quilt of Night (Hopkinson, 2002)
Almost to Freedom (Nelson, 2003)
Aunt Harriet's Underground Railroad in the Sky (Ringgold, 1995)
Follow the Drinking Gourd (Winter, 1989)

Civil War Era
Li'l Dan, the Drummer Boy: A Civil War Story (Bearden, 2003)
The Blue and the Gray (Bunting, 1996b)
The Wagon (Johnston, 1996a)
Cecil's Story (Lyon, 1991)

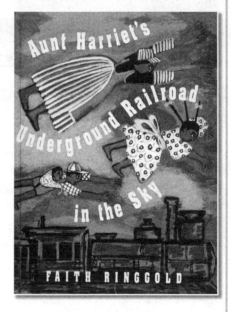

Historical fiction picture books provide a glimpse into the past.

Immigration
How Many Days to America? A Thanksgiving Story (Bunting, 1988)
When Jesse Came Across the Sea (Hest, 1997)
What Zeesie Saw on Delancey Street (Rael, 1996)
Brothers in Hope: The Story of the Lost Boys of Sudan (Williams, 2005a)
The Memory Coat (Woodruff, 1999)

Westward Expansion
Dandelions (Bunting, 1995)
A Packet of Seeds (Hopkinson, 2004)
Sunsets of the West (Johnston, 2002)
Kindle Me a Riddle: A Pioneer Story (Karim, 1999)

Title: _____   **Author:** _____

Guidelines for Selecting Quality Historical Fiction

Title	Author	Classroom Fit?	
Criteria	**Teacher Observations**	**Yes**	**No**
Setting: Accurately detailed and realistic			
Plot: Well developed			
Characters: Believable and well rounded			
Dialogue: Natural, reflects the time period			
Theme: Timely and/or relevant			
Style: Engaging, fits the novel			
Tells a good story that offers insights into values and beliefs from the past			
If present, illustrations extend the story line and reflect realistic details of the times			
Overall appeal and suitability for students			
Informative author's notes			

Adapted from Galda & Cullinan, 2006; Hillman, 2002; Huck et al., 2004

PART 2 LINKING LITERATURE AND LEARNING

The Reading Connection

Connections with the past might begin with picture books (Fuhler, Farris, & Nelson, 2006; Beck et al., 2000). You have read that comprehension is facilitated when there is a base to which new knowledge can be connected (Anderson & Pearson, 1984; Block & Pressley, 2002; Harvey & Goudvis, 2007). Use that knowledge by reading one or two books to examine an issue or to give readers a sense of time and place. Choose titles to build an understanding of historical events that are to be covered in an upcoming unit of study or in a book to be read for a whole-class literature study. Jennifer Soalt (2005) tells us how valuable it is to pair historical fiction with informational texts. When we do, students are building background knowledge and developing pertinent vocabulary. In addition, they are likely to be more motivated to learn about the upcoming topic. Added together, this step improves overall comprehension. It would also be fun and beneficial to read some of the titles aloud, strengthening listening and thinking skills.

Primary Lesson Plan: Creating Mental Images— Visualizing Another Time and Place

Purpose:

In addition to building background knowledge for the historical events that are part of our social studies curriculum, well-written historical fiction picture books are helpful when teaching students how to visualize or make mental images to strengthen their comprehension. Debbie Miller (2002) points out that readers make mental images during and after reading by utilizing their five senses, emotional responses, and their background knowledge.

Materials/Preparation:

+ *Dandelions* (Bunting, 1995) or another favorite historical fiction title
+ Copy of Mental Image Response Sheet (see page 164) for each student in your class

DANDELIONS

Written by
EVE BUNTING

Illustrated by
GREG SHED

Use Eve Bunting's book to help readers visualize the past.

Mini-Lesson

1. Choose a historical fiction picture book that matches your curriculum and your students' learning needs.

2. Read it aloud without displaying illustrations, stopping at key points for students to record mental images on the response sheet.

3. Once students have completed their Mental Image Response Sheet, ask them to share their thoughts, images, and feelings with a partner.

4. The example that follows (page 163) uses the book *Dandelions* by Eve Bunting.

Teacher Modeling Using *Dandelions* (Bunting, 1995)

Teacher: We've been learning about life long ago and how it compares to life today. Many things have changed since people drove west in their covered wagons to begin a new life. Today we are going to read a picture book about one family's journey. While we are reading, we are going to use our mental images to picture what is happening in *Dandelions*.

"It was made of sod, chunks like bricks cut from the ground, and it had one door and one window that Mr. Svenson had bought for $1.25 in town. He kept touching the window as if he couldn't believe it was there" (unpaged).

Teacher: How is the Svenson's home different from yours? Can you visualize what it might look like? Draw a sketch in the first box of your image of the Svensons' home.

"Wagons and mule teams and horses and people filled the street. My ears rang with the noise of voices and the shinnying and braying of the animals" (unpaged).

Teacher: Draw a picture in the second box showing what sounds Zoe and her father heard as they rode into town.

"Oh, the licorice smell that wafted from her breath. It made my mouth water" (unpaged).

Teacher: Imagine what it would have been like to have a candy treat only once in a great while. Draw your image of Zoe's sister's treat in the third box.

After planting the treasured dandelions she brought home for her mom, Zoe looks on the roof and observes, "I'd wanted to see a golden blaze so dazzling it would hurt our eyes. But above us there was only a green stubble with a patch or two of wilted yellow" (unpaged).

Teacher: How would you feel if you went to all the trouble to plant the dandelions and that was how they turned out? Write about or draw your feeling in the last box.

Name _____ Date _____

Mental Image Response Sheet

What do you see?	What do you hear?
What do you smell, taste or touch?	How would you feel?

Intermediate Lesson Plan: Building Comprehension by Promoting Higher-Level Thinking Skills—Using the "Bloom Ball"

Purpose:

This activity encourages students to consider the book they're reading in a variety of ways, striving for higher-level thinking as they complete the steps. You are upping the comprehension ante by moving thinking into the higher levels of Bloom's taxonomy (1956) as students deepen comprehension and review story elements as a part of the process. As the students complete this activity, making a ball out of paper on which they've written a literary critique, emphasize that it isn't enough to just finish each segment of the ball. They must be prepared to discuss their responses with their classmates at some point. Because "publishing" is an important part of sharing a completed project, Bloom Balls should be displayed for classmates to enjoy. Try this at the conclusion of literature circles or after a class study of the historical fiction genre.

Materials/Preparation:

♦ Make a chart titled "Levels of Thinking" to reinforce the fact that readers need to move beyond the first two to be critical thinkers.

♦ For each student, print out 12 circles from a previously prepared file on your computer or collect 12 previously printed circles. It will be easier to work on each circle when it is still on the sheet rather than cutting them out at this point. Use one circle for each of the following activities. (See diagram on page 167.)

Mini-Lesson:

Introduce this activity before the students begin reading their books so they can work on the circles a little at a time, gathering pertinent information along the way. To teach the series of steps, be sure to model them by using a book that the class is familiar with or that you have read and want to share. Use the following directions to guide your readers through the process.

Before Reading:

Circle 1: *Write the title and author of your book. Arrange the lettering in a visually appealing manner. Be attentive to accurate spelling.*

Circle 2: *Use the Internet to research your author. Write down four essential or interesting facts about the author.*

During Reading:

Circle 3: *Draw a picture or make a map of the setting of the story. Write a sentence or two describing the integral setting. Use your writer's eye to make the sentences descriptive.*

Circle 4: *Find and copy two examples of the use of figurative language. Explain the imagery being used by the author. Be ready to tell the class how the author's style enhances an event or the story.*

Circle 5: *List the values, attitudes, beliefs, and/or themes addressed throughout the story.*

After Reading:

Circle 6: *Write a short paragraph describing the main character of the story. Include both physical, emotional, and personality characteristics. Be prepared to discuss with the class how you came to know the character through the author's words.*

Circle 7: *Summarize the plot, including key ideas and important events.*

Circle 8: *Draw a picture of a scene from the story that was particularly significant to you. Be prepared to explain the role that setting played in the story.*

Circle 9: *Write a poem about the story, highlighting a specific part of the plot or describing the main character in a different way.*

Circle 10: *Write a succinct paragraph to explain how this book relates to your life or to life in today's world.*

Circle 11: *Discuss your text-to-self connections to the book. How did you feel immediately after finishing the book? Write a brief explanation.*

Circle 12: *Critique the book. What criteria are you using to make your decisions? Tell why you would or would not recommend this title to a friend.*

Completing the Bloom Ball

Students can decorate the folds using a theme from the book or another design at this point. Next, cut out the circles and fold on the lines, making certain that all of the folds are facing up. Then, begin gluing the circles together. For the most professional looking project, be patient with the gluing process. After you glue several circles together, let them dry for several minutes. Do not try to complete the ball all at once. Finally, be ready to share an overview of the completed ball or select several circles to highlight with your literature circle group or the whole class.

Assessment

Develop a rubric (below) that will pinpoint how adequately each student made personal connections to the book at various levels of Bloom's taxonomy. Then, take effort into account, consider visual appeal, monitor for neatness, and highlight accurate mechanics. In addition, class discussions will indicate each student's ability to explain his or her connections to the particular book that was read.

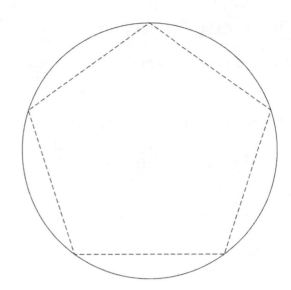

Levels of Thinking (Bloom's Taxonomy)

Evaluate: To judge something against a standard. Key terms: *evaluate, debate, criticize, conclude.*

Synthesize: To create or design something that did not previously exist; to put things together in a new way. Key terms: *invent, combine, create, design.*

Analyze: To break down complex information or ideas into simple parts to see how the parts relate to one another or are organized. Key terms: *classify, outline, diagram.*

Apply: To use learned material to solve novel or real-life situations. Key terms: *construct, change, solve.*

Comprehend: To grasp the meaning of text. Key terms: *translate, interpret, extrapolate.*

Know: To recall information straight from the text. Key terms: *list, match, name.*

The Writing Connection

Primary Lesson Plan: Creating a World With Words

Purpose:

Effective writers can create a distinct world with words. Detailed description helps the reader visualize the setting of a story. To help primary students use descriptive words when writing about a setting, try the following mini-lesson.

Materials/Preparation:

Create a chart with familiar settings, including weather, time, and place (see page 169).

Mini-Lesson

1. Select a combination of a weather word, a time word, and a place. Model how to describe that particular setting using images. (See examples below.)

2. Encourage students' responsibility by creating a description using a shared writing format. Next, divide students into pairs. Provide each pair with a different setting combination. Working with their partners, students write a short description of their setting without using the setting words. For example:

   A sunny afternoon at the beach
   As we lay on our towels we could feel the hot sand on our feet and hear the crash of the waves hitting the shore.

   A stormy night at a haunted house
   The door creaked as we slowly walked into the house. When the lightning flashed, we caught a glimpse of the cobweb-filled rooms.

3. Finally, partners read their descriptions aloud while the rest of the class tries to guess their setting. Students can continue to practice describing settings in their writer's notebook.

Familiar Settings		
Weather Words	**Time Words**	**Places**
sunny	morning	beach
stormy	afternoon	haunted house
windy	evening	circus
rainy	sunrise	zoo
cloudy	sunset	farm
snowy	springtime	playground
misty	autumn	classroom
foggy	winter	city
damp	summertime	forest
chilly	Fourth of July	jungle
frosty		

Intermediate Lesson Plan: Discovering Various Authors' Styles

Purpose:

Take a minute to review the explanation of style in Chapter 1. Remember that when you examine a writer's style, you are typically listening for his or her distinct voice. That voice is heard most clearly when words are cleverly arranged or when rich, colorful language is used. If you are working with the six traits of writing in your classroom, the components of voice and word choice will be your focus because they contribute to one's style.

Materials:

A selection of your favorite novels or picture books that demonstrate an author's distinctive style. Consider these:

♦ *Crispin: At the Edge of the World* (Avi, 2006), novel

♦ *By the Sword* (Castrovilla, 2007), picture book

♦ *Rodzina* (Cushman, 2003), novel

♦ *That Dadblamed Union Cow* (Fletcher, 2007), picture book

♦ *Fair Weather* (Peck, 2001), novel

Mini-Lesson:

1. One of the best ways to appreciate an author's particular style is to read the story aloud (Huck et al., 2004). Before you read personally selected samples of text to the class, review the importance of imagery. Done well, it describes for our senses what is happening or how things look as we read.

2. Display and read through the following questions. Students will use them to gauge the effectiveness of a particular style:
    Does the passage read smoothly?
    If there is dialogue, is it natural?
    How is imagery, including similes, alliteration, onomatopoeia, or repetition, used effectively?
    Do sentences vary in length to add interest?

3. Model the process. Read short passages from several favorites, taking time to show how you would answer the questions.

4. Student application: Students are to find exemplary parts of the book they are reading and read two of them aloud to a classmate. Working in pairs, readers will evaluate and record their observations by using the Investigating Style Checklist (page 171) to think carefully about the style. Share a sampling of the discoveries with the rest of the class to underscore how the wise use of style is essential to crafting memorable writing.

Investigating Style Checklist

Directions: Select a favorite passage from a book you are reading. Examine how the author's style impacts the writing by completing the chart below. Share the results with a classmate.

Criteria	Evaluation and Support
The text reads smoothly.	Example:
The dialogue between characters is natural and believable.	Example:
Sentence length varies to provide a rhythm for the story.	Example:
There is evidence of figurative language that helps the reader visualize elements of the story. Types:	Example:
The vocabulary reflects the time and place accurately.	Example:
Additional observations:	

Literature Is Back! © Copyright: © 2007 by Carol J. Fuhler and Maria P. Walther, Scholastic Teaching Resources

Four Fine Web Sites

4kids.org

www.4kids.org
This is a student-focused site that combines Internet know-how with a weekly newsletter, challenging games, and engaging areas for kids.

National Council for the Social Studies

www.socialstudies.org/resources/notable
Notable Trade Books for Young People is a superb resource that includes fiction and nonfiction titles across the grades. Download and print the lists.

American Library Association's Great Web Sites for Kids

www.ala.org/great websites
Come here to find safe, engaging, student-friendly sites.

Readers Theater Scripts and Plays

www.teachingheart.net/readerstheater.htm
Use the teacher's guides and tips for writing your own Readers Theater scripts to bring history to life in your classroom.

Summary

Historical fiction relates a realistic story about life long ago. It affects its readers on different levels, from providing the simple enjoyment of reading a well-told story to offering insights into the past and promoting fresh perspectives about ways to solve age-old dilemmas. The engaging books in this genre are authored by writers that readers can emulate as they pen their own tales. These titles present opportunities for you to thread literacy skills across the curriculum, as reading, writing, and higher-level thinking are tied to the facts that history affords us. As such, historical fiction needs a home on the shelves and in the hands of learners in our classrooms.

Chapter 7

Nonfiction

IT'S A NECESSITY!

 Non-fiction books are great places too. I especially like books about extraordinary people. Learning about why they are famous is fun. I try to find something that my mom and dad don't know and pass it on to them,

Michael's essay continues . . .

PART 1

BUILDING BACKGROUND FOR TEACHING WITH NONFICTION

Exploring the World of Nonfiction

Animals, space travel, rocks, bugs, plants, famous historical figures, and much, much more. Books that are brimming with information about topics such as these fly off the library shelves. Children are intrigued by the world of nonfiction; the wealth of engaging titles in this genre motivates many students to read and enjoy experiences with books (Kiefer, Hepler, & Hickman, 2007). Nonfiction not only inspires children to pick up a book, it also spurs them on to other titles as they continue their quest for knowledge. As such, "Nonfiction enhances our understanding. It allows us to investigate the real world and inspires us to dig deeper to inquire and better understand" (Harvey, 2002, p. 13). When we examine our literacy habits both inside and outside of school, we discover that much of the reading and writing we do involves informational text. This fact, coupled with the enjoyment students get from such titles, underscores the need to increase the number of nonfiction literacy opportunities in our classrooms. In this chapter, we will explore the ever-expanding world of quality nonfiction titles for elementary-grade students. Join us as we climb mountains, rocket into space, examine the tiniest bugs, meet famous men and women, and learn how a book is made.

What Are Nonfiction Books?

The main purpose of nonfiction books is to inform the reader. In addition, authors of nonfiction aim to engage, inspire, and impel readers to question and then pursue answers. Sally Walker, 2006 Sibert Informational Book Medal winner, shares her aspirations for readers: "I hope my book will spark readers' senses of adventure, motivate them to ask questions, and stimulate them to seek answers" (Jacobs, Mitchell, & Livingston, 2006. p. 392). Fortunately, writers of nonfiction books for children can choose from a universe of topics to research and explain. Consequently, the content of nonfiction books emphasizes documented facts about the natural and social world. To illuminate these topics, authors of this genre write in an expository format, carefully explaining the content to their readers (Lynch-Brown & Tomlinson, 2005). The genre of nonfiction is characterized by authenticity, accuracy, and up-to-date knowledge (Hillman, 1999). In addition, nonfiction titles that are carefully designed, include rich detail, and examine topics from unusual viewpoints are appealing to young readers (Jacobs & Tunnell, 2004).

The design of nonfiction books is different from those in other genres. When we read a narrative picture book, we see that the purpose of the illustrations is to enhance and extend the story, adding to the reader's enjoyment. In contrast, the purpose of visual information in a nonfiction text is to inform, illustrate a point, extend the information in the text, build visual literacy, and/or guide the reader through the text (Chapman & Sopko, 2003). To entice students into this genre, we look for books with visual aspects that grab the reader. Primary-grade students who are fascinated with animals will be amazed and informed as they examine Nic Bishop's striking, close-up photographs in *Red-Eyed Tree Frog* (Cowley, 1999) and *Chameleon, Chameleon* (Cowley, 2005). Intermediate-grade readers are often drawn to books with photographs as well. The stunning photographs in *Children of the Great Depression* (Freedman, 2005), *Dive! My Adventures in the Deep Frontier* (Earle, 1999), or the 2007 Orbis Pictus Award winner *Quest for the Tree Kangaroo: An Expedition to the Cloud Forest of New Guinea* (Montgomery, 2006) illuminate information in ways that text just can't do. To find other eye-catching titles, look for authors of nonfiction books who have a reputation for using remarkable photographs to enhance their texts, such as Sandra Markle and Seymour Simon. Another such author is graphic artist Steve Jenkins. His Web site, www.stevejenkinsbooks.com, features a short video of how he creates the stunning images in books like *Actual Size* (2004), where readers see the actual size of 18 animals and insects. Some of the species are so huge he can only show the size of one of their body parts. Fortunately, the authors and illustrators of informational titles have capitalized on the latest technology to produce books on all topics that are visually pleasing and inviting.

Nic Bishop's striking photographs invite young readers into the world of nonfiction.

Another aspect that sets nonfiction apart from the other genres in this book is the content. Accurate, authentic, and up-to-date information is a must. Many interested learners are intrigued by little-known facts. They enjoy amazing their friends and family with interesting tidbits of knowledge about what they are learning. Readers in the intermediate grades enjoy Patricia Lauber's fact-filled yet humorous look at plumbing throughout the ages in *What You Never Knew About Tubs, Toilets, & Showers* (2001). Pair this text with *Toilets, Bathtubs, Sinks, and Sewers: A History of the Bathroom* (Colman, 1994) and you are sure to learn something new about the history of personal hygiene. For a series of books highlighting amazing facts, sample Melvin and Gilda Berger's titles *Hurricanes Have Eyes but Can't See: And Other Amazing Facts About Wild Weather* (2004b) or *Fish Sleep but*

> "Certainly the basic purpose of nonfiction is to inform, to instruct, hopefully to enlighten. But that's not enough. An effective nonfiction book must animate its subject, infuse it with life. It must create a vivid and believable world that the reader will enter willingly and leave only with reluctance."
>
> (Russell Freedman, Newbery Medal Winner, 1992, p. 3)

Don't Shut Their Eyes: And Other Amazing Facts About Ocean Creatures (2004a). When you consider the multitude of informational books available, there is sure to be a fact-filled treasure for every child in your classroom.

Curious authors of nonfiction are on the lookout for unusual topics to share with their readers. To hook your reluctant readers, consider offering them books written about obscure topics such as dust or salt. The picture book *Stars Beneath Your Bed: The Surprising Story of Dust* (2005) by April Pulley Sayre introduces readers to the concept of dust. Ann Jonas's watercolor illustrations complement Sayre's text as she explains little-known facts about this substance that surrounds us. *The Story of Salt* (Kurlansky, 2006) offers intermediate-grade readers a historical look at the flavoring we sprinkle on our food. To sum up, nonfiction titles are written in an expository format to inform and, hopefully, inspire the reader. Exemplary texts in this genre are visually appealing, with attention to detail and unusual topics to hook readers.

Nonfiction is the largest single genre of children's literature (Lynch-Brown & Tomlinson, 2005), making it a challenge to select exemplary books to highlight in this chapter. To narrow our focus and assist you as you integrate literacy into your science and social studies lessons, we will turn to the standards that drive our curriculums. First, as outlined by the National Council for the Social Studies (1994), we will feature books and ideas from the following strands: Culture and Cultural Diversity and Time, Continuity, and Change (History). Then, we will highlight two of the "big ideas" identified by the National Science Education Standards (NRC, 1996): Life Science and Earth and Space Science. It is our hope that you will find titles to inform and inspire your learners as you inquire about the fascinating world in which we live.

Nonfiction: Infusing Reading and Writing Into the Content Areas

We know that nonfiction propels our students to think, question, and expand their knowledge base. We want to give it equal billing in our classrooms, but the question is, *"How do we find the time?"* One way to infuse nonfiction texts throughout your day is to select texts that will extend the learning that is taking place during your social studies and science curriculums. Then, while reading these texts to or with your students, teach them the specific strategies they need in order to comprehend and compose informational texts.

Social Studies

Unfortunately, the social studies textbooks we have in our classrooms have often been around for a number of years. Those texts might contain a chapter or less about the subject matter in your curriculum, thereby limiting the depth of coverage that is possible for most topics. In addition, some of your students are simply turned off by textbooks (Dunn, 2000). To spark your students' interest and extend their understanding of upcoming content, add nonfiction read-alouds to your social studies lessons. This is an ideal way to raise curiosity, build background, and teach essential strategies for unraveling nonfiction text.

During nonfiction read-alouds, you can teach your children two strategies developed by Linda Hoyt (2002). The first is "I Remember." While reading an engaging title, stop at appropriate places during the text to invite students to say something about what they have heard and remembered. This activity helps students get in the habit of stopping to think and recall along the way. The next strategy is "Say Something." To use this strategy, pause while reading to provide students a minute or two to reflect and comment or expand on what they have heard. As with any new strategy, take the time to model, practice, and reinforce appropriate discussion techniques. Reading aloud is just one way to incorporate books into your social studies teaching. Let's take a look at two social studies standards to find other appealing titles and teaching ideas.

Culture and Cultural Diversity

The students who inhabit our classrooms come from different backgrounds and cultures. Helping students understand, appreciate, and respect diverse backgrounds is one of the goals of social studies instruction. Sharing accurate nonfiction titles about diverse cultures is one way to deepen this understanding. In the primary grades, holiday celebrations are an important part of many children's lives. Consider taking time around the winter holidays of Christmas, Hanukkah, and Kwanzaa to invite all children in your classroom to share their families' customs and traditions by presenting a brief oral report. This literacy activity boosts your students' speaking and listening skills. If students in your intermediate-grade classroom commemorate Ramadan, Diane

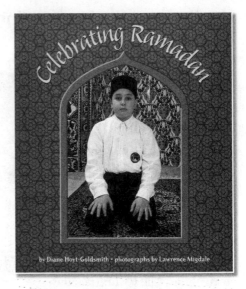

Read books to help students gain an understanding of the cultures and customs of their peers.

Hoyt-Goldsmith's (2001) photo-essay *Celebrating Ramadan* will provide your class with background information about this special month. This author has also penned titles about other religious holidays, including *Celebrating Passover* (2000) and *Three Kings Day: A Celebration of Christmastime* (2004). This is an engaging step toward building acceptance across cultures.

Along with highlighting multicultural celebrations, nonfiction books take us on trips to faraway lands to discover the cultures of different places through reading. For young students, the concept of our global community is explored in the book *Be My Neighbor* (Ajmera & Ivanko, 2004). With words of wisdom from the late Fred Rogers, this book helps children see the similarities among neighborhoods across the globe. Intermediate readers might take such a journey as they follow a young girl's life in Iraq in *Thura's Diary* (al-Windowi, 2004). Others can sample *Water Buffalo Days* (Huynh, 1999) to learn about daily life in Vietnam. Then, during the study of World War II, interested readers can meet *Hitler Youth: Growing Up in Hitler's Shadow* (Bartoletti, 2005). Learning will be enriched by these encounters.

Time, Continuity, and Change (History)

Understanding the events of the past helps students be better prepared to face the challenges of the future. In every class we have a student or two who is a history buff.

He or she can name every president of the United States or tell you intriguing details about the Civil War. Students often amaze us with their knowledge. To build on their enthusiasm and spark interest in historical events for all of our students, share nonfiction texts that bring history to life. When talking with teachers who used innovative strategies to enliven social studies instruction, Mary Ann Dunn remarks, "Photographs, literature and primary sources bring history to life and attach human emotions and perspective to people who died so long ago that they might seem to students never to have lived at all" (Dunn, 2000, p. 133). To help students make text-to-self connections between historical events and their own lives, choose books written through the eyes of a child. Older readers will glean a riveting picture of the San Francisco earthquake in 1906 while reading *A Day That Changed America: Earthquake!* (Tanaka, 2005). The words of four young survivors will have today's readers wondering what they would do in such a situation or relating their own experiences in a harrowing circumstance. Don't miss the voices of children who made an impact on history in *We Were There, Too!: Young People in U.S. History* (Hoose, 2001). After reading such books, encourage students to look for other titles written from a child's point of view. During writing workshop, ask your students to research a historical event and write about it as if they had been there.

As we teach our social studies content, we want history to come alive for our students; otherwise, many will view history merely as a random collection of dates and facts. When children are presented with high-quality nonfiction books about historical events, it helps them visualize the past (Norton, 2003). For example, Rhonda Blumberg gives us a different perspective on the Lewis and Clark expedition through an American slave's eyes in *York's Adventures With Lewis and Clark: An African-American's Part in the Great Expedition* (2004), while Jim Murphy illuminates the tragedy of rampant disease in *An American Plague: The True and Terrifying Story of the Yellow Fever Epidemic of 1793* (2003). Moving through time, *Dust to Eat: Drought and Depression in the 1930s* (Cooper, 2004) explains the struggles of families who could no longer eke out a living on the nation's farms. In addition to other titles mentioned in the chapter, there

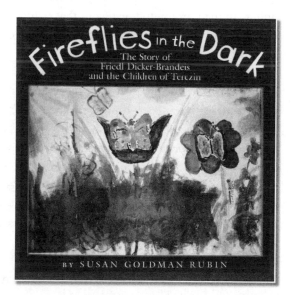

Children's art from a concentration camp brings history to life with no trace of sensationalism.

is a wealth of material to deepen one's understanding of World War II. One suggestion is *Fireflies in the Dark: The Story of Friedl Dicker-Brandeis and the Children of Terezin* (Rubin, 2000) or, closer to home, *The Children of Topaz* (Tunnell & Chilcoat, 1996), which reveals the story of life in a Japanese-American internment camp. Be assured that there is many a good title to flesh out those facts and dates. In the upcoming pages you will see that science, too, can be infused with life in the same way.

Science

Scientists predict outcomes, generate questions, observe, make hypotheses, summarize their learning, and use collected data to draw conclusions. Likewise, effective readers engage in similar mental processes (Yopp & Yopp, 2006). As we help students build background for the study of science by reading engaging nonfiction titles, we can also strengthen their reading skills. Hallie and Ruth Yopp (2006) share an effective before-reading strategy called Preview-Confirm-Predict, designed to activate students' schema and develop their vocabulary knowledge. To teach this strategy, select a nonfiction book that is brimming with visuals, such as *Growing Up Wild: Penguins* (Markle, 2002) or *Sea Horse: The Shyest Fish in the Sea* (Butterworth, 2006). Begin with a picture walk through the text. Invite students to work with partners or in small groups to write down vocabulary words they predict will appear in the text based upon their survey of the visuals. Once they have a collection of words, ask them to sort and classify their words. Finally, each group identifies one of their words that they think every group recorded, one that is unique to their group, and one word that sparks their curiosity. One by one, groups share their three words, and a discussion ensues. This discussion helps set a purpose and builds anticipation for reading the text.

We've seen how well-chosen nonfiction titles help breathe life into history lessons; in the same way, we can use books to open doors into the world of scientific thought. To deepen students' understanding of the thought processes scientists employ, Donna Farland (2006) suggests collecting nonfiction books that portray scientists at work, the struggles they face, and their determination and perseverance in their quest for answers. A few titles that meet her criteria include Aliki's portrayal of George Washington Carver in *A Weed Is a Flower* (1988) and Peter Sis's biography of Galileo Galilei, *Starry Messenger* (1996). Let's take a look at two areas of science, along with a wealth of titles to grab your students' interest and extend their learning beyond the classroom.

Life Science

Through the study of life science, students gain a deeper understanding of plants, living things, and their habitats. As you explore topics such as plant growth and the life cycle of a butterfly in your classroom, surround learners with quality nonfiction books to further their knowledge. If the study of butterflies and the amazing story of monarch migration has piqued your learners' interest, share the book *The Journey: Stories of Migration* (Rylant, 2006). Rylant's words flow as she describes the migratory habits of a locust, gray whale, American silver eel, monarch butterfly, caribou, and Arctic tern. Then, don't miss the work of the next three authors.

Jim Arnosky is a prolific life-science writer whose picture books are accurate and reader friendly. He has written many books about animals and their habitats. Some of his books include *All About Lizards* (2004), *All About Sharks* (2003), *All About Turkeys* (1998), and *All About Owls* (1995). Sandra Markle's books can match the interests of both primary- and middle-grade readers as she investigates a variety of animals, some gentle, others fierce. Popular books include *A Mother's Journey* (Markle & Marks, 2005) about the

Explore topics such as migration with Cynthia Rylant's poetic book.

Emperor penguin; *Porcupines* (2006), about the prickly woodlands inhabitant, and *Zebras* (2007), a look at the curiously garbed animal seen by most of us only in a zoo. In addition, Steve Jenkins' informative books include *Almost Gone: The World's Rarest Animals* (2006). Jenkins has organized this book into three sections describing endangered animals and the number of that species that are still alive, extinct creatures, and those species that are coming back because their habitats are finally being protected. Add *A Pinky Is a Baby Mouse, and Other Baby Animal Names* (Ryan, 1997) and you have a collection of books about creatures large and small. Animal enthusiasts are fortunate indeed that so many fine writers are creating books to satisfy their quest for knowledge.

Earth and Space Science—Fossils, Sun, Moon, and Stars

As we enrich our science curriculum with literature, it is important to guide our students as they uncover the differences between narrative picture-book illustrations of scientific phenomena and information collected through careful observations. By integrating inquiry-based instruction in science and nonfiction literature, we can help students become informed, critical readers. To illustrate this integration, we've included a lesson that addresses the National Science Education Standards (NRC, 1996) and helps students overcome common misunderstandings about the cycle of moon phases. The following engaging lesson, *Reading the Moon*, was developed by Kathy Cabe Trundle and Thomas H. Troland (2005).

> **Try This!** **Reading the Moon**
>
> During a unit on the moon, share some classic picture books such as *Papa, Please Get the Moon for Me* (Carle, 1986) and *Moon Bear* (Asch, 1978). These books are engaging read-alouds, but they also contain *incorrect* representations of the phases of the moon. To lead students to discover this, begin by showing them how to gather and record moon observations. Provide students with a moon calendar, including a circle for a drawing and a spot to record the date, time, and direction in which their observation was made. Once students have collected data for about nine weeks, reread the picture books, asking questions to guide their thinking. Compare the illustrations in the books to their collected data. After reading, students write a summary of their comparisons. In addition, consider sharing some of the moon books found in the Glance Chart that follows.

Glance Chart

Text Sets for Science Topics		
Topic	**A Literature Sampling**	**Research-Supported Literacy Activities**
Butterfly Life Cycle (Life Science)	*Waiting for Wings* (Ehlert, 2001) (Gr. K–2) *Monarch Butterfly* (Gibbons, 1989) (Gr. 2–4) *From Caterpillar to Butterfly* (Heiligman, 1996) (Gr. PS–1) *An Extraordinary Life: The Story of a Monarch Butterfly* (Pringle, 1997) (Gr. 4–8) *Becoming Butterflies* (Rockwell, 2002) (Gr. PS–2)	To infuse writing into your science curriculum, have your students make butterfly journals. Model recording your scientific observations with words and illustrations. Invite students to do the same as their caterpillars turn into butterflies.

Text Sets for Science Topics

Topic	A Literature Sampling	Research-Supported Literacy Activities
Dinosaurs (Life Science)	*Did Dinosaurs Eat Pizza?: Mysteries Science Hasn't Solved* (Hort, 2006) (Gr. 1–3) *Prehistoric Actual Size* (Jenkins, 2005) (Gr. PS–5) *The Dinosaurs of Waterhouse Hawkins* (Kerley, 2001) (Gr. 2–5) *Boy, Were We Wrong About Dinosaurs!* (Kudlinski, 2005) (Gr. 2–4) *Dinosaur Parents, Dinosaur Young: Uncovering the Mystery of Dinosaur Families* (Zoehfeld, 2001) (Gr. 4+)	Invite students to choose two or three books on dinosaurs. Then, using a double-entry journal, students take notes on information of interest in the left-hand column. Write questions or reactions in the right-hand column. When completed, learners use the data to write a short report entitled "I Used to Think, But Now I Know…" Finally, they can present it in poster format or using PowerPoint.
The Earth's Moon (Earth and Space Science)	*What the Moon Is Like* (Branley, 2000) (Gr. 1–3) *The Moon and You* (Krupp, 1993) (Gr. 3–5) *If You Decide to Go to the Moon* (McNulty, 2005) (Gr. K–3) *The Moon* (Simon, 2003) (Gr. 2+) *Team Moon: How 400,000 People Landed Apollo 11 on the Moon* (Thimmesh, 2006) (Gr. 5+)	Using the book *Postcards From Pluto: A Tour of the Solar System* (Leedy, 1993) as a model, provide students with a blank "postcard" and invite them to write a postcard to a family member from the moon. Encourage them to include interesting facts about this fascinating place.
Weather (Earth and Space Science)	*Flash, Crash, Rumble, and Roll* (Branley, 1999) (Gr. K–4) *It's Raining Cats and Dogs: All Kinds of Weather and Why We Have It* (Branley, 1987) (Gr. 3+) *The Kids' Book of Weather Forecasting* (Breen & Friestad, 2000) (Gr. 3–5) *The Weather Detectives* (Eubank, 2004) (Gr. 3+) *Weather Words and What They Mean* (Gibbons, 1990) (Gr. K–2)	To incorporate the weather words they have learned and the observations they have gathered, teach students how to summarize their learning using a favorite form of poetry. See Chapter 8 for a list of poetry books on science topics to help inspire your writers.

Pairing Fiction and Nonfiction

When we look for ways to incorporate nonfiction into our busy day, pairing fiction with nonfiction titles simply makes sense. Consider pairing the zany picture book *Sweet Dream Pie* (Wood, 1998) with *Be My Neighbor* (Ajmera & Ivanko, 2004) to offer students two different views of neighborhood life. In intermediate-grade social studies class units on American history, you might begin with *Night Boat to Freedom* (Raven, 2006) and then share *Moses: When Harriet Tubman Led Her People to Freedom* (Weatherford, 2006). Together you will experience the bravery behind dreams of freedom. When learning about life on the prairie, read Eve Bunting's *Dandelions* (1995) paired with the slightly longer *The Prairie Builders* (Collard, 2005) for a view of prairies past and present that will also integrate history and geography. Then, geography and its related plant and animal life can be introduced through the rhythmic *Welcome to the Sea of Sand* (Yolen, 1996) coupled with Wright-Frierson's fabulous sketches in *A Desert Scrapbook* (1996). Addressing the social studies standards will be an exciting prospect through such paired titles. In addition, fiction titles often lead students to ask questions that are quickly answered by doing a little research. Having paired sets of books at your fingertips makes this a bit easier. And by reading aloud nonfiction titles, we are balancing the types of books we read to children. Consider also how this works in the science curriculum (see chart, page 185).

> "The writer of compelling nonfiction does not simply collect and display facts, but weaves information and details into a vision that reveals the subject in a way that readers find irresistible."
>
> (Jacobs & Tunnell, 2004, p. 148)

Outstanding Authors of Nonfiction

There are many stellar authors that we could have included in this list. We tried to balance those who write mainly for the primary grades and those whose books are geared toward intermediate grades and beyond.

Aliki: Aliki writes and illustrates picture books for younger readers. Some of her nonfiction books include *My Five Senses* (1962) and *My Visit to the Zoo* (1997).

Paired Science-Related Fiction and Nonfiction Picture Books

Fiction	Nonfiction
Animals	
Diary of a Worm (Cronin, 2003)	*Wiggling Worms at Work* (Pfeffer, 2004)
The Great White Man-Eating Shark (Mahy, 1990)	*Amazing Sharks* (Thomson, 2005)
Bats at the Beach (Lies, 2006)	*Zipping, Zapping, Zooming Bats* (Earle, 1995)
Weather	
The Rain Came Down (Shannon, 2000)	*Down Comes the Rain* (Branley, 1997)
Cloudy With a Chance of Meatballs (Barrett, 1978)	*How Does the Sun Make Weather?* (Williams, 2005)
The Wind Blew (Hutchins, 1974)	*I Face the Wind* (Cobb, 2003)
It Looked Like Spilt Milk (Shaw, 1947)	*The Cloud Book* (dePaola, 1975b)
Trees	
A Tree Is Nice (Udry, 1956)	*Be a Friend to Trees* (Lauber, 1994)
A Grand Old Tree (DePalma, 2005)	*Sky Tree* (Locker, 1995)
Bugs	
The Bee Tree (Polacco, 1993)	*Honey in a Hive* (Rockwell, 2005)
Insects Are My Life (McDonald, 1995)	*Buzz! A Book About Insects* (Berger, 2000)
Hey! Little Ant (Hoose & Hoose, 1998)	*Ant Cities* (Dorros, 2000)
Super Fly Guy (Arnold, 2006)	*Flies Are Fascinating* (Wilkinson, 1994)
Butterfly Count (Collard, 2002)	*Becoming Butterflies* (Rockwell, 2002)
Butterfly House (Bunting, 1999)	*From Caterpillar to Butterfly* (Heiligman, 1996)

Russell Freedman: Freedman is an award-winning author of nearly 50 books on topics ranging from animal behavior to people in history. Intermediate-grade history buffs will savor *Freedom Walkers: The Story of the Montgomery Bus Boycott* (2006a), *Lincoln: A Photobiography*, (1987), and *Give Me Liberty!: The Story of the Declaration of Independence* (2000).

Gail Gibbons: Gibbons' richly illustrated nonfiction texts enlighten primary-grade readers about their favorite topics, including *Ice Cream: The Full Scoop* (2006), *Horses* (2005), and *Penguins* (1998).

James Cross Giblin: Giblin writes informational chapter books about everyday items, as in *Be Seated: A Book About Chairs* (1993); mysteries of science, as with *The Mystery of the Mammoth Bones: And How It Was Solved* (1999); and other intriguing topics for intermediate-grade readers, such as *The Secrets of the Sphinx* (2004).

Patricia Lauber: Lauber's collection of books for science enthusiasts includes an assortment of topics. Many of her books are part of the Let's-Read-and-Find-Out Science series from HarperCollins publishers.

Seymour Simon: Simon, a former teacher, has written more than 200 highly acclaimed science books for children about the human body, space, planets, stars and the universe, our planet, animals, and much more. He has a series of easy readers titled See More Readers, appropriate for students in kindergarten through second grade.

Michael's essay, Part 3

> My favorite books explain all parts of the person's life from when they were little, until they were old, including funny things. I liked one story about when Albert Einstein was a child. He didn't talk until he was four years old, when his soup was too hot. They asked why he didn't talk before. He said "Everything was perfect!" That's a funny kid.
>
> It is also interesting to learn what the world was like when these famous people lived. One book, "Who was Helen Keller", talks about how hard it was to be deaf and blind back when she lived. There were only ten or twenty schools for the deaf people or blind people back then. Now we have more teachers and schools to help blind and deaf students.

Literature Is Back!

Have You Read These?

A FEW OF OUR FAVORITE SERIES SCIENCE BOOKS

Earthworks (Boyds Mills Press) (Gr. K–2)

♦ *Glaciers: Nature's Icy Caps* (Harrison, 2006)

♦ *Volcanoes: Nature's Incredible Fireworks* (Harrison, 2002)

Let's-Read-and-Find-Out Science 1 (Gr. PK–1) and 2 (Gr. 1–4) (HarperCollins)

♦ *Air Is All Around You* (Branley, 2006)

♦ *Dinosaur Tracks* (Zoehfeld, 2007)

Nature Watch (Lerner) (Gr. 3–5)

♦ *Baboons* (Stewart, 2007)

♦ *Carnivorous Plants* (Johnson, 2007)

On My Own Science (Millbrook Press) (Gr. 3–6)

♦ *Shipwreck Search: Discovery of the H. L. Hunley* (Walker, 2006)

♦ *Mystery Fish* (Walker, 2006a)

See More Readers (Chronicle Books) (Gr. 1–3)

♦ *Planet Mars* (Simon, 2006)

♦ *Amazing Bats* (Simon, 2005)

Sally Walker: Walker is the winner of the 2006 ALSC Robert F. Sibert Informational Book Medal for her book *Secrets of a Civil War Submarine: Solving the Mysteries of the* H. L. Hunley (2005). Although *Secrets* is written for middle-school readers, Walker has written more than 20 books, including some for readers in grades 2 through 4, such as *Rocks* (2007) and *Sea Horses* (2004).

A Glance at Biography and Autobiography

Biographies written for children have an interesting history. Early biographies penned in the 17th through 19th centuries had didactic themes and were written by biographers who believed the books should be vehicles for religious, political, or social education. In the mid-1800s biographies shifted from religious vehicles to political tools highlighting people who had acquired power, fame, and wealth. In the early 20th century, driven by new insights into child development, biographers protected children from the indiscretions of their subjects. Also, during this time period, few biographies were written about women and members of minority groups. Biographies published about political leaders through the early 1960s included omissions and distortions to allow authors to highlight what they believed were important contributions (Norton, 2003). Fortunately, by the late 1960s and 1970s, the face of the biography shifted once again. Authors like Jean Fritz began to change the content of biographies with authentic, dynamic, and readable titles such as *Why Don't You Get a Horse, Sam Adams?* (1974).

Today's biographies highlight stories of people from all walks of life.

Children today are able to read unique and interesting biographies about a diverse collection of people. In *Where Lincoln Walked* (1998) and *Where Washington Walked* (2004), for example, Raymond Bial's photo-essays offer students a glimpse into the lives of the two presidents by focusing on the places where they lived and worked. Each book includes a list of places to visit so that you can walk in their footsteps. Along with titles about famous men and women, there are numerous books penned about amazing human beings who were not as well known, such as *Mary Anning: Fossil Hunter* (Walker, 2001), about the

> "Biographies of all types give children a glimpse into other lives, other places, other times. The best of them combine accurate information and fine writing in a context that children enjoy—the story that really happened." (Kiefer et al., 2007, p. 653)

young English girl who discovered a dinosaur fossil. Likewise, students can read about people who may spark controversy among readers (Kiefer et al., 2007).

The hallmarks of well-written biographies for children include accurate information and a quick-paced narrative. Biographies should be objectively written, presenting various points of view, as Candace Fleming offers intermediate-grade readers in her biography *Our Eleanor: A Scrapbook Look at Eleanor Roosevelt's Remarkable Life* (2005). Biographies for children are written in different formats. Enjoy learning about people from various backgrounds alongside your students as you read and reflect on the life stories illuminated in the pages of a book.

Have You Read These?

A FEW OF OUR FAVORITE BIOGRAPHIES AND AUTOBIOGRAPHIES OF AUTHORS/ILLUSTRATORS

- *Under the Royal Palms: A Childhood in Cuba* (Ada, 1998) (Gr. 3–5)

- *Prairie Girl: The Life of Laura Ingalls Wilder* (Anderson, 2004) (Gr. 2–5)

- *The Journey That Saved Curious George: The True Wartime Escape of Margaret and H. A. Rey* (Borden, 2005) (Gr. 4–8)

- *The Boy on Fairfield Street: How Ted Geisel Grew Up to Become Dr. Seuss.* (Krull, 2004b) (Gr. 1+)

- *Looking Back: A Book of Memories* (Lowry, 1998) (Gr. 5+)

- *Tomás Rivera* (Medina, 2004) (Gr 1–2)

- *Bill Peet: An Autobiography* (Peet, 1989) (Gr. 3+)

Types of Biographies and Autobiographies

Types/Description	A Literature Sampling	Research-Supported Literacy Activities
Partial Biographies Provide an in-depth look at one part of the person's life. These are also known as phase biographies.	*Coming Home: From the Life of Langston Hughes* (Cooper, 1994) (Gr. K–4) *My Brother Martin* (Farris, 2003) (Gr. 1–4) *Why Don't You Get a Horse, Sam Adams?* (Fritz, 1974) (Gr. 3+) *Frederick Douglass: The Last Days of Slavery* (Miller, 1995) (Gr. K–3)	To create a living history museum, each student selects a person to research. After researching, each student pens a brief biography script written in the first-person point of view. Students rehearse their scripts and create costumes. Invite students from other classes to the museum. When they touch a student's hand, he or she shares that person's life story.
Complete Biographies Recount a person's life from birth to present, or to the person's death, if he or she is deceased.	*Knockin' on Wood: Starring Peg Leg Bates* (Barasch, 2004) (Gr. 1–4) *The Adventures of Marco Polo* (Freedman, 2006b) (Gr. 5+) *Helen Keller: A Determined Life* (MacLeod, 2004) (Gr. 3–6) *Sequoyah: The Cherokee Man Who Gave His People Writing* (Rumford, 2004) (Gr. 1–4)	To help students understand the chronological organization of complete biography and identify the main events, teach students how to make a timeline. Divide students into small groups or pairs. Each group will construct a timeline of key events in the person's life.

Glance Chart

Types of Biographies and Autobiographies

Types/Description	A Literature Sampling	Research-Supported Literacy Activities
Collective Biographies Describe the lives of several people with a common thread.	*Adventurous Women: Eight True Stories About Women Who Made a Difference* (Colman, 2006) (Gr. 5+) *Let It Shine: Stories of Black Women Freedom Fighters* (Pinkney, 2000) (Gr. 4+) *Extraordinary Asian Americans and Pacific Islanders* (Sinnott, 2003) (Gr. 3–5) *Hooray for Inventors!* (Williams, 2005b) (Gr. 3–6)	Compare and contrast two people in a book using a Venn diagram or H chart. Moss (2004) also suggests using retellings to help students understand the organization of expository text. Readers select a favorite person and retell the information about her/him, focusing on key facts. This will also strengthen their comprehension skills.
Auto-biographies/ Memoirs A person writes about his or her own life.	*Reaching for the Moon* (Aldrin, 2005) (Gr. 1–4) *Through My Eyes* (Bridges, 1999) (Gr. 4+) *26 Fairmount Avenue* (dePaola, 1999) (Gr. 2–4) *Don't Tell the Girls: A Family Memoir* (Giff, 2005a) (Gr. 3–5)	To build background for the text before reading, collect artifacts that will promote a discussion about the time period or person. Using these artifacts, discuss students' prior knowledge and any vocabulary words that may be helpful for students as they read the autobiography.

Why Is Nonfiction Important to My Students?

We have provided the groundwork for an understanding of the value and benefits of nonfiction titles wisely integrated throughout your teaching day and offered tempting options for personal reading. The following research-based merits merely underscore our beliefs in the potential of this genre.

Nonfiction books:

- Satisfy and ignite students' natural curiosity about the world
- Serve as a springboard for thinking and learning about the world
- Offer new perspectives on familiar topics
- Help readers identify with people different from themselves
- Include the broadest collection of topics, subjects, people, events, and thoughts to explore
- Expand students' vocabulary
- Build learners' background knowledge, which, in turn, increases their engagement

(Harvey, 2002; Kiefer et al., 2007; Kurkjian, Livingston, & Cobb, 2006; Norton, 2003; Temple et al., 2002)

Endings and Beginnings

As our nonfiction adventure draws to a close, we invite you to browse your shelves to locate your favorite titles. Ask the school librarian for stellar titles to boost the offerings you use to spark student interest in upcoming units of study. Don't forget to encourage your students to do book talks of their favorites. Together you will spread the news that nonfiction makes for fascinating reading.

Guidelines for Selecting Quality Nonfiction

Accuracy and Authenticity	Yes	No	Somewhat
Look at the "About the Author" page, book jacket, or introduction. Is the author qualified to write about the topic?			
Has the manuscript been checked by authorities in the field? Has the author provided a reference list of cited sources?			
Are the facts accurate according to other sources?			
Check the copyright date. Does the book include current information?			
Comments:			

Content	Yes	No	Somewhat
Is the topic age-appropriate for students?			
Is the topic adequately covered?			
Does the book lead readers to inquire further?			
Comments:			

Style	Yes	No	Somewhat
Is the information presented clearly and directly?			
Does the author use vivid and interesting language?			
Does the author invite readers to get involved with the text by generating interest in and enthusiasm about the topic?			
Comments:			

Organization	Yes	No	Somewhat
Does the author's choice of organizational structure clarify content?			
Are the scope and organization of the topic appropriate for students?			
If the book is divided into sections or chapters, and are they clearly structured with appropriate headings?			
Does the book include easy-to-access features, such as a table of contents, index, and glossary?			
Comments:			

Illustrations	Yes	No	Somewhat
Is the book visually appealing to your students?			
Do the illustrations complement, clarify and/or extend the text?			
Does the choice of media match the purpose of the illustration?			
Comments:			

(Adapted from Kiefer et al., 2007; Temple et al., 2002)

PART 2

LINKING LITERATURE AND LEARNING

The Reading Connection

Barbara Moss (2004) reminds us that it is critical to teach our students the literacy skills needed to succeed in an increasingly demanding Information Age. In order to master the onslaught of nonfiction materials in texts and on the Internet, every one of our literacy learners must understand the demands of reading and writing informational texts. How might we do that?

The following lessons demonstrate how naturally nonfiction fits into your classroom. Packed with information, these titles are perfect choices for teaching valuable reading and writing skills. Because they are constructed differently from narrative texts, these expository titles need to be unpacked through direct teaching and plenty of engaging, ongoing practice.

Primary Lesson Plan: Questioning Before, During, and After Reading Nonfiction Texts

Purpose:

Young children walk into kindergarten with endless questions. We can capitalize on this natural curiosity by helping them navigate nonfiction texts. Stephanie Harvey (2002) underscores the importance of questioning as the strategy that propels learners forward. To employ this strategy successfully, it is essential that students see models of experts engaged in reading, thinking, and questioning their way through a nonfiction text.

Materials/Preparation:

- Engaging nonfiction texts

- Prepared sticky notes for use during your read-aloud/think-aloud lesson

- Sticky notes or a chart for recording students' questions during a read-aloud/think-aloud lesson

Mini-Lesson:

1. Prepare questions to share with students before, during, and after reading. Taking a few moments to do this ahead of time will help you focus your questions on the teaching points you want to highlight. Remember to ask questions to increase comprehension as well as questions to foster awareness of the author's craft. See the questions below based on the book *Lily Pad Pond* (Lavies, 1989).

2. Once students have watched as you read, think,

Choose an engaging nonfiction book to model asking questions before, during, and after reading.

Before-reading questions:

♦ *Hmmm! I wonder which creature pictured on the cover is the subject of this book?*

♦ *How has the author organized the information?*

During-reading questions:

♦ *After reading the word* nymph: *I wonder what this word* nymph *means? I'll keep reading to try to figure it out.*

♦ *Wow! That's an interesting fact. How did the author make me feel so excited?*

♦ *I don't understand this sentence. What is it about? I'm going to reread and look at the picture to try to figure it out.*

♦ *What a smart way to end the book. How did the author let me know the book was over?*

After-reading questions:

♦ *I wonder what the author wanted me to understand?*

♦ *This book made me curious about bullfrogs. Where could I learn more about this creature?*

and model your questioning, they are ready to join in. Maria's first graders generated the before-, during-, and after-reading questions on page 196 while listening to the book *Chameleon, Chameleon* (Cowley, 2005).

3. Continue to practice this strategy with small groups of students during guided reading to reinforce and extend their learning. Finally, provide students with three sticky notes to record their own questions as they read nonfiction titles on their own.

Before-reading questions:

What is the chameleon going to do?
When do chameleons change colors?
Why is it spiky?
Does a chameleon change colors when it eats something?

During-reading questions:

Why does it have small eyes?
What does "peaceful colors" mean?
How does it know when food is nearby?

After-reading questions:

What are a chameleon's enemies?
Why didn't the chameleon change colors?

Intermediate Lesson Plan: Determining Important Information

Purpose:

Stephanie Harvey and Anne Goudvis (2007) give us some pointers on helping our students determine important information when reading nonfiction text. They suggest that students look for the key concepts and essential ideas first, and then go back and savor the engaging details.

Materials:

♦ Enlarged Finding Big Ideas chart (see page 197)

♦ Short nonfiction picture books

Mini-Lesson:

1. To help students master this skill, model the process of locating the big ideas using a favorite nonfiction picture book. Thinking aloud as you determine the key concepts, demonstrate how you separate the details from the big ideas. Using a shorter text enables you to focus easily on each step.

2. Use the Finding Big Ideas reproducible on page 197 or write each step on chart paper as a handy reference for students. Check for understanding as you complete each section. Clarify the process as needed.

<table>
<tr><td colspan="2">**Finding Big Ideas**
Directions: After selecting a book, complete the chart below. Discuss your learning with your class.</td></tr>
<tr><td>Book Title:</td><td>Author:</td></tr>
<tr><td>Before reading: What do I already know about this topic?</td><td>Notes:</td></tr>
<tr><td>During reading: What do I think the author is trying to tell me? (big ideas)</td><td>Notes:</td></tr>
<tr><td>What key facts/details from the text support the big ideas?</td><td>Notes:</td></tr>
<tr><td>After reading: What have I learned?</td><td>Notes:</td></tr>
</table>

3. Next, involve learners in pairs practice. Ask them to think aloud together as they pull out key concepts from fascinating details (Robb, 2004). Direct them to a collection of fascinating nonfiction picture books gathered ahead of time, letting them choose a topic of mutual interest.

4. Once the work is done, be certain to highlight the efforts of each pair through discussion. This gives you an opportunity to assess understanding and for the students to highlight a particularly interesting book for potential readers.

5. Finally, challenge readers to work independently on other content-related material.

The Writing Connection

Throughout this chapter, we highlight well-crafted nonfiction books that offer student writers models of rich expository writing in which the author's passion for the topic shines through. When we ask our learners to write about such texts, they are given the opportunity to work with the new ideas they are learning as well as to practice the writer's craft (Moss, Leone, & DiPillo, 1997). One of the ways to help students enhance their nonfiction pieces is by adding the features that are found in informational books.

Another way is to teach and support students as they frame their writing within the commonly used text structures inherent in expository text.

Primary Lesson Plan: Exploring the Features of Nonfiction Texts

Purpose:

The writers of nonfiction texts provide readers with many supportive text features to assist them in understanding the information. Knowledgeable readers who know how to access visual information found in nonfiction text features are better equipped to read and comprehend the material.

Materials/Preparation:

A collection of nonfiction texts that contain prominent nonfiction features, such as a table of contents, headings, diagrams, labels, captions, a glossary, an index, and so on

Mini-Lesson:

1. Read aloud a nonfiction text. As you are reading, point out and discuss the unique features and the purpose for each feature.

2. Record each feature and its purpose on a chart. (See chart above.)

3. Once students are familiar with these features, divide them into pairs or small groups and give each pair or group three or four sticky notes.

4. Send each group on a scavenger hunt through books to look for new features.

5. Share and discuss features and their purposes and continue to add to the chart.

6. Once students are familiar with these features, encourage them to include the features in their own nonfiction writing.

First graders go on a scavenger hunt for nonfiction features.

Nonfiction Features	Purpose
Table of Contents	Find what we want to learn about.
Heading	Tell us what the part is going to be about.
Caption	Tells about the picture
Label	Tells about a picture, photograph or its parts
Close-up	See the details of small things
Cutaway/Cross-Section	Look at the inside of things
Bold Print Italics	the word is important
Amazing Fact Boxes	facts that make the reader say, "wow!"
Pronunciation Guide	Chunk the word so you can sound it out

A chart of nonfiction features and their purposes.

Literature Is Back!

Intermediate Lesson Plan: Exploring Expository Text Structures

Purpose:

When children are able to navigate expository text structures, they have more success comprehending and retaining the information found in nonfiction books (Dymock, 2005; Pearson & Duke, 2002; Temple et al., 2002). The lesson below will get you started as you explicitly teach students how expository text structures work. Expository text structures offer readers a map to help guide them through the text and grasp the author's intended message (Moss, 2004).

Materials/Preparation:

♦ Blank Expository Text Structures chart (page 200)

♦ A nonfiction book that exemplifies the text structure you want to explore

♦ Enlarged graphic organizers for whole-group lesson (see pages 201–205)

♦ Sample texts and graphic organizers for each small group of students

Mini-Lesson:

1. Select a book with an expository text structure that you would like to highlight. Read the book aloud once for enjoyment. On the second reading, work with the students to chart the signal words.

2. Next, demonstrate how to diagram the text using the appropriate graphic organizer. This portion of the lesson allows students to "see" how the author has organized the information (Dymock, 2005).

3. After completing the graphic organizer, collaborate with your students to write a definition of this type of expository text.

4. Once you are confident your students understand this text structure, divide them into small groups. Give each group a sample text that is at their independent reading level and the appropriate graphic organizer. Students will read the text and then work together to complete the graphic organizer. Once they have completed the graphic organizer, each student will write a short summary or retelling of what they have learned from the text.

5. Now that students have had experience reading and analyzing the text structure, they are ready to write.

6. Model and think aloud as you write an expository essay that follows the text structure. Invite students to write their own expository pieces using the text structure you have studied.

Expository Text Structures

Structure	Description	Sequence	Compare and Contrast	Cause and Effect	Problem and Solution Question and Answer
Definition	Presents and describes a topic by detailing characteristics, highlighting features, and providing examples	Organizes facts, events, or concepts in numerical or chronological order	Identifies the similarities and differences between two or more facts, concepts, or ideas	Explains one or more causes and the resulting effects	States a problem and lists one or more solutions for the problem
Signal Words	for example, characteristics include, such as, like, by observing	first, next, last, before, after, finally, then, until	same as, alike, similar to, resembles, compared to, different from, unlike, on the other hand	If___then___, because of, as a result, since, therefore, due to, thus, consequently	problem is, puzzle is solved, one reason for that outcome is
Sampling of Titles	I See Animals Hiding (Arnosky, 2000) Bats (Gibbons, 2000) Be a Friend to Trees (Lauber, 1994)	Turtle Crossing (Chrustowski, 2006) The Race to Save the Lord God Bird (Hoose, 2004) The Life and Times of the Apple (Micucci, 1992)	Elephants Can Paint, Too! (Arnold, 2005) Toad or Frog, Swamp or Bog? (Graham-Barber, 1994) A Wasp Is Not a Bee (Singer, 1995)	What Do You Do When Something Wants to Eat You? (Jenkins, 1997) Quest for the Tree Kangaroo (Montgomery, 2006) What Stinks? (Singer, 2006)	How Do Frogs Swallow Their Eyes? Questions and Answers About Amphibians (Berger & Berger, 2002) What Do You Do With a Tail Like This? (Jenkins & Page, 2003) The Cod's Tale (Kurlansky, 2001)

Compare and Contrast

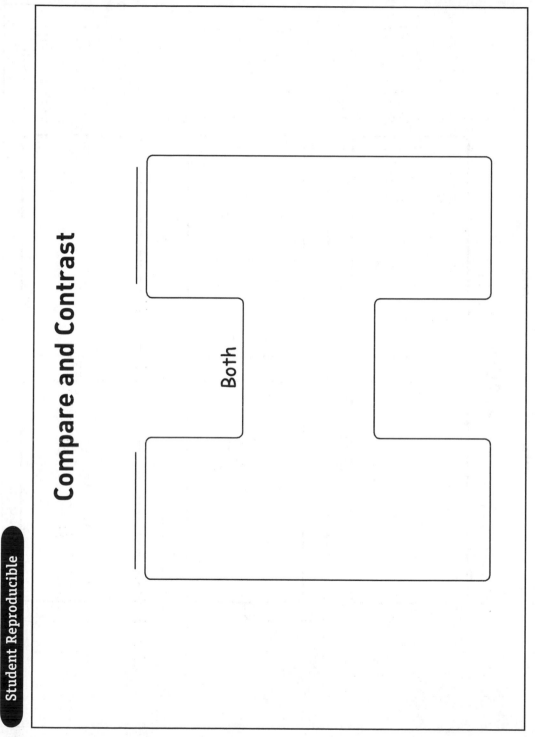

Both

Literature Is Back! © Copyright: © 2007 by Carol J. Fuhler and Maria P. Walther, Scholastic Teaching Resources

Sequence

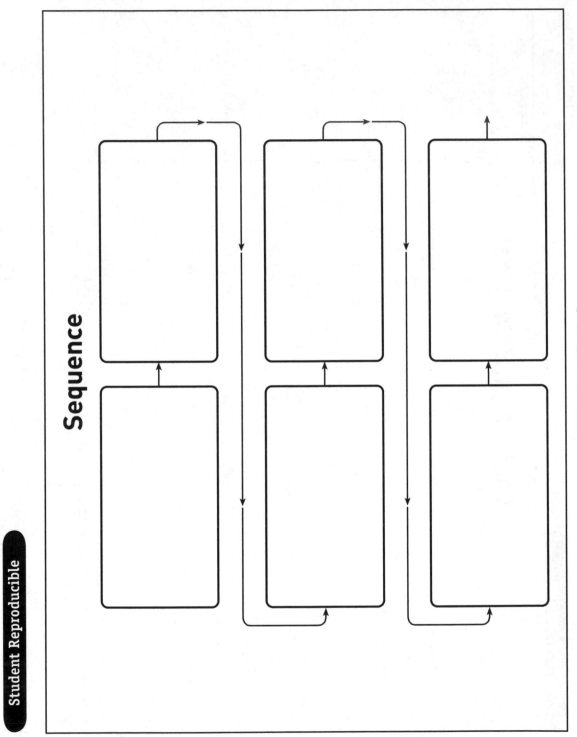

Cause and Effect

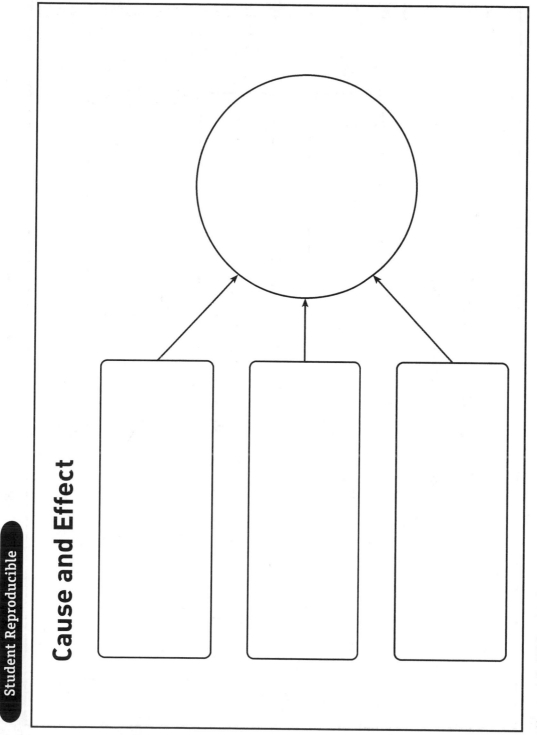

Literature Is Back! © Copyright © 2007 by Carol J. Fuhler and Maria P. Walther, Scholastic Teaching Resources

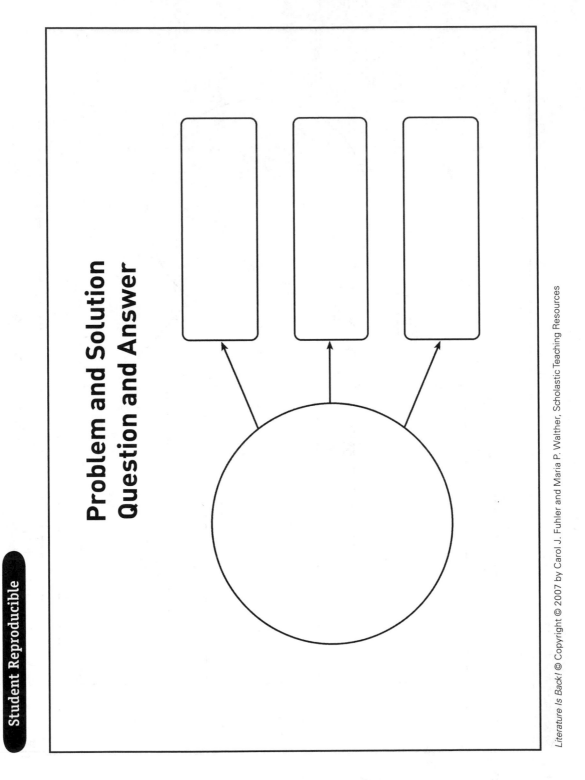

Problem and Solution Question and Answer

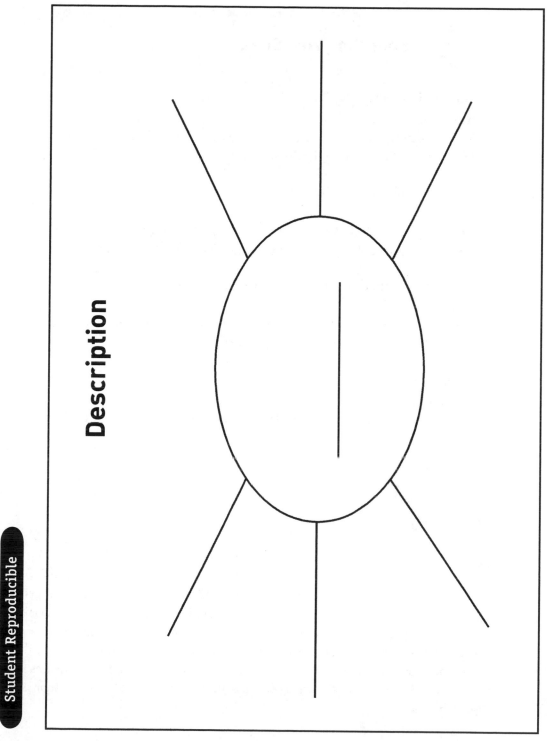

Description

Four Fine Web Sites

National Geographic

www.nationalgeographic.com

In the educators' section of this Web site, you can access a collection of lesson plans that are tied to the Geography for Life standards.

National Science Teachers Association

www.nsta.org

On this site you will find a list of the "highest quality, most engaging and scientifically accurate books for children" published each year, along with other resources.

National Council for the Social Studies

www.ncss.org

Access this site for a yearly list of Notable Trade Books for Young People. The site also offers lesson plans and ideas for teaching current events.

PBS

www.pbs.org

Click on the Kids pages for interactive learning and information on a variety of topics.

Summary

Nonfiction books capture our students' attention, offer answers to their unending questions, and motivate them to expand their knowledge by seeking out more information. The world of nonfiction literature for children has improved and multiplied, giving us a wealth of titles from which to choose. In order to make every instructional minute count, we select books to enhance our content area curriculum while at the same time teaching essential literacy understandings. Students with a rich background of nonfiction reading and writing experiences are on the road to successful experiences in school and in life in an era when being on top of the exploding world of information is an absolute necessity.

Chapter 8

Poetry

CHANGING THE TEMPO IN YOUR CLASSROOM

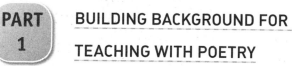

PART 1 — BUILDING BACKGROUND FOR TEACHING WITH POETRY

Introducing Rhymes, Rhythms, and Quiet Places

When words come trip, trip, tripping over your tongue, then hop down to tease your toes into tap, tap, tapping out their rhythms, poetry has come to call. Don't hesitate. Open your classroom door to this welcome guest. Sometimes short, other times long, perhaps silly, even somber—there's sure to be a poem for every student in your classroom. How do we teach all students to appreciate what poetry has to offer? Donald Graves (2003) says to surround them with poetry. Ronald Cramer (2001) and Jim Trelease (2006) join others, in urging us to read it aloud. Laura Robb (2003) reminds us to weave poetry across the curriculum. Informative, amusing, and even reassuring, it adds a spark to science, social studies, and math. Imagine beginning your lesson on the scientific method with the innovative "Scientific Method at Bat," from *Science Verse* (Scieszka, 2004):

> The outlook wasn't brilliant for my
> experiment that day;
> The only way to graduate was to
> come up with an A.
> So when my lab exploded and
> turned to blackish gunk,
> My chance of passing anything went
> Titanic—you know, sunk.
> (unpaged)

Poetry begs to be read aloud.

It won't take long to realize that first-hand experience with poetry can foster a love for this genre (Galda & Cullinan, 2006; Heard, 1989). Join us as we work together to develop a positive "poetitude," the belief that poetry has a number of values as a teaching and learning tool for all of our students (Parr & Campbell, 2006, p. 36). A bounty of exceptional books and sound teaching ideas await you.

What Is Poetry?

Poetry eludes a simple definition. It may be easier to define through actual experiences than by written explanations. However, it does have some distinctive characteristics to help us investigate its inner workings. First, poetry is compact; every word counts. Second, the arrangement of words and their sounds adds flavor to each poem. Then, whether the poem rhymes or is in free verse, a natural rhythm is required (Glazer & Giorgis, 2005). Hillman (2002) explains that poetry is often "… patterned. It has more intensity than prose, it uses more figurative language, and it sometimes follows rather strict structures" (p. 137). Yet, there are ballads, narratives, and lyrical poetry that tell a story, so the length does vary. Finally, poetry captures a moment of our emotions, eliciting a smile, a knowing sigh, or a reflective pause. In the process, it gives us an opportunity to see life a little differently or to use our imaginations in playful ways (Galda & Cullinan, 2006; Kiefer, Hepler, & Hickman, 2007). With these characteristics as our background, let's take a brief look at Mother Goose rhymes. They play a role in developing language skills and forging early connections with poetry (Opitz, 2000).

> *"Poetry splashes the page in a rainbow of words and images. Poetry is a mystery of moods and tones, of thoughts and feelings. In the end, it cannot be satisfactorily explained; it must be felt."*
>
> (Cramer, 2001, p. 302)

The nursery rhymes we learned as children are a readily accessible introduction to poetry (Lukens, 2007; Lynch-Brown & Tomlinson, 2005). Heard over and over again, chanted at home and in primary grades, these verses become a part of a child's early acquaintance with such familiar elements of poetry as rhythm, rhyme, and sound patterns. Children from varying cultural backgrounds are raised with such familiar, playful rhymes. Can you finish these old favorites?

> There was an old woman who lived in a shoe…
> or
> This little piggie went to market,
> This little piggie stayed home…

No doubt the concluding lines popped right into your mind. If not, find them in the colorful *Random House Book of Mother Goose* (Lobel, 1986). Another steppingstone to poetry involves jump-rope rhymes. You'll hear voices carrying favorite rhymes across the playground at recess as ropes whirl and feet slap the ground. To add variety to what students already know, share a few new verses from Joanna Cole's *Anna Banana: 101 Jump Rope Rhymes* (1989) or read aloud the delightful picture book *Jump Rope Magic* (Scruggs, 2000). From these upbeat beginnings, the next pages will examine the particular elements that are the very fiber of poetry. Used inventively, they become the threads with which poets weave their magic.

What Are the Elements of Poetry?

When poets pen their lines, they have commonly used tools at hand. The following elements are an integral part of the poems you and your students enjoy. With a better understanding of what they are and how they can be applied, you will use them with confidence when you and your class read and write poetry together.

Try This!   Tips for Teaching Poetry

1. Examine your poetry experiences and attitude, and work with your students to develop an upbeat, positive approach to sharing and composing poetry.

2. Read your favorite poems aloud to surround your students with the sounds of language.

3. Question the poet.

4. Look for poetry in everyday life.

5. Write your own poems.

6. Read your poems to an audience.

7. Borrow a poetry lesson from a book, Web site, or colleague.

8. Integrate what you know about teaching writing and reading into your poetry lessons.

9. Focus on the process of writing poetry.

10. Create your own poetry lessons.

11. Cultivate a safe classroom environment in which your students can share their poems with others.

12. Collaborate with colleagues to collect successful poetry lessons.

13. Publish your lessons and ideas.

(Linaberger, 2004/2005; Parr & Campbell, 2006)

Literature Is Back!

Rhythm and Rhyme

Children are drawn to poetry as they match their innate natural rhythms to those inside a poem (Huck et al., 2004). All poems have rhythm to one degree or another. Sometimes the beat may be hand-clapping strong as in this sampling of "Mother Doesn't Want a Dog" by Judith Viorst:

> Mother doesn't want a dog.
> Mother says they smell,
> And never sit when you say sit,
> Or even when you yell.
> And when you come home late at night
> And there is ice and snow,
> You have to go back out because
> The dumb dog has to go… (Prelutsky, 1983, p. 133)

This makes you want to read the rest, doesn't it? Then, rhythm may be gentle, as found in "April Rain Song" by Langston Hughes:

> Let the rain kiss you.
> Let the rain beat down upon your head with silver liquid drops.
> Let the rain sing you a lullaby.
> The rain makes still pools on the sidewalk.
> The rain makes running pools in the gutter.
> The rain plays a little sleep-song on our roof at night—
> And I love the rain. (Kennedy, 2005, p. 63)

However a poet chooses to use rhythm, it is done with an eye to creating meaning (Galda & Cullinan, 2006). Develop an ear for the rhythms of poems by reading them aloud. Ask children to point out words that are stressed strongly or lightly. Snap or clap, briskly or softly, as students listen and study how poets use this particular element. Before you know it, young writers will be deftly adding this element to their poems.

The most familiar element of poetry, needing little explanation, is rhyme. Children love the rhymes in poems, typically listening for ending rhymes (Cramer, 2001). They often despair when they try it themselves, however, for rhyming is difficult. As a result, one of the first lessons to teach budding poets is that while rhymes are enjoyable to hear, not every poem has to rhyme. Although they also focus on rhythm, the preceding two poems are perfect examples of poems with and without rhyme. Invite students to bring samples of both kinds to a Listening Circle from time to time. As you savor selections, cue students into the way rhythm and rhyme work together to create the musical quality of poetry.

Sound Patterns

In Chapter 1 we discussed style, looking at the way authors use their words in narrative writing. The same sound patterns that impact style now reappear in poetry, carrying even more weight. They are revisited briefly here with an illustration of how they work.

Listen to how alliteration and consonance work as you read the first verse of "Multilingual Mynah Bird" by Jack Prelutsky (2006, p. 44):

> Birds are known to cheep and chirp
> and sing and warble, peep and purp,
> and some can only squeak and squawk
> but the mynah bird is able to talk…

Then, try the primary lesson on onomatopoeia (page 229) to practice this device with your students. You'll enjoy an opportunity to play with "noisy" words. You can easily adapt the lesson to engage intermediate-grade learners as well.

Imagery

Poets have a way of showing us everyday things in an entirely different light. They use imagery to draw on our senses to generate vivid pictures in our minds as our eyes sample their words (Cramer, 2001; Lukens, 2007). The constant challenge is to create images that are fresh and unique. For example, have you ever thought about "sunflakes" as imagined by Frank Asch in these opening lines?

> Sunflakes
> If sunlight fell like snowflakes,
> gleaming yellow and so bright,
> we could build a sunman,
> we could have a sunball fight,
> we could watch the sunflakes
> drifting in the sky.
> (de Regniers, Moore, White, & Carr, 1988, p. 27)

- • *alliteration:* repetition of the first letter or consonant blends in one or more words in a line
- • *consonance:* like alliteration but attention is on the close placement of final consonants
- • *assonance:* vowel sounds are repeated in one or more words in a line
- • *onomatopoeia:* words that sound like their meanings as in the *sizzle* of bacon, the *roar* of a lion, or a *crack* of thunder

Find a selection of your favorite poems that vividly shows imagery at work. Read a poem aloud and ask the students to sketch what they see, hear, taste, or feel depending on the poet's words. Try another one. Visualizing is an important comprehension strategy that can be practiced effortlessly within the world of poetry, especially when imagery is masterfully done.

Figurative Language

In the process of helping us perceive the world a little differently, poets often compare one thing we readily recognize with another, presenting us with quite an attention-grabbing surprise. They reach for similes—indirect comparisons and metaphors (direct comparisons) to delight and entertain readers. Enjoy the *simile* found in the first verse of "The Power Shovel" by Rowena Bennett (Hopkins, 1987, p. 9):

> The power digger
> Is much bigger
>> Than the biggest beast I know.
> He snorts and roars
>> Like dinosaurs
> That lived long ago.

A vivid *metaphor* is found in the description of March in *January Rides the Wind* (Otten, 1997, unpaged):

> March eats the winter;
> icicles drip from its mouth
> to fall on secret gardens.

Readers can go on a hunt for other examples of figurative language, periodically reading their discoveries aloud for the class to enjoy. They might collect a sampling in their writers' notebooks for future reference as they learn from the experts.

Finally, *personification,* when used skillfully, is another powerful tool for young poets. In this case, poets take inanimate objects or animals and enliven them with human characteristics. Notice how effective this device is in "Flight Practice," from the beautiful *Hummingbird Nest: A Journal of Poems* (George, 2004, unpaged):

> Four curled feet grip
> the top of the nest.
> Two tiny motors
> rev up for wing test.

Two aviators
Begin to lift off…
　　　　Uh-oh!
They quickly adjust
Wing speed back to slow…
Two student pilots
not yet ready
　　　to
　　　　　　let
　　　　　　　　　go.

Place the focus on figurative language by showcasing each element on an attention-getting, student-created bulletin board. Students can collect poems that highlight each device effectively. Add interpretive student illustrations. The end result will be a captivating spot for readers to stop, browse, and discover the writer's craft as it is tied to poetry.

Shape

Sometimes poets use the shape of their poems to add to the visual experience and to extend the meaning of the poem (Grandits, 2005). Words might swirl like water as a fish swims through it or stretch out long and thin like a giraffe's neck. When the shape clearly represents the topic of the poem, we have created concrete poems. The clever use of shape invites student creativity. Look at how effective this is in Jack Prelutsky's poem "A Triangular Tale."

I
DO
NOT
KNOW
AT ALL HOW
I GOT STUCK
INSIDE THIS PIECE
OF PIE AND I'M
UNSURE HOW TO
BEGIN TO GET OUT
OF THE FIX I'M IN. THIS
TRIANGLE IS SIMPLY NOT
AN ENTERTAINING SORT
OF SPOT SO I CAN SAY WITHOUT
A DOUBT I'D LIKE TO LEAVE AND **WOW**….
I'm out!
(Prelutsky, 1996, p. 60)

Bring in numerous examples of the innovative use of shape. Sample the titles in the chart on page 216 and find others in anthologies and theme-related poetry books. It won't be long before you are savoring students' efforts as they bring their own poems to life through shape.

Children's Poetry Preferences

When you share poetry in your classroom, what kinds of poems do your students prefer? If you study the research, you'll learn that both primary- and intermediate-grade students have their favorites. Children usually prefer these forms:

♦ Narrative poems rather than lyric poems

♦ Limericks rather than free verse and haiku

♦ Poems with different sound patterns, especially rhyming poems

♦ Poems with a distinct rhythm

♦ Humorous poems, animal poems, and poems about families

♦ Contemporary poems and those that express familiar and positive emotions (Fisher & Natarella, 1982; Terry, 1974)

While there are no clearly drawn lines because personal taste varies, it seems that primary students tend to enjoy poems about strange and fantastic events, animals, and other children. Students in the intermediate grades are more apt to select poems with realistic topics about family experiences and animals with a liberal dose of humor mixed in. Both groups of children have found figurative language confusing (Lynch-Brown & Tomlinson, 2005). Practical advice is to begin with those poems your students like. Gradually extend their knowledge and experiences with others that are more challenging (Lukens, 2007; Parr & Campbell, 2006).

Have You Read These?

A FEW OF OUR FAVORITE HUMOROUS POETRY BOOKS

♦ *Laugh-eteria* (Florian, 1999)

♦ *Oh No! Where Are My Pants? And Other Disasters* (Hopkins, 2005)

♦ *Kids Pick the Funniest Poems* (Lansky, 1991)

♦ *For Laughing Out Loud: Poems to Tickle Your Funnybone* (Prelutsky, 1991)

♦ *Behold the Bold Umbrellaphant* (Prelutsky, 2006)

♦ *Frankenstein Makes a Sandwich* (Rex, 2006)

♦ *Where the Sidewalk Ends* (Silverstein, 1974)

♦ *Runny Babbit: A Billy Sook* (Silverstein, 2005)

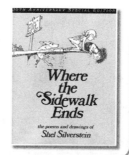

Poetry by Popular Preferences

Subject	A Literature Sampling	Research-Supported Literacy Activities
Animals	*Carnival of the Animals* (Chernaik, 2005) *Bugs: Poems About Creeping Things* (Harrison, 2007) *Yellow Elephant: A Bright Bestiary* (Larios, 2006) *Who Swallowed Harold? And Other Poems About Pets* (Pearson, 2005) *Butterfly Eyes and Other Secrets of the Meadow* (Sidman, 2006a) *Eric Carle's Animals, Animals* (Whipple, 1989)	Encourage students to build fluency through repeated readings with the goal of reading a favorite animal poem aloud. For book-length poems, work in pairs or triads to perfect and present the poem in an engaging listening experience for classmates. Form a poetry troupe and perform for other classes.
Family and Friendship	*Hopscotch Love* (Grimes, 1999) *Danitra Brown Leaves Town* (Grimes, 2002 *Very Best (Almost) Friends: Poems of Friendship* (Janeczko, 1999) *You and Me: Poems of Friendship* (Mavor, 1997) *In Daddy's Arms I Am Tall* (Steptoe, 1997)	Have students pick a friend or family member to write about. Use imagery and figurative language to bring the person to life in the mind of listeners and other readers. A second choice is to write about an experience shared with a friend or one's family.
School	*Don't Read This Book, Whatever You Do!* (Dakos, 1993) *Mathematickles* (Franco, 2003) *Danitra Brown, Class Clown* (Grimes, 2005) *School Supplies: A Book of Poems* (Hopkins, 1996b) *If Kids Ruled the School* (Lansky, 2004)	Model the writing process through a class-composed poem. Brainstorm school topics and select a favorite. Work together to create a poem. Then, revise to underscore its importance in creating a polished poem. Reinforce the fact that words can be manipulated until they are just right.

Poetry: Types, Titles, and Teaching Ideas

When discussing the different types of poetry, we have chosen to concentrate on six types: narrative, lyrical, limericks, free verse, haiku, and concrete poems. See the Glance Chart Forms of Poetry (pages 220–221) for a brief description of each type, exemplary books to get you started, and a relevant teaching idea. Whatever type you are teaching, remember to model, model, model. Choose examples that you personally enjoy, and you'll easily present them with genuine enthusiasm. If you would like to build your confidence and broaden your understanding of teaching and writing poetry, turn to the experts. Try Georgia Heard's (1998) *Awakening the Heart: Exploring Poetry in Elementary School* or any of the titles in Helpful Resources for Teaching Poetry (page 224). These experts are creative, congenial teachers.

Here is another innovative idea. To heighten your students' interest in an upcoming theme or topic, Pam Nelson (2005) suggests gathering a collection of items, each with an accompanying poem or poetry book, and placing them in a suitcase, bag, or box. Invite students to choose an item from the container. Then, they are to read the poem aloud that matches the item. Several possible items and poems include:

- **Dinosaurs**—A model dinosaur, plus *Tyrannosaurus Was a Beast: Dinosaur Poems* (Prelutsky, 1988)

- **Geography**—A mango, plus *Is It Far to Zanzibar?* (Grimes, 2000)

- **Sports**—A baseball, plus *Opening Days: Sports Poems* (Hopkins, 1996a)

You will have a wonderful time collecting items and scouring books for poems. That wonder will transfer to your students as they get into the spirit of making poetry connections with the subject matter soon to be taught.

Why Is Poetry Important to My Students?

When you think about poetry, think flexibility. Use poetry to enrich your students' learning in different content areas and to vary your teaching options to reach children of all abilities. Then, always add a few verses to energize your day, never losing sight of the fact that poetry is downright fun.

A Boon to Struggling Readers

While poetry is an inviting tool to help all young children build language skills, it is particularly helpful for struggling readers and second language learners (Hadaway, Vardell, & Young, 2001; Wicklund, 1989). Why? The concise text is less intimidating than many books offer. It reinforces the sounds in words to be mastered, builds needed vocabulary, and is perfect for the supportive practice of choral reading. These are but a few advantages. In addition, poetry is particularly effective in strengthening oral language development. To use poetry to the benefit of every child, try these strategies:

Concrete poems about the seasons fill this colorful picture book.

- ◆ Enthusiastically read poems aloud, displaying the words on an overhead or chart.

- ◆ Invite students to join in on a repeated line or refrain.

- ◆ Choose shorter, rhythmic poems to read in unison with students.

- ◆ Divide students into two groups and use the "call and response" method.

- ◆ If there are multiple stanzas, create multiple groups to read them.

- ◆ Vary voices by assigning individual solo lines.

- ◆ Read poems in two to four voices using books like *Joyful Noise* (Fleischman, 1988) or *Big Talk* (Fleischman, 2000).

- ◆ Combine music and poetry and sing poems.
  (Farris, Fuhler, & Walther, 2004; Hadaway et al., 2001; Wicklund, 1989)

With such a variety available, poems can easily be matched to the interests and experiences of every student in a personally motivating manner.

Literature Is Back!

Poetry Across the Curriculum

To build upon the idea of flexibility, think about Laura Robb's (2003) suggestion to reach across the curriculum with poetry. For instance, understanding that math is difficult for others will catch the attention of a hesitant student who hears the opening lines of "Math Is Brewing and I'm in Trouble" (at right) from *If You're Not Here, Please Raise Your Hand* (Dakos, 1990).

Other tempting titles can be found in Poetry Across the Curriculum, below. Add your favorites to this starter list.

Numbers single,

Numbers double.

Math is brewing

And I'm in trouble.

If I could mix a magic brew,

Numbers, I'd take care of you! (p. 4)

Poetry Across the Curriculum

Science:

• *Erni Cabat's Magical World of Dinosaurs* (Cabat & Butler, 1989) (Gr. 3–6)

• *Spectacular Science: A Book of Poems* (Hopkins, 1999) (Gr. 2–6)

• *Bone Poems* (Moss, 1997) (Gr. 3–5)

• *Earthshake: Poems From the Ground Up* (Peters, 2003) (Gr. 1–6)

• *Song of the Water Boatman & Other Pond Poems* (Sidman, 2005) (Gr. K–5)

• *Feathers: Poems About Birds* (Spinelli, 2004) (Gr. 2–5)

• *Bird Watch* (Yolen, 1990) (Gr. 2+)

Social Studies:

• *When Horses Ride By: Children in the Times of War* (Greenfield, 2006) (Gr. 2–6)

• *Maples in the Mist: Children's Poems From the Tang Dynasty* (Ho, 1996) (Gr. 3+)

• *My America: A Poetry Atlas of the United States* (Hopkins, 2000) (Gr. 3–8)

• *Hand in Hand: An American History Through Poetry* (Hopkins, 1994) (Gr. 3–6)

• *Festivals* (Livingston, 1996) (Gr. K–4)

• *Mural on Second Avenue and Other City Poems* (Moore, 2005) (Gr. K–2)

• *…I Never Saw Another Butterfly: Children's Drawings and Poems from Terezin Concentration Camp, 1942–1944* (Volavkova, 1994) (Gr. 4–6)

Forms of Poetry

Form of Poetry/Description	A Literature Sampling	Research-Supported Literacy Activities
Narrative These lengthier poems must tell a story complete with the familiar literary elements.	*All by Herself: 14 Girls Who Made a Difference* (Paul, 1999) *Heartland* (Siebert, 1989) *'Twas the Night Before Christmas* (Tavares, 2006) *I Have Heard of a Land* (Thomas, 1998)	Invite students to make puppets or use other props and dramatize a story to enhance comprehension and build oral language skills. Present productions on parents' night or for a school assembly.
Lyrical Lyrical poems capture feelings, a moment, or a scene, and are descriptive. Emotions drive this type of poetry.	*Honey, I Love* (Greenfield, 1995) *This Place I Know: Poems of Comfort* (Heard, 2002) *Poems in Black and White* (Miller, 2007) *Hailstones and Halibut Bones* (O'Neill, 1961)	Students can compose a short story using a poem as the story starter. Follow the Writers' Workshop process. Practice reading the poem and story aloud and then share it in small groups or as a whole-group author celebration.
Free Verse Subtle rhythm, a reflective stance, and absence of rhyme, are hallmarks of free verse.	*In for Winter, Out for Spring* (Adoff, 1991) *Fold Me a Poem* (George, 2005) *The Dream on Blanca's Wall: Poems in English and Spanish* (Medina, 2004) *Canto Familiar* (Soto, 1995)	Teach students to foster connections by asking themselves: —What do I like about this poem? —Does it remind me of anything I have experienced? —What do I think the poet is trying to say to me? Then, discuss poems in small groups. Finally, capture your learning by writing a poem.

Forms of Poetry

Form of Poetry/ Description	A Literature Sampling	Research-Supported Literacy Activities
Limericks Made popular by Edward Lear, these are short nonsense verses that follow a five-line pattern. The first, second, and fifth lines rhyme. Each has three distinct beats. The third and fourth lines rhyme and have two clear beats.	*The Hopeful Trout and Other Limericks* (Ciardi, 1992) *Lots of Limericks* (Livingston, 1991) *The Book of Pigericks* (Lobel, 1983) *One at a Time: His Collected Poems for the Young* (McCord, 1986)	Highlight the humor with artistic connections. Students pick a limerick, add a fitting illustration, then present the creation to the class. Display on a bulletin board highlighting the delights of limericks. Preserve the work later in a class book.
Concrete Poet uses the shape of the words on the page to underscore the meaning or idea behind the poem.	*Outside the Lines: Poetry at Play* (Burg, 2002) *Flicker Flash* (Graham, 1999) *Technically, It's Not My Fault* (Grandits, 2004) *A Poke in the I: A Collection of Concrete Poems* (Janeczko, 2001) *Doodle Dandies: Poems That Take Shape* (Lewis, 1998) *Come to My Party and Other Shape Poems* (Roemer, 2004) *Meow Ruff: A Story in Concrete Poetry* (Sidman, 2006b)	Invite students to try their hand at concrete poetry. Encourage them to begin with a familiar object such as a shape, animal, or household item.
Haiku Japanese verse that typically uses nature as a theme and reflects a brief thought or emotion. Poems follow a pattern of 3 lines and 17 syllables: First line – 5 Second line – 7 Third line – 5	*Don't Step on the Sky: A Handful of Haiku* (Chaikin, 2002) *Cool Melons—Turn to Frogs!: The Life and Poems of Issa* (Gollub, 1998) *One Leaf Rides the Wind: Counting in a Japanese Garden* (Mannis, 2002) *If Not for the Cat: Haiku* (Prelutsky, 2004) *Spring: A Haiku Story* (Shannon, 1996) *Grass Sandals: The Travels of Basho* (Spivak, 1997)	Strengthen word recognition skills as students examine potential words for their poems. They must recognize and count syllables and consider word meanings as they judge words for their ability to communicate exactly the mood.

Building Blocks of Literacy: The Sounds of Language

Very young children love to play with the sounds of language. They build imaginatively upon the rhymes and verses they have heard, making up their own giggle-producing versions (Glazer & Giorgis, 2005; Opitz, 2000). In the process, they are developing vital skills in phonemic awareness, the alphabetic principle, and language patterns (Farris et al., 2004). This is an opportune time to augment the joy of wordplay, making poetry a natural part of the life of each learner. In the process your children will polish fluency skills, a critical component in reading comprehension (Fountas & Pinnell, 1996). Older students are continuing to strengthen their literacy skills in a myriad of ways, including expanding their vocabulary. Poetry is an invitation to keep at it. Bobbi Katz (Janeczko, 2002) offers learners the following encouragement: "Remember: words are a poet's basic tools. Collect vocabulary. Eat your words! Explore the taste as well as the sound of words. Does a word hum to you? Does it invite you to play? Does it beg you to repeat it? To rhyme it? The more words you know, the easier it will be to find the lines to create the images you want and to carry them where you want them to go" (p. 59).

Guidelines for Selecting Poetry

As with books in the other genres, poetry offerings vary in quality. Use the guidelines below to help you find the most appropriate, irresistible poems:

- The ideas and feelings shared in the poem are interesting, unique, and imaginative.

- The poem is appropriate for your students and does not preach to them.

- The poem looks at the world from a child's perspective.

- The poem expresses ordinary ideas and feelings in unique ways.

- Poetry collections are judged on the literary merit of selected poems first and illustrations second.

- Poetry exhibits a fresh, natural use of language, and rhymes are not contrived.

(Glazer & Giorgis, 2005; Lynch-Brown & Tomlinson, 2005)

Endings and Beginnings

Poetry is a gift you give yourself and your students every time you share a poem. It is a vehicle to teach reading, writing, fluency, listening, and to simply savor wonderful words. It celebrates our laughter, quiet times, and sorrow, binding us together into a community of learners who share similar experiences inside and outside of the classroom. Have we convinced you to polish your "poetitude" by now? Do make this flexible genre an integral part of life in your classroom.

Have You Read These?

A FEW OF OUR FAVORITE POETRY ANTHOLOGIES

- *A Jar of Tiny Stars: Poems by NCTE Award-Winning Poets* (Cullinan, 1996)
- *Sing a Song of Popcorn* (de Regniers, Moore, White, & Carr, 1988)
- *Good Books, Good Times!* (Hopkins, 1990)
- *A Family of Poems: My Favorite Poetry for Children* (Kennedy, 2005)
- *Talking Like the Rain: A First Book of Poems* (Kennedy & Kennedy, 1992)
- *More Spice Than Sugar: Poems About Feisty Females* (Morrison, 2001)
- *The Beauty of the Beast: Poems From the Animal Kingdom* (Prelutsky, 2006)
- *The Random House Book of Poetry for Children* (Prelutsky, 1983)
- *Here's a Little Poem: A First Book of Poetry* (Yolen & Peters, 2007)

Helpful Resources for Teaching Poetry

- *For the Good of the Earth and Sun: Teaching Poetry* (Heard, 1989)
  Heard shows teachers how to make classrooms havens for poetry writers.

- *Poetry Matters: Writing a Poem From the Inside Out* (Fletcher, 2002)
  Fletcher guides experienced intermediate-grade poets through the process of creating and improving their poems.

- *A Kick in the Head: An Everyday Guide to Poetic Forms* (Janeczko, 2005)
  This clever book explains the rules of 29 poetic forms with accessible examples.

- *Seeing the Blue Between: Advice and Inspiration for Young Poets* (Janeczko, 2002)
  Thirty-two poets write a bit of advice to students and include a sampling of poems.

- *Read a Rhyme, Write a Rhyme* (Prelutsky, 2005)
  This collection of poems on ten popular themes includes a "poemstart" for each theme and suggests how readers may continue the poem.

- *The Adventures of Dr. Alphabet: 104 Unusual Ways to Write Poetry in the Classroom and in the Community* (Morice, 1995)
  You and your students will be challenged to write a variety of inventive poems as you read this book.

LINKING LITERATURE AND LEARNING

The Reading Connection

LaDonna Wicklund (1989) reminds us of the potential of shared reading when she demonstrates the values of adapting it to a shared poetry approach (Fountas & Pinnell, 1996). Effective with her struggling readers, it is applicable to all students. Begin by using a classroom chart or overhead to read and study a poem together. Discuss unusual words, build vocabulary, and increase fluency as you read a poem over and over again together. In addition, sharing a poem in this manner is a great confidence builder as you scaffold learning when you are trying a new type of poetry on for size. Notice how this shared poetry approach can work in the upcoming mini-lessons.

Primary Lesson Plan: Sing a Song, Read a Rhyme—Increasing Phonemic Awareness and Phonics Skills

Purpose:

As young children sing along to a familiar tune, they are making discoveries about the sound system of language. As we sing with our children, we can capitalize on the teaching opportunities by pointing out specific language features (Opitz, 2000). These language features may take the form of rhymes such as those found in familiar tunes, made into picture books like *Row, Row, Row Your Boat* (Goodhart, 1997).

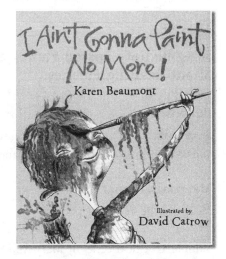

Materials/Preparation:

♦ Your favorite song picture books. Here are a few of our favorites that feature catchy rhythms and rhymes:

I Ain't Gonna Paint No More! (Beaumont, 2005)
Give a Dog a Bone (Kellogg, 2000)
We All Go Traveling By (Roberts, 2003)

Mini-Lessons:

Each of the following mini-lesson ideas is designed to assist you in using songs to build your students' phonological awareness and phonics skills.

- Share songs throughout the day. Use them to help students make the transition from one activity to the next. Sing as you wait for the bell to ring at the end of the day.

- Divide students in two groups and teach them how to sing "Row, Row, Row Your Boat" in a round.

- Type the words to the songs for students to sing and read at home.

- Invite students to create their own verses to add to their favorite songs.

- Use familiar tunes to rewrite songs about various topics.

- Provide students with musical instruments to play along to reinforce the rhythm of the tune.

A song about turtles written to the familiar tune of "Camptown Races."

Intermediate Lesson Plan: How to Develop Oral and Silent Reading Fluency

Purpose:

A smile-inducing way to develop oral reading fluency is to make choral reading a part of your day. Begin with these samples and go on a quest to discover your own favorites.

Materials/Preparation:

A copy of the following poems:

Sample 1: "Clickbeetle" by Mary Ann Hoberman (Prelutsky, 1983, p. 193)

> Clickbeetle
> Clackbeetle
> Snapjack black beetle

Glint glitter glare beetle
Pin it in your hair beetle
Tack it to your shawl beetle
Wear it at the ball beetle
Shine shimmer spark beetle
Glisten in the dark beetle
Click beetle
Clack beetle

Sample 2: "Song of the Train" by David McCord (1980, p. 107)
Clickety-clack,
Wheels on the track,
This is the way
They begin the attack:
Click-ety-clack,
Click-ety-clack,
Click-ety, *clack*-ety,
Click-ety
Clack.

Clickety-clack,
Over the crack,
Faster and faster
The song of the track:
Clickety-clack,
Clickety-clack,
Clickety-clackety,
Clackety
Clack.

Riding in front,
Riding in back,
Everyone hears
The song of the track:
Clickety-clack,
Clickety-clack,
Clickety, *clickety*,
Clackety
Clack.

Mini-Lesson: Oral Reading Fluency

1. Print out the entire sample of each poem. Display one on chart paper, ELMO,™ or an overhead transparency.

2. Model reading the poem aloud with expression.

3. Practice reading through it with the class several times until students are comfortable with the words and rhythm.

4. Break into two groups and read it as a round. Direct the second group to begin after the first two lines. Try it again because once is not enough!

5. After some practice, read the poem at a faster pace. Then, break into three groups and read it briskly. The words will fairly fly around the room. Next, try the second example.

After this shared experience, notice the high energy level in the classroom when you are done reciting. Active participation in poetry does that.

Mini-Lesson: Silent Reading Fluency

To improve silent reading fluency, give students time to read a variety of poetry. As with other types of reading, the more they read, the better they get.

1. Have students select and reread some of their favorite poems. With each careful reading, students are becoming more comfortable with the vocabulary, content, phrasing, and emotions underlying the poems.

2. Caution students to pay attention to the meaning of the poems rather than just trying to read them at a faster rate with each rereading (Worthy & Prater, 2002).

3. Give students an incentive to practice. Encourage them to showcase their fluent interpretation of a favorite poem by scheduling periodic Poetry Reads where students sign up ahead of time to read a well-digested poem to the class. Enjoy a coffeehouse atmosphere at another time. Serve hot chocolate, a few munchies, add a microphone, and invite poets to participate. This is a wonderful, change-of-pace way to strengthen important literacy skills.

The Writing Connection

Young children delight at the sounds of language. They love joining in with their favorite authors or poets when they use onomatopoeia to add punch to their writing. The following primary mini-lesson will help you introduce this clever writing technique to your budding authors. In the intermediate lesson, learn how you can tie social studies and writing together by having students write a poem about a historical person or an everyday hero. In this case, you start with a narrative and end with a poem.

Primary Lesson Plan: Adding a SPLASH to Your Writing!

Purpose:

To teach children what techniques like onomatopoeia can do for their writing.

Materials/Preparation:

Any of the following picture books and poems that include a rich variety of sounds:

♦ *Slop Goes the Soup: A Noisy Warthog Word Book* (Edwards, 2001)

♦ *Barnyard Banter* (Fleming, 1994)

♦ *Hoot, Howl, Hiss* (Koch, 1991)

Mini-Lesson:

1. Write the following examples of onomatopoeia on a chart or chalkboard: *pop, chomp, slam, crunch, splash, hoot.* Ask students to share what they notice about the words. Discuss the definition of onomatopoeia, a word that sounds just like the noise it is describing.

2. Read some samples from the above books. Remind children to listen for the use of onomatopoeia.

3. Make a list of examples of onomatopoeia that can be used as students write or revise a piece of work. For example, when writing a piece about school, we listed all onomatopoeia possibilities, in our environment, such as:
Whirr goes the pencil sharpener.
Bounce goes the ball.

4. Encourage students to use or add an appropriate onomatopoeia to their piece.

Add Onomatopoeia!

creak ▫   bubble °°
slurp ⊖   tick-tock ⊕
crackle   whoosh ⊂⟋
groan   toot-toot
click-clack hiccup
squeak   splash ∵∵
squirt   boom
tweet   smash
pitter-patter crash
pop ∪
boink

A collection of onomatopoeia.

Intermediate Lesson Plan: From Narrative to Poetry—Writing Biographical Poems

Purpose:

Reading and writing biographical poems reinforces personal connections.

Materials/Preparation:

Use a selection of books such as these:

- *Heroes and She-roes: Poems of Amazing and Everyday Heroes* (Lewis, 2005)
- *How Smart We Are* (Nikola-Lisa, 2006)
- *All By Herself: 14 Girls Who Made a Difference* (Paul, 1999)
- *Hoop Kings* (Smith, 2004)
- *Hoop Queens* (Smith, 2003)

For additional writing material, look for a collection of picture book biographies or other short biographies, copies of *Sports Illustrated for Kids*, or appropriate Internet sites.

Mini-Lesson:

1. Read a selection of poems from the above titles. Make text-to-self or text-to-text connections by asking students what they know about the person in each poem.

2. Bring in an appropriate collection of picture book biographies or other relevant materials with relatively short text. Short text provides just enough information to work with during the first attempts to write poetry from narrative material.

3. Model the writing process by reading one of the picture books aloud. Demonstrate how you select tidbits of interest to work into a poem.

4. Decide on the type of poem best suited to the subject matter. Ask the students to contribute as you write together.

5. Divide into pairs and let each pair take the first draft to the next stage.

6. Share and discuss the various refined drafts. Students can choose to continue to revise this attempt or to set it aside and try a fresh poem on their own.

7. Finally, let students read and write, circulating through the class to offer support as needed.

8. Polish and publish in an eye-catching way.

Four Fine Web Sites

PoetryTeachers.com

www.poetryteachers.com

Enjoy an exceptional site for a myriad of ideas and resources for teaching poetry.

Poetry for Kids: Giggle Poetry

www.gigglepotz.com/kidspoetry.htm

Find teaching tips, favorite poets, and poetry lesson plans here.

Poetry4Kids.com

www.poetry4kids.com

Kenn Nesbitt's Poetry Playground includes poems, games, lessons, links, and more.

Potato Hill Poetry

www.potatohill.com

Here is a perfect site on which you can to publish your students' poetry along with your own.

Summary

Poetry. Our classrooms are not complete without it. Because some of us have not had much experience with this genre, it might be neglected. Do not be fearful of new or uncommon materials that can bring excitement to your classroom day. Partner with a colleague to pool resources and expertise, perfect your "poetitude," and give your students the gift of poetry. Read aloud or sampled silently, poetry can enrich students' reading and writing lives, from the youngest listener to the budding intermediate-grade writer, and can inspire teachers as well. Life in your classroom will be rich, rollicking, and rewarding when you infuse poetry throughout your reading, writing, and content area curriculum.

Chapter 9

Using Children's Literature

IN THE CLASSROOM

> My favorite place is
> inside a book for many
> reasons. It is a place I
> can vist without paying anything
> or traveling anywhere. It
> is open all the time and
> I can go whenever I want.
> I really like when my mom
> and dad read to me because
> I can just rest and listen
> to the story.

Michael's essay, Part 4

So Many Books, So Little Time

So many books, so little time. This slogan stretches across the front of T-shirts and on canvas bags at our favorite bookstores. Without a doubt, finding ways to lessen the frantic pace in classrooms is a quandary. Our curriculum is jam-packed. How, then, do we efficiently use the time available to meet our students' needs and to teach essential literacy skills and strategies? We make decisions. Throughout a typical teaching day, we make a multitude of instructional decisions. We continually ask ourselves tough questions such as these: *What is the best way to reach a reluctant learner? Why is a student having difficulty comprehending or composing text? How can I meet the needs of my struggling readers and writers and those who excel? When will I have time to plan for instruction, gather materials, and teach the lessons that are vital to my students' growth as literacy learners?* Fortunately, we have the words of knowledgeable experts to steer us in the right direction. To frame our thinking, we look to the National Board for Professional Teaching Standards (2001) and their standards for accomplished educators. Their five core propositions tell us that effective teachers:

- commit themselves to students and their learning
- know the subjects they teach and how to teach those subjects to students
- manage and monitor student learning
- think systematically about their practice and learn from experience
- participate in learning communities

In this chapter we will use those five core propositions as a framework to guide you in making instructional choices that will positively impact your readers and writers. We've translated them into a set of helpful guidelines for integrating the wealth of material found in this text into your daily classroom practice.

Make every student count.
- Know your literacy learners.
- Know the qualities of exemplary classroom teachers.

Make every minute count.
- Know your curriculum standards and expectations.
- Recognize the hallmarks of proficient readers and writers.
- Use instructional time to its fullest.

Make every lesson count.
- Be an active reader and writer.
- Reflect, question, and continue to learn.

Make every book count.
- Create excitement for a book.

With this concluding chapter, we offer a big-picture look at literacy instruction. We suggest ideas coupled with some of our favorite teaching resources, should you wish to dig deeper. Since it is impossible for us to share everything you need to know about teaching reading and writing in one short chapter, we offer a stepping-off point as you continue to use the best books to teach your readers and writers.

Make Every Student Count

How do we choose the right book from the wealth of resources that are available in the world of children's literature? How do we choose teaching techniques that will enhance student learning? Again, it comes down to informed decision making. Our instructional choices are driven by the needs of our learners. This is easy to forget when we are faced with daunting curricular demands. Certainly, following your school's curriculum and standards is important; however, students' needs must be placed at the forefront when selecting the best books, materials, and approaches.

Know Your Literacy Learners

Allot plenty of time to get to know your students and their literacy learning needs. Dick Allington underscores the importance of knowing students when he says that effective teaching "is all about finding out what works best for the individual child and the group of children in front of you" (2005, p. 462). Set aside a few minutes each day to chat with a student or two about books. Jotting anecdotal notes during such informal conferences will add to your understanding of students' needs. You may want to use a small spiral notebook for each child; however, if you like all the information in one spot, fill a three-ring binder with loose leaf paper and slip in a divider labeled with each child's name. If you prefer a form rather than a blank piece of paper, you may choose to use something similar to the Reading Conference Form provided below.

Getting to know your students as writers is as simple as putting a blank piece of paper in front of them. On one of the first days of school, invite your students to write. To set the stage, model and think aloud while composing your own piece. You may want to write a bit about yourself, and then request that students do the same. As you read their written work, not only will you learn about your students as writers, but you will also get a snapshot of their lives outside of school. For further reading on the topic of getting to know your students, consider Donald Graves' book *Sea of Faces* (2006). Informal data collected from

Reading Conference Form			
Date	Title	Observations of Reading Behaviors	Interests/ Favorite Books

anecdotal records and analysis of writing samples along with formal assessment data present a clear picture of students' strengths and weaknesses. The more you know about your students, the easier it will be to design and implement effective instruction.

Know the Qualities of Exemplary Classroom Teachers

The choices we make as knowledgeable professionals have a profound impact on our literacy learners. Dick Allington (2002) studied exemplary educators and found six common features of teachers who deliver effective literacy instruction. They include the following.

♦ *Time:* Dedicate ample time to real reading and writing because "extensive practice provides the opportunities for students to consolidate the skills and strategies teachers often work so hard to develop" (p. 742).

♦ *Texts:* Choose texts carefully, keeping the readers' ability in mind. Children "need a rich supply of books they can actually read" (p. 743).

♦ *Teaching:* Be an active teacher. Model and demonstrate strategies that good readers and writers employ.

♦ *Talk:* Talk *with* your students, not *at* your students. Ask open-ended, higher-level questions that lead to meaningful discussions with and among students.

♦ *Tasks:* Design meaningful assignments that offer students choice within structure.

♦ *Testing:* Evaluate student work based on effort and improvement rather than simply on achievement.

How do we put Allington's "six Ts" into practice? By using the wealth of information and mini-lessons in this book to their fullest potential. To that end, we echo the recommendations of experts in advocating the gradual-release-of-responsibility approach to teaching reading and writing.

Gradual Release of Responsibility

The gradual-release-of-responsibility approach (Harvey & Goudvis, 2007; Miller, 2002) or optimal learning model (Routman, 2003) provides students with the support needed to learn and apply new literacy skills and strategies. As we nudge our readers and writers along on the road toward independence, we carefully plan our instruction to scaffold their learning. Applying the gradual-release-of-responsibility approach to our literacy lessons simply makes sense. If you glance back at the mini-lessons in this book, you will find that we offered many suggestions for teacher modeling and thinking aloud. Whether children are just beginning to understand how print works or are learning how to synthesize, they need an expert to guide the way. You are the expert in your classroom. Letting students

> "Students learn what we show them. If we take the time to model the writing process and share writer's secrets, they will get an insider's view of what they are expected to do and have a better chance of doing it for themselves."
>
> (Culham, 2005, p. 65)

have a peek inside your head to see what you do when you come to a word you don't know or how you interact with text is beneficial. To think aloud while reading, stop periodically to highlight your thought processes and make teaching points. This is the time to explicitly show students how good readers think strategically in order to comprehend text. Laura Robb assists intermediate-grade teachers with this important teaching tool in her book *Teaching Reading With Think Aloud Lessons* (2007). The same holds true for teaching writing. Students benefit from demonstration lessons in which we model the author's craft.

After modeling, practice the strategy or writing technique together with your students in guided situations. This might include shared reading/writing and discussion, scaffolding students' learning during small-group or individual reading/writing conferences, and encouraging students to share their thinking during partner reading and sharing, literature circle discussions, and whole-class discussions. Once students have had ample time to practice with support, they can try to apply the strategy on their own. Finally, to cement understanding, students will benefit from the challenge of applying the strategy to a new genre or format or effectively using the strategy in a more challenging text (Harvey, 2002). Students improve with careful guidance and specific comments geared to nudge them forward as literacy learners. Our time is better spent on

Have You Read These?

A FEW OF OUR FAVORITE RESOURCES ON READING AND WRITING WORKSHOP

+ *The Reading Zone* (Atwell, 2007)
+ *Writing Workshop: The Essential Guide* (Fletcher & Portalupi, 2001)
+ *Reading With Meaning* (Miller, 2002)
+ *Revisiting the Reading Workshop* (Orehovec & Alley, 2003)
+ *Reading Essentials* (Routman, 2003)
+ *Writing Essentials* (Routman, 2004)

Literature Is Back!

meaningful interactions with our students than on assigning tasks simply to keep them busy. Meaningful interactions such as those described in the gradual-release-of-responsibility model are emphasized during reading and writing workshops.

Reading and Writing Workshops

The structure of the reading and writing workshops puts the gradual-release-of-responsibility model into action. The components of a workshop approach lend themselves to scaffolded instruction and provide ample time for students to engage in meaningful practice.

Knowing the importance of making time for reading and writing workshop is just part of the challenge; finding time is the issue we will address next.

The Components of a Reading or Writing Workshop

10–15 minutes may include:
* Read-aloud/think-aloud
* Write-aloud/think-aloud
* Mini-lesson

20–60 minutes may include:
* Independent reading or writing
* Individual or group conferences
* Small-group guided lessons

5–15 minutes:
* Sharing

Make Every Minute Count

Tick, tock, tick, tock. The hands on the clock on your classroom wall continue to move. Some days it seems that the dismissal bell rings and you've only scratched the surface of what you wanted to teach. Your lesson plans are filled with circles and arrows, shifting Monday's mini-lessons to Tuesday, then Wednesday, and so on. Each summer your administration shares a new program for you to implement, a new plan for helping students achieve. How do you make the precious minutes count? Begin by examining your beliefs. What do you believe students should know and be able to do when they leave your classroom? How do your beliefs translate into the tone you set, the language you use, and the lessons you teach? What are the beliefs of your school or district? Do they have a mission and vision statements to which you can refer? Before reading on, take a few moments to jot down your beliefs.

Know Your Curriculum Standards and Expectations

Along with analyzing your beliefs, it is critical that you know the goals for learning set out by your school, district, and state standards. For a global set of standards, review the 12 Standards for the English Language Arts set forth by the International Reading Association

> "Like writing, reading is an act of composition. When we write, we compose thoughts on paper. When we read, we compose meaning in our minds. Thoughtful, active readers use the text to stimulate their own thinking and engage with the mind of the writer."
>
> (Harvey, 2002, p. 14)

(IRA) and the National Council of Teachers of English available at www.ncte.org or www.readwritethink.org. As you glance at the standards, it will be apparent that the lessons contained in this book reflect the essence of those standards. We've designed lessons that will help you and your students explore a wide range of texts across genres, both classic and contemporary. Through meaningful interactions with well-written books, children apply comprehension strategies. Using texts as models for exemplary writing, young authors learn how to write for different purposes and to different audiences.

We've demonstrated how, by interacting with texts, children gain an understanding of life and of our world. We've offered research-based ways to help your learners participate as "knowledgeable, reflective, creative, and critical members in a variety of literacy communities" (NCTE/IRA, 1996, p. 3). Now, we invite you to expand on the lessons in this text as you continue to use fine literature to meet standards in your classroom.

Recognize the Hallmarks of Proficient Readers and Writers

In order to nurture literacy learners, we have to recognize the hallmarks of proficient readers and writers. Studies have shown that proficient readers are better able to understand when they think and read at the same time. If you teach the primary grades, you know that quite a bit of time is spent exploring the world of words, while at the same time teaching readers how to comprehend text. As teachers of readers and writers, we model, teach, and provide time for students to practice the skills and strategies needed to read and write fluently, to understand written material, and to express their thoughts clearly in writing. When you choose how to allocate your instructional time, plan meaningful activities that will advance the proficiency of your literacy learners. See the summary chart on page 240.

Use Instructional Time to Its Fullest

To maximize instructional time, we offer a few tried and true techniques to enhance your literacy instruction, including turn and talk, interactive journaling, reader response, and Readers Theater. To begin, let's take a look at an effective way to boost discussion and thinking skills during your read-alouds. This strategy (see box, page 239) is called "turn and talk" (Miller, 2002; Routman, 2003). As with any routine you are going to begin,

Try This! Enhance Read-Alouds With "Turn and Talk"

During read-alouds, stop along the way to pose the following queries to students.

Reading Like a Writer Across Genres

- Where do you think this author got his/her ideas?

- Did the lead this author use make you want to read the story?

- Did you hear any words that you want to remember and use in your writing?

- Did you notice the way the sentences flow? Talk about how the writer did that.

- Does this writing have voice? Why or why not?

Reading Fiction

- What do you predict will happen next? What evidence have you seen or heard to prove your prediction?

- Do you have any questions at this point?

- Is the setting important to the story?

- Why do you think the character is acting this way?

- How might the story end? Why do you think that will happen?

- What was the big idea of this story? What was the author's message?

Reading Nonfiction

- How has the author organized the information?

- What is one interesting way the author or illustrator helps you learn the information?

- Tell your partner something you have learned.

- Do you have a question about the part I just read? Let's discuss.

Reading Poetry

- What images did you visualize during this poem?

- What language did the poet use that you especially liked?

(Miller, 2002; Routman, 2003)

Hallmarks for Proficient Readers and Writers

Proficient Readers	Proficient Writers
Develop an understanding of how words work.	Apply their growing knowledge of words as they stretch out words and spell them using the sounds they know.
Use decoding or fix-up strategies flexibly to figure out unknown words.	Apply strategies and utilize resources to figure out how to spell words while writing.
Activate their schema and build background knowledge for a wide variety of texts.	Are active collectors of ideas for writing through careful observation and wide reading.
Understand the meaning of the vocabulary in the books they read.	Choose interesting words when they write.
Construct meaning while reading by applying effective reading strategies.	Convey meaning through writing by knowing their audience and purpose.
Read with fluency and expression.	Write with fluency and expression.
Adjust their reading based on their purpose, the genre, and the type of text.	Design their written work to match their purpose and audience.

Have You Read These?

A FEW OF OUR FAVORITE BOOKS FOR FOSTERING PROFICIENT READERS AND WRITERS

- *6 + 1 Traits of Writing: The Complete Guide for the Primary Grades* (Culham, 2005)
- *6 + 1 Traits of Writing: The Complete Guide (Grades 3 and Up)* (Culham, 2003)
- *Phonics They Use* (Cunningham, 2005)
- *Strategies That Work* (Harvey & Goudvis, 2007)
- *Choice Words* (Johnston, 2004)
- *Teaching Writing: Balancing Process and Product* (Tompkins, 2007)

you'll want to model "turn and talk" with another adult or student. Once students have observed you, consider assigning children a "turn and talk" partner or small group.

Another technique that integrates reading, writing, thinking, and discussion is "interactive journaling" (Hoyt, 1999). To do this with your students, group students into triads, give each student a blank piece of paper, and select a thought-provoking book or topic for discussion. Then, give the directions in the Try This! box (page 242).

A third technique that helps readers comprehend text is "meaningful response." This book contains numerous specific ideas for readers' response. Something to consider when asking students to respond is the balance between the time spent reading and the time spent responding. If students do not have to write extensively, responding in writing is less

Provide opportunities for students to read, write, and talk about books.

intimidating and doesn't distract from the act of reading. One option is to encourage response to the text they are reading using those ever-handy sticky notes to make connections at appropriate parts of their books (Harvey & Goudvis, 2007). Then, pair readers and let them use those noted passages to begin a discussion about their books. If you are focusing on a particular literary element, have readers post a sticky note in their books when they find an exemplary passage that underscores what you have taught and want them to practice. Pair and share to strengthen learning. In addition, you can use sticky notes as a way to assess readers' understanding and guide them in their thinking. For example, if you are working on the strategy of prediction, ask students to post their predictions in the text as they are reading. Before they leave, remind them to open their book to the prediction they would like to share with you. As you read their predictions, you will be able to determine whether they understand how to use the clues in the text to guide their predictions. If not, you can add a comment or two to guide them for the next day's reading.

Readers Theater is another way to celebrate books while at the same time building students' oral reading fluency. It does not require a lot of preparation. The only material needed is a copy of a script for each performer. There are many scripts available on the Internet, including those found at StoryCart Readers Theatre, www.storycart.com. Furthermore, students can hone their writing skills by adapting their favorite tales into Readers Theater scripts.

 Integrating Reading, Writing, Thinking, and Discussion

1. Have students divide their papers into quarters.

2. Have them number each section, then write their name on the back.

3. Say, "Today I'm going to share the book _____ with you. We will be thinking about the book and writing our thoughts on paper for others to read." Read the text.

4. After reading, continue with: "In section one, write or draw your thoughts about the book. How did the book make you feel? Did you make any connections? Do you have any questions?"

5. Tell students to pass their thoughts to the teammate on the right. Each should read the paper he or she just received. Ask: "If this person said this to you what would you say back?" Students should write a response in section two.

6. Once again, they pass the paper to the person on the right. Now, each reads sections one and two. Discuss. In section three, students should respond to what was written or add a new thought.

7. Finally, have students pass the paper back to its original owner. In section four, have students reflect on the thoughts of the two partners, then discuss how their thinking was changed as they read and talked about the reflections of others. (Hoyt, 1999)

Literature Is Back!

Make Every Lesson Count

When planning lessons, we want to meet our students' needs, nudge them to the next level, and provide them with research-based literacy strategies that will continue to help them long after they leave our classrooms. To do this effectively, we need to understand how readers and writers think.

Be an Active Reader and Writer

Each day we ask our students to read and write for a variety of purposes. To understand the underlying processes that students employ, it is important that we keep our reading and writing skills honed. If you are asking your students to keep a reading log, consider starting one of your own. Inspired by Regie Routman's book *Reading Essentials* (2003), Maria and her daughter, Katie, each began her own reading log in the fall of 2002. Five years and nearly 200 books later, Katie continues to keep track of her independent reading. What a treasure to have this record of her own reading.

Likewise, Maria's reading journal is something she shares with her students to model book selection and reading across genres. Moreover, a reading log is a helpful resource when you are standing in the bookstore wondering to yourself, "Did I already read that book?"

Katie's reading log.

It seems for many of us that being an active reader is a bit easier to sustain than
being an active writer. As teachers we do quite a bit of expository writing. Specifically, we
write narrative reports about student progress, complete stacks of forms, and correspond
with parents and others. The time to write for pleasure is limited, and the importance
of writing on a regular basis is something we tend to overlook. If finding time to write
outside of school is a challenge, take a few minutes at the beginning of writing workshop
to pen a short piece. Encourage your administrators to make writing a regular part of
faculty meetings. Try out Linda Rief's book *100 Quickwrites* (2003), designed for middle-
school writers, which offers powerful pieces that encourage written response in a two- to
three-minute time frame. The sharing and discussion that follow will not only help you
learn about one another as writers but will foster an understanding of what we ask of our
students. If your students take a standardized writing test, do a sample test under the
same conditions. After the experience, debrief with colleagues to brainstorm strategies
to help students succeed in the same situation. Activities such as these will help you be a
better teacher of writing.

Reflect, Question, and Continue to Learn

In our isolated classrooms we often forget that we are surrounded by innovative and
insightful educators. At a recent seminar, Debbie Miller, author of *Reading With Meaning*
(2002), spoke about creating a culture of thinking in the classroom. It was apparent as
she spoke about her experiences that she was fortunate to have been part of a culture of
thinking outside her classroom. She met with colleagues, read and discussed difficult
books, and engaged in deep discussions about students, their learning, and the best way

to help them understand. Maria and her teammates do the same. Maria shares, "One of the most powerful professional activities I engage in that improves student learning is my 'Tuesday Night Team' meeting. This weekly meeting provides each of us with an opportunity to reflect on the lessons we teach and the interactions we have with our students to examine how they are impacting student learning. I get feedback from other teachers who are using the same strategies and can hear about what they would change and how they would change it. It provides all of us with deeper insight into our teaching. When one of us is struggling with a student, we have other knowledgeable professionals to offer strategies and ideas." We encourage you to find a community of colleagues to support and enrich your teaching. Consider meeting once a month to discuss a book, a powerful quote, or an innovative teaching strategy. If you are fortunate enough to work in a school where reflective discussions are occurring, celebrate! Share your ideas with others. Spread the word.

Make Every Book Count

This book is filled with enticing titles to share with your students. Knowing that our time with learners is limited, we strive to select each book carefully. When you have two books from which to choose, select the one that exemplifies the traits of good writing, or reach for the book that will encourage students to think, debate, and discuss. To that end, it is helpful if you keep current with the world of children's books. Ask your school librarian what resources she has available, read children's literature reviews, locate lists of award-winning books, and consult the valuable resources we have listed on page 247.

Have You Read These?

A FEW OF OUR FAVORITE RESOURCES ABOUT THE CRAFT OF WRITING

- *The Art of Teaching Writing* (Calkins, 1994)
- *Writing: Teachers & Children at Work* (Graves, 2003)
- *Writing Toward Home: Tales and Lessons to Find Your Way* (Heard, 1995)
- *Cracking Open the Author's Craft* (Laminack, 2007)
- *Bird by Bird: Some Instructions on Writing and Life* (Lamott, 1995)
- *Nonfiction Writing: From the Inside Out* (Robb, 2004)

Create Excitement for a Book

As soon as you finish the last page of an engaging read-aloud and place it on the shelf, eager hands snap it up, wanting to read it again and again. The simple act of sharing a book creates excitement for that particular title. Other ways to create book-generated enthusiasm in your classroom include book talks and guest readers.

Book Talks

Book talks are an effective way to introduce children to books in different genres and generate excitement for a book. For a sampling of ready-to-use book talks, log on to nancykeane.com/booktalks. In addition, many publishers, such as Scholastic and Random House, have a collection of book talks on their Web sites to get you started. Of course, the best book talks are the ones you create yourself. Tips for successful book talks include the following.

- Create interest by sharing an exciting or amusing anecdote from the book.

- Be specific when talking about the contents.

- Talk about titles you enjoy. Your excitement will shine through!

- Have a few copies of the book handy so children can begin reading it right away. (Kiefer, Hepler, & Hickman, 2007)

Guest Readers and Authors

Inviting parents, community members, former students, and others into your classroom to read to students not only demonstrates the importance of reading, but also promotes books. You might begin a guest reader program in your classroom in which family members of students come in once during the year to share a book. In addition, inviting authors to visit and talk about their craft enlightens students about the writer's world. The Society of Children's Book Writers and Illustrators (www.scbwi.org) is a helpful resource that provides names of local authors and illustrators who do author visits. If hiring an author to visit is not in your school's budget, check out the author's Web site for resources or videos to bring the writer to life for your students.

Guest readers promote the importance of reading.

> I like reading books because it helps me learn and is relaxing. Through books I can feel what other people feel and visit places I have never been. I wonder where my next book will take me?

Michael's essay, Part 5: The End

The End

What a journey it has been! We stepped off with trumpets blaring, parading through picture book land. Soon after, the whispers of voices from long ago accompanied us on our traditional literature trek. Without stopping to catch a breath, we were introduced to the ambassador of modern fantasy along with his fanciful friends and foes. Narrowly escaping the clutches of a dragon, an open window appeared that led us into the familiar world of realistic fiction. Well rested and recharged, we had our passports stamped with dates from long ago, explored the world of nonfiction, and ended by listening to the rhythms, rhymes, and quiet places found within the lines of a favorite poem. Thank you for joining us on this pleasurable foray through the world of children's literature. We wish you the best as you continue your journey by reaching for book, after book, after book…

Children's Literature Cited

Aardema, V. (1991). *Borreguita and the coyote.* (P. Mathers, Illus.). New York: Knopf.

Ada, A. R. (1998). *Under the royal palms: A childhood in Cuba.* New York: Atheneum.

Adler, D. (1997). *Chanukah in Chelm.* (K. O'Malley, Illus.). New York: Morrow.

_____. (2005). *Joe Louis: America's fighter.* (T. Widener, Illus.). San Diego: Harcourt.

Adoff, A. (1991). *In for winter, out for spring.* (J. Pinkney, Illus.). San Diego: Harcourt Brace Jovanovich.

Ajmera, M., & Ivanko, J. D. (2004). *Be my neighbor.* Watertown, MA: Charlesbridge.

Alarcón, F. X. (1997). *Laughing tomatoes and other spring poems/Jitomates risueños y otros poemas de primavera.* (C. Gonzalez, Illus.). San Francisco, CA: Children's Book Press.

_____. (2005). *Poems to dream together/Poemas para soñar juntos.* (P. Barragan, Illus.). New York: Lee and Low.

Aldrin, B. (2005). *Reaching for the moon.* (W. Minor, Illus.). New York: HarperCollins.

Alexander, L. (1964). *The book of three.* New York: Holt.

Aliki. (1962). *My five senses.* New York: Crowell.

_____. (1983). *A medieval feast.* New York: HarperCollins.

_____. (1988). *A weed is a flower.* New York: Aladdin Library.

_____. (1997). *My visit to the zoo.* New York: HarperCollins.

Allen, S., & Lindaman, J. (2006). *Written anything good lately?* (V. Enright, Illus.). Minneapolis, MN: Millbrook.

al-Windowi, T. (2004). *Thura's diary.* New York: Viking.

Andersen, H. C. (2002). *The nightingale.* Retold by Stephen Mitchell. (B. Ibatoulline, Illus.). Cambridge, MA: Candlewick.

_____. (2005). *Thumbelina.* Retold by Amy Ehrlich. (S. Jeffers Illus.). New York: Dutton.

Anderson, W. (2004). *Prairie girl: The life of Laura Ingalls Wilder.* (R. Graef, Illus.). New York: HarperCollins.

Andrede, G. (1999). *Giraffes can't dance.* (G. Parker-Rees, Illus.). New York: Orchard.

Arnold, K. (2005). *Elephants can paint, too!* New York: Atheneum.

Arnold, T. (2006). *Super fly guy.* New York: Scholastic.

Arnold, T., et al. (2006). *Why did the chicken cross the road?* New York: Dial.

Arnosky, J. (1995). *All about owls.* New York: Scholastic.

_____. (1998). *All about turkeys.* New York: Scholastic.

_____. (2000). *I see animals hiding.* New York: Scholastic.

_____. (2003). *All about sharks.* New York: Scholastic.

_____. (2004). *All about lizards.* New York: Scholastic.

Aruego, J. (2006). *The last laugh.* New York: Dial.

Asch, F. (1978). *Moon bear.* New York: Scribner.

Avi. (1994). *The barn.* New York: Orchard.

_____. (1999). *Ragweed.* New York: Avon.

_____. (2005). *The book without words: A fable of medieval magic.* New York: Hyperion.

_____. (2006). *Crispin: At the edge of the world.* New York: Hyperion.

Babbitt, N. (1975). *Tuck everlasting.* New York: Farrar, Straus and Giroux.

Bang, M. (1980). *The grey lady and the strawberry snatcher.* New York: Four Winds.

_____. (1983). *Ten, nine, eight.* New York: Greenwillow.

Bang-Campbell, M. (2004). *Little Rat rides.* (M. Bang, Illus.). Orlando, FL: Harcourt.

Banyai, I. (1995). *Zoom.* New York: Viking.

Barasch, L. (2004). *Knockin' on wood: Starring Peg Leg Bates.* New York: Lee & Low.

Barrett, J. (1978). *Cloudy with a chance of meatballs.* (R. Barrett, Illus.). New York: Atheneum.

Barrie, J. (1911). *Peter Pan.* (N. S. Unwin, Illus.). New York: Scribner.

Barron, T. A. (1996). *The lost years of Merlin.* New York: Philomel.

Barry, D., & Pearson, R. (2004). *Peter and the starcatchers.* (G. Call, Illus.). New York: Hyperion.

Bartoletti, S. C., (2005). *Hitler youth: Growing up in Hitler's shadow*. New York: Scholastic.

Base, G. (2001). *The water hole*. New York: Harry N. Abrams.

Bearden, R. (2003). *Li'l Dan, the drummer boy: A Civil War story*. (H. L. Gates, Jr., Illus.). New York: Simon & Schuster.

Beatty, P. (1988). *Charley Skedaddle*. New York: Troll.

Beaumont, K. (2005). *I ain't gonna paint no more!* (D. Catrow, Illus.). Orlando, FL: Harcourt.

Berger, M. (2000). *Buzz! A book about insects*. New York: Scholastic.

Berger, M., & Berger, G. (2002). *How do frogs swallow their eyes?: Questions and answers about amphibians*. New York: Scholastic.

_____. (2004a). *Fish sleep but don't shut their eyes: And other amazing facts about ocean creatures*. New York: Scholastic.

_____. (2004b). *Hurricanes have eyes but can't see: And other amazing facts about wild weather*. New York: Scholastic.

Bial, R. (1998). *Where Lincoln walked*. New York: Walker & Company.

_____. (2004). *Where Washington walked*. New York: Walker & Company.

Bierhorst, J. (1987). *Doctor coyote: A Native American Aesop's fables*. (W. Watson, Illus.). New York: Macmillan.

Birdsall, J. (2005). *The Penderwicks: A summer tale of four sisters, two rabbits, and a very interesting boy*. New York: Knopf.

Blackstone, S. (2005). *Alligator alphabet*. (S. Bauer, Illus.). Cambridge, MA: Barefoot.

Bloom, B. (1999). *Wolf!* (P. Biet, Illus.). New York: Orchard.

Blos, J. (1990). *Old Henry*. Ontario, Canada: Mulberry.

Blumberg, R. (2004). *York's adventures with Lewis and Clark: An African-American's part in the great expedition*. New York: HarperCollins.

Blume, J. (1970). *Are you there God? It's me, Margaret*. New York: Simon & Schuster.

Bodkin, O. (1998). *The crane wife*. (G. Spirin, Illus.). San Diego: Voyager/Harcourt.

Boling, K. (2004). *January, 1905*. San Diego: Harcourt.

Borden, L. (2000). *Sleds on Boston Common: A story from the American Revolution*. (R. A. Parker, Illus.). New York: McElderry.

_____. (2005). *The journey that saved Curious George: The true wartime escape of Margaret and H. A. Rey*. (A. Drummond, Illus.). Boston: Houghton Mifflin.

_____. (2006). *Across the blue Pacific: A World War II story*. (R. A. Parker, Illus.). Boston: MA: Houghton Mifflin.

Bowdish, L. (2000). *Brooklyn, Bugsy, and me*. (N. Carpenter, Illus.). New York: Farrar, Straus and Giroux.

Bradby, M. (1995). *More than anything else*. (C. Soentpiet, Illus.). New York: Orchard.

Bragg, M. C. (1930). *The little engine that could*. (retold by W. Piper). New York: Platt & Munk.

Branley, F. M. (1987). *It's raining cats and dogs: All kinds of weather and why we have it*. (T. Kelley, Illus.). Boston: Houghton Mifflin.

_____. (1997). *Down comes the rain*. (J. G. Hale, Illus.). New York: HarperCollins.

_____. (1999). *Flash, crash, rumble, and roll*. (T. Kelley, Illus.). New York: HarperCollins.

_____. (2000). *What the moon is like*. (T. Kelley, Illus.). New York: HarperCollins.

_____. (2006). *Air is all around you*. (J. O'Brien, Illus.). New York: HarperCollins.

Breen, M., & Friestad, K. (2000). *The kid's book of weather forecasting*. (M. Kline, Illus.). New York: Williamson.

Bregoli, J. (2004). *The goat lady*. Gardiner, ME: Tilbury House.

Brett, J. (1989). *The mitten*. New York: Putnam.

_____. (1999). *The gingerbread baby*. New York: Putnam.

_____. (2005). *Honey…honey…lion!* New York: Putnam.

Bridges, R. (1999). *Through my eyes*. New York: Scholastic.

Briggs, R. (1978). *The snowman*. New York: Random House.

Brisson, P. (2006). *I remember Miss Perry*. (S. Jorisch, Illus.). New York: Dial.

Brown, M. (1950). *Dick Whittington and his cat*. New York: Scribner's.

Brown, M. (2004). *My name is Celia: The life of Celia Cruz*. (R. Lopez, Illus.). Flagstaff, AZ: Northland.

Brown, M. W. (1939). *The noisy book*. (L. Weisgard, Illus.). New York: Harper and Row.

_____. (1947). *Goodnight moon*. (C. Hurd, Illus.). New York: HarperCollins.

_____. (1985). *Goodnight moon room: A pop-up book*. (C. Hurd, Illus.). New York: HarperFestival.

Browne, A. (2003). *The shape game*. New York: Farrar, Straus and Giroux.

_____. (2004). *Into the forest*. Cambridge, MA: Candlewick.

Bruchac, J. (1998). *The arrow over the door*. (J. Watling, Illus.). New York: Dial.

Bruel, N. (2005). *Bad kitty*. New Milford, CT: Roaring Brook.

Bruss, D. (2001). *Book! Book! Book!* (T. Beecke, Illus.). New York: Arthur A. Levine.

Bryan, A. (2003). *Beautiful blackbird*. New York: Atheneum.

Buehner, C. (2004). *Superdog: The heart of a hero*. (M. Buehner, Illus.). New York: HarperCollins.

Bunting, E. (1988). *How many days to America? A Thanksgiving story*. (B. Peck, Illus.). New York: Clarion.

_____. (1990). *The wall*. (R. Himler, Illus.). New York: Clarion.

_____. (1991). *Fly away home*. (R. Himler, Illus.). New York: Clarion.

_____. (1994). *A day's work*. (R. Himler, Illus.). New York: Clarion.

_____. (1994). *Smoky night*. (D. Diaz, Illus.). San Diego: Harcourt Brace.

_____. (1995). *Dandelions*. (G. Shed, Illus.). San Diego: Harcourt.

_____. (1996a). *The Wednesday surprise*. (D. Carrick, Illus.). New York: Clarion.

_____. (1996b). *The blue and the gray*. (N. Bittinger, Illus.). New York: Scholastic.

_____. (1996c). *Train to somewhere*. (R. Himler, Illus.). New York: Clarion.

_____. (1998). *So far from the sea*. (C. Soentpiet, Illus.). New York: Clarion.

_____. (1999). *Butterfly house (G. Shed, Illus.)*. New York: Scholastic.

_____. (2003). *Anna's table*. Chanhassen, MN: Northword.

Burg, B. (2002). *Outside the lines: Poetry at play*. (R. Gibbon, Illus.). New York: G. P. Putnam's Sons.

Burkhard, D. (2005). *Riddle in the mountain*. Fort Collins, CO: Dogtooth.

Burnett, F. H. (1962). *The secret garden*. New York: HarperCollins.

Burnford, S. E. (1961). *The incredible journey*. (C. Burger, Illus.). Boston: Little, Brown.

Burton, V. L. (1942). *The little house*. Boston: Houghton Mifflin.

Butterworth, C. (2006). *Sea horse: The shyest fish in the sea*. (J. L. Lawrence, Illus.). Cambridge, MA: Candlewick.

Byars, B. C. (1988). *The burning questions of Bingo Brown*. New York: Viking Penguin.

_____. (2002). *The keeper of the doves*. New York: Viking.

Byng, G. (2002). *Molly Moon's incredible book of hypnotism*. New York: HarperCollins.

Cabat, E., & Butler, L. (1989). *Erni Cabat's magical world of dinosaurs*. Tucson, AZ: Great Impressions.

Cameron, A. (1998). *The secret life of Amanda K. Woods*. New York: Frances Foster.

Carle, E. (1979). *The very hungry caterpillar*. New York: Philomel.

_____. (1986). *Papa, please get the moon for me*. Natick, MA: Picture Book Studio.

_____. (1987). *The tiny seed*. Natick, MA: Picture Book Studio.

_____. (1990). *The very quiet cricket*. New York: Philomel.

_____. (2004). *Mister Seahorse*. New York: Philomel.

_____. (2005). *10 little rubber ducks*. New York: HarperCollins.

Carroll, L. (1999). *Alice's adventures in Wonderland*. (Retold and illustrated by Helen Oxenbury.) Cambridge, MA: Candlewick.

Carus, M. (Ed.). (2002). *Fire and wings: Dragon tales from East and West*. (N. Mistry, Illus.). Chicago: Cricket.

Castrovilla, S. (2007). *By the sword*. (B. Farnsworth, Illus.). Honesdale, PA: Boyds Mills Press.

Catling, P. S. (1979). *The chocolate touch*. (M. Apple, Illus.). New York: Morrow.

Chaikin, M. (2002). *Don't step on the sky: A handful of haiku.* (H. Nakata, Illus.). New York: Henry Holt.

Chernaik, J. (Ed.). (2005). *Carnival of the animals: Poems inspired by Saint-Saens' music.* (S. Kitamura, Illus.). Cambridge, MA: Candlewick.

Cherry, L. (1990). *The great kapok tree.* New York: Harcourt Brace.

Child, L. (2005). *Clarice Bean spells trouble.* Cambridge, MA: Candlewick.

Christclow, E. (1999). *What do illustrators do?* New York: Clarion.

Chrustowski, R. (2006). *Turtle crossing.* New York: Henry Holt.

Ciardi, J. (1992). *The hopeful trout and other limericks.* (S. Meddaugh, Illus.). Boston: Houghton Mifflin.

Clark, C. G. (2003). *Hill hawk Hattie.* Cambridge, MA: Candlewick.

_____. (2005). *Hattie on her way.* Cambridge, MA: Candlewick.

Cleary, B. (1955). *Beezus and Ramona.* (L. Darling, Illus.). New York: Morrow.

_____. (1965). *The mouse and the motorcycle.* (L. Darling, Illus.). New York: Morrow.

_____. (1983). *Dear Mr. Henshaw.* (P. O. Zelinsky, Illus.). New York: Morrow.

_____. (1999). *Ramona's world.* (A. Tiegreen, Illus.). New York: Morrow.

Clements, A. (1996). *Frindle.* (B. Selznick, Illus.). New York: Simon & Schuster.

_____. (1999). *The Landry News.* (B. Selznick, Illus.). New York: Aladdin.

_____. (2001). *The school story.* (B. Selznick, Illus.). New York: Simon & Schuster.

_____. (2002). *A week in the woods.* New York: Simon & Schuster.

_____. (2006). *Room one: A mystery or two.* (C. Blair, Illus.). New York: Simon & Schuster.

Clinton, C. (2005). *Simeon's fire.* Cambridge, MA: Candlewick.

Cobb, V. (2003). *I face the wind.* New York: HarperCollins.

Codell, E. R. (2003). *Sahara special.* New York: Hyperion.

_____. (2005). *Hanukkah, Shmanukkah!* (L. Pham, Illus.). New York: Hyperion.

_____. (2005). *Diary of a fairy godmother.* (D. Kozjan, Illus.). New York: Hyperion.

Coerr, E. (1993). *Sadako.* (E. Young, Illus.). New York: G. P. Putnam's Sons.

Cole, J. (1989). *Anna Banana: 101 jump rope rhymes.* (A. Tiegreen, Illus.). New York: HarperTrophy.

Collard, S. B. (2002). *Butterfly count.* (P. Kratter, Illus.). New York: Holiday House.

_____. (2005). *The prairie builders: Reconstructing America's lost grasslands.* Boston: Houghton Mifflin.

Colman, P. (1994). *Toilets, bathtubs, sinks, and sewers: A history of the bathroom.* New York: Atheneum.

_____. (2006). *Adventurous women: Eight true stories about women who made a difference.* New York: Henry Holt.

Connor, L. (2004). *Miss Bridie chose a shovel.* (M. Azarian, Illus.). Boston: Houghton Mifflin.

Conrad, P. (1989). *The tub people.* (R. Egielski, Illus.). New York: Harper & Row.

Coolidge, O. (2001). *Greek myths.* Boston: Houghton Mifflin.

Coombs, K. (2006). *The runaway princess.* New York: Farrar, Straus, & Giroux.

Cooney, B. (1982). *Miss Rumphius.* New York: Viking.

Cooper, F. (1994). *Coming home: From the life of Langston Hughes.* New York: Philomel.

Cooper, M. L. (2004). *Dust to eat: Drought and depression in the 1930s.* New York: Clarion.

Cooper, S. (1991). *Matthew's dragon.* (J. A. Smith, Illus.). New York: McElderry.

_____. (2005). *The magician's boy.* (S. Riglietti, Illus.). New York: McElderry.

Coville, B. (1991). *Jeremy Thatcher, dragon hatcher.* (G. A. Lippincott, Illus.). San Diego: Jane Yolen Books.

_____. (1994). *The dragonslayers.* (K. Coville, Illus.). New York: Pocket Books.

Cowley, J. (1999). *Red-eyed tree frog.* (N. Bishop, Illus.). New York: Scholastic.

_____. (2005). *Chameleon, chameleon.* (N. Bishop, Illus.). New York: Scholastic.

Craft, C. (1999). *King Midas and the golden touch.* (K. Y. Craft, Illus.). New York: Morrow.

Craft, M. F. (2002). *Sleeping beauty.* (K. Y. Craft, Illus.). New York: North-South.

Craig, R. (1995). *Malu's wolf*. New York: Orchard.

Creech, S. (2000). *The wanderer*. New York: Scholastic.

_____. (2001). *Love that dog: A novel*. New York: Joanna Cotler.

_____. (2002). *Ruby Holler*. New York: HarperCollins.

Crews, D. (1978). *Freight train*. New York: Greenwillow.

_____. (1986). *Ten black dots*. New York: Greenwillow.

Crews, N. (2004). *The neighborhood Mother Goose*. New York: Greenwillow.

Crimi, C. (2005). *Henry and the buccaneer bunnies*. (J. Manders, Illus.). Cambridge, MA: Candlewick.

Cronin, D. (2000). *Click, clack, moo: Cows that type*. (B. Lewin, Illus.). New York: Simon & Schuster.

_____. (2003). *Diary of a worm*. (H. Bliss, Illus.). New York: Joanna Cotler.

_____. (2006). *Click, clack, splish, splash: A counting adventure*. (B. Lewin, Illus.). New York: Atheneum.

Cullinan, B. (Ed.). (1996). *A jar of tiny stars: Poems by NCTE award-winning poets. (A.* Macleod & M. Nadel, Illus.). Honesdale, PA: Boyds Mills Press.

Curtis, C. P. (1995). *The Watsons go to Birmingham—1963*. New York: Delacort.

_____. (1999). *Bud, not Buddy*. New York: Delacorte.

Cushman, D. (1996). *The ABC mystery*. New York: HarperCollins.

Cushman, K. (1996). *The ballad of Lucy Whipple*. New York: Clarion.

_____. (2003). Rodzina. New York: Clarion.

Cuyler, M. (2000). *100th day worries*. (A. Howard, Illus.). New York: Simon & Schuster.

D'Aulaire, I., & D'Aulaire, E. P. (1962). *D'Aulaires' book of Greek myths*. New York: Doubleday.

_____. (1986). *D'Aulaires' Norse gods and giants*. New York: Doubleday.

Dahl, R. (1961). *James and the giant peach*. (N. E. Burke, Illus.). New York: Knopf.

_____. (1991). *The Minpins*. New York: Viking.

Dakos, K. (1990). *If you're not here, please raise your hand: Poems about school*. (G. B. Karas, Illus.). New York: Four Winds Press.

_____. (1993). *Don't read this book, whatever you do!* (G. B. Karas, Illus.). New York: Simon & Schuster.

Dalgliesh, A. (1954). *The courage of Sarah Noble*. (L. Weisgard, Illus.). New York: Scribners.

Danneberg, J. (2000). *First day jitters*. (J. Love, Illus.). Watertown, MA: Charlesbridge.

Danziger, P. (1994). *Amber Brown is not a crayon*. (T. Ross, Illus.). New York: Putnam.

_____. (2002). *Get ready for second grade, Amber Brown*. (T. Ross, Illus.). New York: Putnam.

Davol, M. W. (1997). *The paper dragon*. (R. Sabuda, Illus.). New York: Atheneum.

Day, A. (1985). *Good dog, Carl*. New York: The Green Tiger Press.

Deedy, C. A. (1994). *The library dragon*. (M. P. White, Illus.). Atlanta: Peachtree.

Demi. (1990). *The empty pot*. New York: Holt.

_____. (1997). *Buddha stories (Jataka tales)*. New York: Holt.

DePalma, M. N. (2005). *A grand old tree*. New York: A. A. Levine.

dePaola, T. (1975a). *Strega Nona: An old tale*. New York: Little Simon.

_____. (1975b). *The cloud book*. New York: Holiday House.

_____. (1979). *Big Anthony and the magic ring*. San Diego: Harcourt Brace.

_____. (1980). *The knight and the dragon*. New York: Putnam.

_____. (1991). *Now one foot, now the other*. New York: Putnam.

_____. (1999). *26 Fairmount Avenue*. New York: Putnam.

de Regniers, B. S. (1985). *So many cats*. New York: Houghton Mifflin.

de Regniers, B. S., Moore, E., White, M. M., & Carr, J. (Eds.). (1988). *Sing a song of popcorn: Every child's book of poems*. (Nine Caldecott Illustrators). New York: Scholastic.

DeTerlizzi, T., & Black, H. (2003). *The field guide*. New York: Simon & Schuster

De Young, C. C. (1999). *A letter to Mrs. Roosevelt*. New York: Delacorte/Random House.

DiCamillo, K. (2000). *Because of Winn-Dixie*. Cambridge, MA: Candlewick.

_____. (2002). *The tiger rising*. Cambridge, MA: Candlewick.

_____. (2003). *The tale of Despereaux*. (T. B. Ering, Illus.). Cambridge, MA: Candlewick.

_____. (2006). *The miraculous journey of Edward Tulane*. (B. Ibatoulline, Illus.). Cambridge, MA: Candlewick.

Doherty, B. (1997). *Tales of wonder and magic*. (J. Wijngaard, Illus.). Cambridge, MA: Candlewick.

Dorris, M. (1994). *Guests*. New York: Hyperion.

Dorros, A. (2000). *Ant cities*. New York: Crowell.

_____. (2005). *Julio's magic*. (A. Grifalconi, Illus.). New York: HarperCollins.

Duffey, B. (2001). *Fur-ever yours, Booker Jones*. New York: Viking.

DuPrau, J. (2003). *The city of Ember*. New York: Random House.

Earle, A. (1995). *Zipping, zapping, zooming bats*. (H. Cole, Illus.). New York: HarperCollins.

Earle, S. A. (1999). *Dive! My adventures in the deep frontier*. New York: Scholastic.

Eccles, M. (2001). *By Lizzie*. New York: Dial.

Edwards, M. (2005). *Stinky Stern forever*. Orlando, FL: Harcourt.

Edwards, P. D. (2001). *Slop goes the soup: A noisy warthog word book*. (H. Cole, Illus.). New York: Hyperion.

Ehlert, L. (1988). *Planting a rainbow*. San Diego: Harcourt Brace Jovanovich.

_____. (1989). *Color zoo*. New York: Lippincott.

_____. (2001). *Waiting for wings*. San Diego: Harcourt.

_____. (2002). *In my world*. San Diego: Harcourt.

_____. (2005). *Leaf man*. San Diego: Harcourt.

Ehrlich, A. (1996). *When I was your age: Original stories about growing up*. Cambridge, MA: Candlewick.

Ellis, S. (2003). *The several lives of orphan Jack*. (B. St. Aubin, Illus.). Berkeley, CA: Douglas & McIntyre.

Emberley, B. (1967). *Drummer Hoff*. (E. Emberley, Illus.). New York: Aladdin Paperbacks.

Erdrich, L. (1999). *The birchbark house*. New York: Hyperion.

Ernst, L. C. (2004). *The turn-around, upside-down alphabet book*. New York: Simon & Schuster.

Estes, E. (1944). *The hundred dresses*. (L. Slobodkin, Illus.). San Diego: Harcourt Brace.

Eubank, M. E. (2004). *The weather detectives*. (M. A. Hicks, Illus.). Layton, UT: G. Smith.

Falwell, C. (1996). *Dragon tooth*. New York: Clarion.

Farrell, J. (2007). *Stargazer's alphabet: Night-sky wonders from A to Z*. Honesdale, PA: Boyds Mills Press.

Farris, C. K. (2003). *My brother Martin: A sister remembers growing up with the Rev. Martin Luther King, Jr*. (C. Soentpiet, Illus.). New York: Simon & Schuster.

Ferris, J. (2002). *Once upon a marigold*. San Diego, CA: Harcourt Brace.

Finchler, J., & O'Malley, K. (2006). *Miss Malarkey leaves no reader behind*. New York: Walker & Company.

Fisher, L. E. (2001). *Gods and goddesses of the ancient Norse*. New York: Holiday House.

Fitzhugh, L. (2001). *Harriet the spy*. New York: Delacorte.

Fleischman, P. (1988). *Joyful noise: Poems for two voices*. New York: Harper & Row.

_____. (2000). *Big talk: Poems for four voices*. (B. Giacobbe, Illus.). Cambridge, MA: Candlewick.

_____. (2004). *Sidewalk circus*. (K. Hawkes, Illus.). Cambridge, MA: Candlewick.

Fleming, C. (2003). *Boxes for Katje*. (S. Dressen-McQueen, Illus.). New York: Farrar, Straus, & Giroux.

_____. (2005). *Our Eleanor: A scrapbook look at Eleanor Roosevelt's remarkable life*. New York: Atheneum.

Fleming, D. (1993). *In a small, small pond*. New York: Henry Holt.

_____. (1994). *Barnyard banter*. New York: Holt.

_____. (2005). *The first day of winter*. New York: Henry Holt.

Fleming, V. (1993). *Be good to Eddie Lee*. (F. Cooper, Illus.). New York: Philomel.

Fletcher, S. (2007). *That dadblamed union cow*. (K. B. Root, Illus.). Cambridge, MA: Candlewick.

Florian, D. (1999). *Laugh-eteria*. San Diego: Harcourt.

Flournoy, V. (1985). *The patchwork quilt*. (J. Pinkney, Illus.). New York: Dial.

Fogelin, A. (2000). *Crossing Jordan*. (S. Schultz, Illus.). Atlanta: Peachtree.

Forbes, E. (1943). *Johnny Tremain*. (L. Ward, Illus.). New York: Dell.

Forward, T. (2005). *The wolf's story: What really happened to Little Red Riding Hood*. (I. Cohen, Illus.). Cambridge, MA: Candlewick.

Fox, M. (1984). *Wilfrid Gordon McDonald Partridge*. (J. Vivas, Illus.). New York: Kane/Miller.

_____. (1994). *Tough Boris*. (K. Brown, Illus.). New York: Harcourt.

Franco, B. (2003). *Mathematickles*. (S. Salerno, Illus.). New York: McElderry.

Freedman, R. (1987). *Lincoln: A photobiography*. New York: Clarion.

_____. (2000). *Give me liberty!: The story of the Declaration of Independence*. New York: Holiday House.

_____. (2005). *Children of the Great Depression*. New York: Clarion.

_____. (2006a). *Freedom walkers: The story of the Montgomery bus boycott*. New York: Holiday House.

_____. (2006b). *The adventures of Marco Polo*. (B. Ibatoulline, Illus.). New York: A. A. Levine.

Freeman, D. (1968). *Corduroy*. New York: Viking.

Friedman, L. B. (2004a). *Back to school, Mallory*. (T. Schmitz, Illus.). Minneapolis, MN: Lerner.

_____. (2004b). *Mallory on the move*. (T. Schmitz, Illus.). Minneapolis, MN: Carolrhoda.

Friend, C. (2007). *The perfect nest*. (J. Manders, Illus.). Cambridge, MA: Candlewick.

Fritz, J. (1974). *Why don't you get a horse, Sam Adams?* (T. S. Hyman, Illus.). New York: Coward, McCann.

Funke, C. (2003). *Inkheart*. New York: The Chicken House/Scholastic.

_____. (2004). *Dragon rider*. New York: Scholastic.

_____. (2005). *Inkspell*. New York: The Chicken House/Scholastic.

Gag, W. (1956). *Millions of cats*. New York: Putnam.

Galdone, P. (1970). *The three little pigs*. New York: Clarion.

Gallaz, C., & Innocenti, R. (1985). *Rose Blanche*. (R. Innocenti, Illus.). Mankato, MN: Creative Education.

Gannett, R. S. (1948). *My father's dragon*. (R. C. Gannett, Illus.). New York: Random House.

Gantos, J. (1998). *Joey Pigza swallowed the key*. New York: Farrar, Straus, & Giroux.

Gardiner, J. R. (1980). *Stone fox*. (M. Sewall, Illus.). New York: Crowell.

Garland, M. (2003). *Miss Smith's incredible storybook*. New York: Dutton.

_____. (2006). *Miss Smith reads again*. New York: Dutton.

Gauthier, G. (2001). *The hero of Ticonderoga*. New York: Putnam.

_____. (2004). *Hummingbird nest: A journal of poems*. (B. Moser, Illus.). San Diego: Harcourt.

_____. (2005). *Fold me a poem*. (L. Stringer, Illus.). San Diego: Harcourt.

Gibbons, G. (1989). *Monarch butterfly*. New York: Holiday House.

_____. (1990). *Weather words and what they mean*. New York: Holiday House.

_____. (1998). *Penguins*. New York: Holiday House.

_____. (2000). *Bats*. New York: Holiday House.

_____. (2005). *Horses*. New York: Holiday House.

_____. (2006). *Ice cream: The full scoop*. New York: Holiday House.

Giblin, J. C. (1993). *Be seated: A book about chairs*. New York: HarperCollins.

_____. (1999). *The mystery of the mammoth bones: And how it was solved*. New York: HarperCollins.

_____. (2004). *The secrets of the Sphinx*. (B. Ibatoulline, Illus.). New York: Scholastic.

_____. (2006). *The boy who saved Cleveland: Based on a true story*. (M. Dooling, Illus.). New York: Henry Holt.

Giff, P. R. (1997). *Lily's crossing*. New York: Delacorte.

_____. (2000). *Nory Ryan's song*. New York: Delacorte.

_____. (2002). *Pictures of Hollis Woods*. New York: Scholastic.

_____. (2005a). *Don't tell the girls: A family memoir*. New York: Holiday House.

_____. (2005b). *Willow Run*. New York: Random House.

Goldin, B. D. (1996). *Coyote and the fire stick: A Pacific Northwest Indian tale.* (W. Hillenbrand, Illus.). New York: Gulliver/Harcourt Brace.

Gollub, M. (1998). *Cool melons—turn to frogs! The life and poems of Issa.* (K. G. Stone, Illus.). New York: Lee and Low.

Goodhart, P. (1997). *Row, row, row your boat.* (S. Lambert, Illus.). New York: Crown.

Graham, J. B. (2003). *Flicker flash.* New York: Houghton Mifflin.

Graham, K. (2004). *The reluctant dragon.* (I. Moore, Illus.). Cambridge, MA: Candlewick.

Graham-Barber, L. (1994). *Toad or frog, swamp or bog?: A big book of nature's confusables.* (A. Gillman, Illus.). New York: Four Winds Press.

Grahame, K. (1994). *Wind in the willows.* New York: Puffin Books.

Grandits, J. (2004). *Technically, it's not my fault: Concrete poems.* New York: Clarion.

Greene, S. (2002). *Falling into place.* New York: Clarion.

Greenfield, E. (1995). *Honey, I love.* (J. S. Gilchrist, Illus.). New York: HarperCollins.

_____. (2006). *When the horses ride by: Children in the times of war.* (J. S. Gilchrist, Illus.). New York: Lee & Low.

Gregory, K. (1999). *Cleopatra VII: Daughter of the Nile, Egypt, 57 B.C.* New York: Scholastic.

Griffin, P. R. (2001). *The ghost sitter.* New York: Dutton.

Grimes, N. (1998). *Jazmine's notebook.* New York: Dial.

_____. (1999). *Hopscotch love.* (M. B. Rosales, Illus.). New York: Lothrop, Lee & Shepard.

_____. (2000). *Is it far to Zanzibar? Poems about Tanzania.* New York: Lothrop, Lee & Shepard.

_____. (2001). *A pocketful of poems.* (J. Steptoe, Illus.). New York: Clarion.

_____. (2002). *Danitra Brown leaves town.* (F. Cooper, Illus.). New York: Clarion.

_____. (2005). *Danitra Brown, class clown.* (E. B. Lewis, Illus.). New York: Clarion.

Grossman, B. (1996). *My little sister ate one hare.* New York: Crown.

Guarino, D. (1989). *Is your mama a llama?* (S. Kellogg, Illus.). New York: Scholastic.

Guy, G. F. (1996). *Fiesta!* (R. K. Moreno, Illus.). New York: Greenwillow.

Haas, J. (1995). *A blue for beware.* (J. A. Smith, Illus.). New York: Greenwillow.

Haddix, M. P. (1998). *Among the hidden.* New York: Simon & Schuster.

_____. (1999). *Just Ella.* New York: Simon & Schuster.

_____. (2002). *Because of Anya.* New York: Simon & Schuster.

Hague, M. (1995). *The book of dragons.* New York: Morrow.

Hahn, M. D. (1986). *Wait till Helen comes: A ghost story.* New York: Clarion.

_____. (1994). *A time for Andrew: A ghost story.* New York: Clarion.

Hale, M. (2004). *The truth about sparrows.* New York: Holt.

Hamilton, V. (1982). *Sweet whispers, Brother Rush.* New York: Philomel.

_____. (1988). *In the beginning: Creation stories from around the world.* (B. Moser, Illus.). New York: Harcourt.

_____. (1999). *Bluish.* New York: Scholastic.

_____. (2004). *The people could fly: The picture book.* (L. & D. Dillon, Illus.). New York: Knopf.

Hannigan, K. (2004). *Ida B . . . and her plans to maximize fun, avoid disaster, and (possibly) save the world.* New York: Greenwillow.

Hansen, J. (1997). *I thought my soul would rise and fly.* New York: Scholastic.

Harrison, D. L. (2002). *Volcanoes: Nature's incredible fireworks.* (C. Nathan, Illus.). Honesdale, PA: Boyds Mills.

_____. (2006). *Glaciers: Nature's icy caps.* (C. Nathan, Illus.). Honesdale, PA: Boyds Mills.

_____. (2007). *Bugs: Poems about creeping things.* (R. Shepperson, Illus.). Honesdale, PA: Boyds Mills.

Hawes, L. (2006). *Muti's necklace: The oldest story in the world.* Boston: Houghton Mifflin.

Heard, G. (Ed.). (2002). *This place I know: Poems of comfort.* (18 renowned picture book illustrators). Cambridge, MA: Candlewick.

Heiligman, D. (1996). *From caterpillar to butterfly.* New York: HarperCollins.

Henkes, K. (1997). *Sun & Spoon*. New York: Greenwillow.

Hennessy, B. G. (2006). *Mr. Ouchy's first day*. (P. Meisel, Illus.). New York: Putnam.

Hermes, P. (2001). *Joshua's diary, the Oregon Trail, 1848*. New York: Scholastic.

Herrera, J. P. (2000). *The upside down boy*. (E. Gomez, Illus.). San Francisco: Children's Book Press.

Hesse, K. (2002). *A light in the storm: The Civil War diary of Amelia Martin*. New York: Scholastic.

Hest, A. (1997). *When Jessie came across the sea*. (P. J. Lynch, Illus.). Cambridge, MA: Candlewick.

_____. (2004). *Mr. George Baker*. (J. Muth, Illus.). Cambridge, MA: Candlewick.

_____. (2005). *The private notebooks of Katie Roberts*. (S. Lamut, Illus.). Cambridge, MA: Candlewick.

Ho, M. (1996). *Maples in the mist: Children's poems from the Tang Dynasty*. (J. & M. Tseng, Illus.). Lee & Low.

Hoban, T. (1986). *Shapes, shapes, shapes*. New York: Greenwillow.

Hobbs, W. (2002). *Wild Man Island*. New York: HarperCollins.

Hoffman, M. (1998). *Clever Katya: A fairy tale from Old Russia*. New York: Barefoot.

_____. (2002). *The color of home*. (K. Littlewood, Illus.). New York: Phyllis Fogelman.

Hogrogian, N. (1971). *One fine day*. New York: Simon & Schuster.

Holm, A. (1963). *I am David*. New York: Harcourt. (Note: previously published as *North to Freedom*)

Holm, J. L. (1999). *Our only May Amelia*. New York: HarperCollins.

Hooks, W. H. (2004). *Pioneer cat*. (C. Robinson, Illus.). New York: Random House.

Hoose, P. (2001). *We were there, too!: Young people in U.S. history*. New York: Farrar, Straus, & Giroux.

_____. (2004). *The race to save the Lord God bird*. New York: Farrar, Straus, & Giroux.

Hoose, P., & Hoose, H. (1998). *Hey, little ant*. (D. Tilley, Illus.). Berkeley, CA: Tricycle.

Hopkins, L. B. (Ed.). (1987). *Click, rumble, roar: Poems about machines*. New York: HarperCollins.

_____. (Ed.). (1990). *Good books, good times!* (H. Stevenson, Illus.). New York: HarperCollins.

_____. (Ed.). (1994). *Hand in hand: An American history through poetry*. (P. M. Fiore, Illus.). New York: Simon & Schuster.

_____. (Ed.). (1996a). *Opening days: Sports poems*. (S. Medlock, Illus.). San Diego: Harcourt.

_____. (Ed.). (1996b). *School supplies: A book of poems*. (R. Flower, Illus.). New York: Simon & Schuster.

_____. (Ed.). (1999). *Spectacular science: A book of poems*. (V. Halstead, Illus.). New York: Simon & Schuster.

_____. (Ed.). (2000). *My America: A poetry atlas of the United States*. (S. Alcorn, Illus.). New York: Simon & Schuster.

_____. (Ed.). (2005). *Oh no! Where are my pants? And other disasters*. (W. Erlbruch, Illus.). New York: HarperCollins.

Hopkinson, D. (2002). *Under the quilt of night*. (J. E. Ransome, Illus.). New York: Simon & Schuster.

_____. (2004). *A packet of seeds*. (B. Andersen, Illus.). New York: Greenwillow.

_____. (2006). *Sky boys: How they built the Empire State Building*. (J. E. Ransome, Illus.). New York: Schwartz & Wade.

Hort, L. (2006). *Did dinosaurs eat pizza?: Mysteries science hasn't solved*. New York: Henry Holt.

Horvath, P. (2001). *Everything on a waffle*. New York: Farrar, Straus, & Giroux.

Howe, J. (1990). *Pinky and Rex*. (M. Sweet, Illus.). New York: Atheneum.

_____. (1996). *Pinky and Rex and the bully*. (M. Sweet, Illus.). New York: Atheneum.

Hoyt-Goldsmith, D. (2000). *Celebrating Passover*. (L. Migdale, Illus.). New York: Holiday House.

_____. (2001). *Celebrating Ramadan*. (L. Migdale, Illus.). New York: Holiday House.

_____. (2004). *Three Kings Day: A celebration of Christmastime*. (L. Migdale, Illus.). New York: Holiday House.

Hunt, J. (1989). *Illuminations*. New York: Simon & Schuster.

Hunter, S. H. (1996). *The unbreakable code*. (J. Miner, Illus.). Flagstaff, AZ: Northland.

Hurmence, B. (1982). *A girl called boy*. Boston: Houghton Mifflin.

Hutchins, P. (1971). *Changes, changes*. New York: Simon & Schuster.

_____. (1974). *The wind blew.* New York: Macmillan.

Huynh, Q. N. (1999). *Water buffalo days.* (J. & M. Tseng, Illus.). New York: HarperTrophy.

Hyman, T. S. (1983). *Little Red Riding Hood.* New York: Holiday House.

Jacques, B. (1991). *Mariel of Redwall.* (G. Chalk, Illus.). New York: Philomel.

_____. (1994). *Martin the warrior.* (G. Chalk, Illus.). New York: Philomel.

Janeczko, P. B. (Ed.). (1999). *Very best (almost) friends: Poems of friendship.* (C. Daveneir, Illus.). Cambridge, MA: Candlewick.

_____. (Ed.). (2001). *A poke in the I: A collection of concrete poems.* (C. Raschka, Illus.). New York: Candlewick.

Jarrie, M. (2005). *ABC USA.* New York: Sterling Publishing Company.

Jay, A. (2003). *ABC: A child's first alphabet book.* New York: Dutton.

Jenkins, S. (1997). *What do you do when something wants to eat you?* Boston: Houghton Mifflin.

_____. (2004). *Actual size.* Boston: Houghton Mifflin.

_____. (2005). *Prehistoric actual size.* Boston: Houghton Mifflin.

_____. (2006). *Almost gone: The world's rarest animals.* New York: HarperCollins.

Jenkins, S., & Page, R. (2003). *What do you do with a tail like this?* Boston: Houghton Mifflin.

Johnson, C. (1955). *Harold and the purple crayon.* New York: HarperCollins.

Johnson, R. L. (2007). *Carnivorous plants.* Minneapolis, MN: Lerner.

Johnston, T. (1996a). *The wagon.* (J. E. Ransome, Illus.). New York: Tambourine Books.

_____. (1996b). *My Mexico~Mexico mio.* (F. J. Sierra, Illus.). New York: G. P. Putnam's Sons.

_____. (2002). *Sunsets of the West.* (T. Lewin, Illus.). New York: Putnam.

_____. (2004). *The harmonica.* (R. Mazellan, Illus.). Watertown, MA: Charlesbridge.

Jonas, A. (1983). *Roundtrip.* New York: Greenwillow Books.

Juster, N. (2005). *The hello, goodbye window.* New York: Michael di Capua Books.

Kalman, M. (2002). *Fireboat: The heroic adventures of John J. Harvey.* New York: Henry Holt.

Karim, R. (1999). *Kindle me a riddle: A pioneer story.* (B. Andersen, Illus.). New York: Greenwillow.

Keats, E. J. (1962). *The snowy day.* New York: Penguin.

Kellogg, S. (1977). *The mysterious tadpole.* New York: Dial.

_____. (1981). *The three sillies.* New York: Clarion.

_____. (1986a). *Best friends.* New York: Puffin.

_____. (1986b). *Pecos Bill.* New York: Morrow.

_____. (1988). *Chicken Little.* New York: Morrow.

_____. (2000). *Give a dog a bone.* New York: SeaStar Books.

Kelly, J., & Tincknell, C. (2004). *The mystery of Eatum Hall.* Cambridge, MA: Candlewick.

Kelly, K. (2004). *Lucy Rose, here's the thing about me.* (A. Rex, Illus.). New York: Delacorte.

Kennedy, C. (2005). *A family of poems: My favorite poetry for children.* (J. Muth, Illus.). New York: Hyperion.

Kennedy, X. J., & Kennedy, D. M. (1992). *Talking like the rain: A first book of poems.* (J. Dyer, Illus.). Boston: Little, Brown.

Kerley, B. (2001). *The dinosaurs of Waterhouse Hawkins: An illuminating history of Mr. Waterhouse Hawkins, artist and lecturer.* (B. Selznick, Illus.). New York: Scholastic.

Kimmel, E. (1988). *Anansi and the moss-covered rock.* (J. Stevens, Illus.). New York: Holiday House.

_____. (2001). *Anansi and the magic stick.* (J. Stevens, Illus.). New York: Holiday House.

_____. (2004). *Wonders and miracles.* New York: Scholastic.

King-Smith, D. (1996). *The stray.* (W. Parmenter, Illus.). New York: Crown.

Kipling, R. (2005). *The jungle book.* (Adapted and Illustrated by Nicola Bayley.) Cambridge, MA: Candlewick.

Kline, S. (1985). *Herbie Jones.* New York: Putnam.

Kloske, G. (2005). *Once upon a time, the end.* (B. Blitt, Illus.). New York: Antheneum.

Knowlton, J. (1988). *Geography from A to Z: A picture glossary.* New York: HarperCollins.

Knudsen, M. (2006). *Library lion.* (K. Hawkes, Illus.). Cambridge, MA: Candlewick.

Koch, M. (1991). *Hoot, howl, hiss.* New York: Greenwillow.

Koller, J. F. (2005). *Seven spunky monkeys.* (L. Munsinger, Illus.). San Diego: Harcourt.

Konigsburg, E. L. (1967). *From the mixed-up files of Mrs. Basil E. Frankweiler.* New York: Simon & Schuster/Atheneum.

Krauss, R. (1945). *The carrot seed.* (C. Johnson, Illus.). New York: HarperCollins.

Krinitz, E. N., & Steinhardt, B. (2005). *Memories of survival.* New York: Hyperion.

Krull, K. (2004a). *A pot o' gold: A treasury of Irish stories, poetry, folklore and (of course) blarney.* (D. McPhail, Illus.). New York: Hyperion.

_____. (2004b). *The boy on Fairfield Street: How Ted Geisel grew up to become Dr. Seuss.* (S. Johnson & L. Fancher, Illus.). New York: Random House.

Krupp, E. C. (1993). *The moon and you.* (R. R. Krupp, Illus.). New York: Simon & Schuster.

Kudlinski, K. V. (2005). *Boy, were we wrong about dinosaurs!* (S. D. Schindler, Illus.). New York: Dutton.

Kurlansky, M. (2001). *The cod's tale.* (S. D. Schindler, Illus.). New York: G. P. Putnam's Sons.

_____. (2006). *The story of salt.* (S. D. Schindler, Illus.). New York: G. P. Putnam's Sons.

Kurtz, J. (2000). *Faraway home.* (E. B. Lewis, Illus.). San Diego: Harcourt.

_____. (2003). *Saba: Under the hyena's foot.* (J. P. Tibbles, Illus.). Middleton, WI: Pleasant Company.

LaMarche, J. (2006). *Up.* San Francisco: Chronicle.

Laminack, L. (2004). *Saturdays and teacakes.* (C. Soentpiet, Illus.). Atlanta: Peachtree.

Lansky, B. (1991). *Kids pick the funniest poems.* (S. Carpenter, Illus.). Minneapolis, MN: Meadowbrook.

_____. (Ed.). (2004). *If kids ruled the school.* (S. Carpenter, Illus.). Minneapolis, MN: Meadowbrook.

Larios, J. (2006). *Yellow elephant: A bright bestiary.* (J. Paschkis, Illus.). San Diego: Harcourt.

LaRochelle, D. (2004). *The best pet of all.* (H. Wakiyama, Illus.). New York: Dutton.

_____. (2007). *The end.* (R. Egielski, Illus.). New York: Scholastic.

Lasky, K. (1996). *True north.* New York: Scholastic.

_____. (1998). *The diary of Zipporah Feldman, a Jewish immigrant girl, New York City, 1903.* New York: Scholastic.

_____. (1999). *Elizabeth I: Red rose of the house of Tudor.* New York: Scholastic.

_____. (2003). *A voice of her own: The story of Phillis Wheatley, slave poet.* (P. Lee, Illus.). Cambridge, MA: Candlewick.

_____. (2004). *Kazunomiya: Prisoner of heaven, Japan 1858.* New York: Scholastic.

Lauber, P. (1994). *Be a friend to trees.* (H. Keller, Illus.). New York: HarperCollins.

_____. (2001). *What you never knew about tubs, toilets & showers.* (J. Manders, Illus.). New York: Simon & Schuster.

Lavies, B. (1989). *Lily pad pond.* New York: Dutton.

Lears, L. (1998). *Ian's walk: A story about autism.* (K. Ritz, Illus.). Morton Grove, IL: Albert Whitman.

Leedy, L. (1993). *Postcards from Pluto: A tour of the solar system.* New York: Holiday House.

LeGuin, U. (1988). *Catwings.* (S. D. Schindler, Illus.). New York: Orchard.

Lehman, B. (2004). *The red book.* Boston: Houghton Mifflin.

_____. (2006). *Museum trip.* Boston: Houghton Mifflin.

L'Engle, M. (1962). *A wrinkle in time.* New York: Farrar, Straus, & Giroux.

Lester, H. (1988). *Tacky the penguin.* (L. Munsinger, Illus.). Boston: Houghton Mifflin.

Lester, J. (1987). *The tales of Uncle Remus: The adventures of Brer Rabbit.* (J. Pinkney, Illus.). New York: Dial.

_____. (1994). *John Henry.* (J. Pinkney, Illus.). New York: Dial.

Lewis, C. S. (1950). *The lion, the witch, and the wardrobe.* (P. Baynes, Illus.). New York: Macmillan.

Lewis, J. P. (2002). *Doodle dandies: Poems that take shape.* New York: Aladdin.

_____. (2005). *Heroes and she-roes: Poems of amazing and everyday heroes.* (J. Cooke, Illus.). New York: Dial.

Lewis, N. (2005). *East o' the sun and west o' the moon.* (P. J. Lynch, Illus.). Cambridge, MA: Candlewick.

Lies, B. (2006). *Bats at the beach*. Boston: Houghton Mifflin.

Lind, M. (2003). *Bluebonnet girl*. (K. Kiesler, Illus.). New York: Henry Holt.

Lindberg, R. (1990). *Johnny Appleseed*. (K. Jacobsen, Illus.). Boston: Little, Brown.

Lionni, L. (1959). *Little blue and little yellow: A story for Pippo and Ann and other children*. New York: I. Obolensky.

Livingston, M. C. (1991). *Lots of limericks*. New York: McElderry Books.

———. (1996). *Festivals*. (L. E. Fisher, Illus.). New York: Holiday House.

———. (1997). *Cricket never does*. (K. DeKiefte, Illus.). New York: McElderry.

Lobel, A. (1983). *The book of pigericks*. New York: Harper & Row.

———. (1986). *The Random House book of Mother Goose*. New York: Random House.

Locker, T. (1995). *Sky tree: Seeing science through art*. New York: HarperCollins.

Lombard, J. (2006). *Drita, my homegirl*. New York: Putnam.

Longfellow, H. W. (2001). *The midnight ride of Paul Revere*. (C. Bing, Illus.). New York: Handprint Books.

Look, L. (2004). *Ruby Lu, brave and true*. (A. Wilsdorf, Illus.). New York: Atheneum.

Lord, C. (2006). *Rules*. New York: Scholastic.

Louie, Ai-Ling. (1982). *Yeh-Shen: A Cinderella story from China*. (F. Young, Illus.). New York: Philomel.

Lowell, S. (1994). *The tortoise and the hare*. (J. Harris, Illus.). Flagstaff, AZ: Rising Moon.

Lowry, L. (1979). *Anastasia Krupnik*. Boston: Houghton Mifflin.

———. (1989). *Number the stars*. Boston: Houghton Mifflin.

———. (1998). *Looking back: A book of memories*. Boston: Houghton Mifflin.

Luthardt, K. (2003). *Peep!* Atlanta, GA: Peachtree.

Lyon, G. E. (1991). *Cecil's story*. (P. Catalanotto, Illus.). New York: Orchard.

———. (1998). *A sign*. New York: Orchard.

MacDonald, R. (2003). *Achoo! Bang! Crash!: The noisy alphabet book*. Brookfield, CT: Roaring Brook.

MacLachlan, P. (1985). *Sarah, plain and tall*. New York: HarperCollins.

MacLeod, E. (2004). *Helen Keller: A determined life*. Toronto: Kids Can Press.

Mahy, M. (1990). *The great white man-eating shark: A cautionary tale*. (J. Allen, Illus.). New York: Dial.

Mannis, C. D. (2002). *One leaf rides the wind: Counting in a Japanese garden*. (S. Hartung, Illus.). New York: Viking.

Markle, S. (2002). *Growing up wild: Penguins*. New York: Atheneum.

———. (2006) *Porcupines*. Minneapolis, MN: Lerner.

———. (2007). *Zebras*. Minneapolis, MN: Lerner.

Markle, S., & Marks, A. (2005). *A mother's journey*. Watertown, MA: Charlesbridge.

Marsalis, W. (2005). *Jazz A B Z: An A to Z collection of jazz portraits*. (R. Rogers, Illus.). Cambridge, MA: Candlewick.

Marsden, C. (2005). *Moon runner*. Cambridge, MA: Candlewick.

Marshall, J. (1972). *George and Martha*. Boston: Houghton Mifflin.

Martin, B., Jr. (1992). *Brown bear, brown bear, what do you see?* (E. Carle, Illus.). New York: Henry Holt.

Martin, B. Jr., & Archambault, J. (1989). *Chicka chicka boom boom*. (L. Ehlert, Illus.). New York: Simon & Schuster.

Martin, J. B. (1998). *Snowflake Bentley*. (M. Azarian, Illus.). Boston: Houghton Mifflin.

Martin, R. (1992). *The rough-faced girl*. (D. Shannon, Illus.). New York: Putnam.

Maruki, T. (1980). *Hiroshima no pika*. New York: Lothrop, Lee, & Shepard.

Mathis, S. B. (1975). *The hundred penny box*. (L. & D. Dillon, Illus.). New York: Viking.

Mavor, S. (1997). *You and me: Poems of friendship*. New York: Orchard.

Mayer, M. (1967). *A boy, a dog, and a frog*. New York: Dial.

———. (1998). *Pegasus*. (K. Y. Craft, Illus.). New York: Morrow.

———. (1999). *Shibumi and the kitemaker*. New York: Marshall Cavendish.

McAllister, M. I. (2005). *The Mistmantle Chronicles: Book one*. (O. Rayyan, Illus.). New York: Hyperion.

McCloskey, R. (1941). *Make way for ducklings*. New York: Viking.

McCord, D. (1986). *One at a time: His poems for the young.* (H. B. Kane, Illus.). Boston: Little, Brown.

McDermott, G. (1974). *Arrow to the sun.* New York: Viking.

_____. (1993). *Raven: A trickster tale from the Pacific Northwest.* San Diego, CA: Harcourt.

_____. (2001). *Jabuti, the tortoise: A trickster tale from the Amazon.* San Diego, CA: Harcourt Brace.

_____. (2003). *Creation.* New York: Dutton.

McDonald, M. (1991). *The potato man.* (T. Lewin, Illus.). New York: Scholastic.

_____. (1995). *Insects are my life.* (P. B. Johnson, Illus.). New York: Orchard Books.

_____. (2000). *Judy Moody.* (P. Reynolds, Illus.). Cambridge, MA: Candlewick.

_____. (2003). *All the stars in the sky: The Santa Fe Trail diary of Florrie Mack Ryder.* New York: Scholastic.

_____. (2006). *Stink and the incredible super-galactic jawbreaker.* (P. H. Reynolds Illus.). Cambridge, MA: Candlewick.

McGrory, A. (2005). *Kidogo.* London, England: Bloomsbury.

McKinley, R. (1978). *Beauty: A retelling of the story of Beauty & the Beast.* New York: Eos/HarperCollins.

_____. (1997). *Rose daughter.* New York: Greenwillow Books.

McKissack, P. (2000). *Nzingha: Warrior queen of Matamba, Angola, Africa, 1595.* New York: Scholastic.

_____. (2002). *Goin' someplace special.* (J. Pinkney, Illus.). New York: Atheneum.

McLeod, B. (2006). *SuperHero ABC.* New York: HarperCollins.

McNulty, F. (2005). *If you decide to go to the moon.* (S. Kellogg, Illus.). New York: Scholastic.

McPhail, D. (2000). *Drawing lessons from a bear.* Boston: Little, Brown.

Medina, J. (2004). *The dream on Blanca's wall: Poems in English and Spanish/El sueño pegado en la pared de Blanca: Poemas y ingles y español.* (R. Casilla, Illus.). Honesdale, PA: Wordsong/Boyds Mills.

_____. (2004). *Tomás Rivera.* (E. Martinez, Illus.). Orlando: Harcourt.

Melmed, L. K. (1997). *Little Oh.* (J. LaMarche, Illus.). New York: HarperCollins.

Meyer, C. (2000). *Anastasia: The last Grand Duchess, Russia, 1914.* New York: Scholastic.

Micucci, C. (1992). *The life and times of the apple.* New York: Scholastic.

Mikaelsen, B. (1995). *Stranded.* New York: Hyperion.

Miles, M. (1971). *Annie and the old one.* (P. Parnall, Illus.). New York: Little, Brown.

Miller, A. A. (2003). *Treasures of the heart.* Chelsea, MI: Sleeping Bear.

Miller, K. (2007). *Poems in black and white.* Honesdale, PA: Wordsong/Boyds Mills.

Miller, W. (1995). *Frederick Douglass: The last days of slavery.* (C. Lucas, Illus.). New York: Lee & Low.

_____. (1997). *Richard Wright and the library card.* (G. Christie, Illus.). New York: Lee & Low.

Mills, C. (2006). *Trading places.* New York: Farrar, Straus, & Giroux.

Milne, A. A. (1966). *Winnie-the-Pooh.* (E. H. Shepard, Illus.). New York: Dutton.

Mochizuki, K. (1993). *Baseball saved us.* (D. Lee, Illus.). New York: Lee & Low.

Montgomery, K. (2006). *Quest for the tree kangaroo: An expedition to the cloud forest of New Guinea.* (N. Bishop, Illus.). Boston: Houghton Mifflin.

Moore, C. C. (2006). *'Twas the night before Christmas.* (M. Tavares, Illus.). Cambridge, MA: Candlewick.

Moore, L. (2005). *Mural on Second Avenue and other city poems.* (R. Karas, Illus.). Cambridge, MA: Candlewick.

Mora, P. (1996). *Confetti: Poems for children.* (E. O. Sanchez, Illus.). New York: Lee & Low.

_____. (2002). *A library for Juana.* (B. Vidal, Illus.). New York: Knopf.

_____. (2005). *Dona Flor: A tall tale about a giant woman with a great big heart.* (R. Colon, Illus.). New York: A. A. Knopf.

Morpurgo, M. (1999). *Kensuke's kingdom.* New York: Scholastic.

Morris, C. (2007). *The boy who was raised by librarians.* (B. Sneed, Illus.). Atlanta, GA: Peachtree.

Morrison, L. (2001). *More spice than sugar: Poems about feisty females.* (A. Boyajian, Illus.). Boston: Houghton Mifflin.

Morrow, B. O. (2003). *A good night for freedom.* (L. Jenkins, Illus.). New York: Holiday House.

Moss, J. (1997). *Bone poems.* (T. Leigh, Illus.). New York: American Museum of Natural History/Workman Publishing.

Mowat, F. (1962). *Owls in the family.* (R. Frankenberg, Illus.). New York: Little Brown.

Munsch, R. (1980). *The paper bag princess.* (M. Martchenko, Illus.). Toronto: Annick.

_____. (1985). *Thomas' snowsuit.* (M. Martchenko, Illus.). Toronto, Canada: Annick Press.

Murphy, J. (2003). *An American plague: The true and terrifying story of the Yellow Fever epidemic of 1793.* New York: Clarion.

Murphy, S. (1997a). *Elevator magic.* New York: HarperCollins.

_____. (1997b). *Divide and ride.* New York: HarperCollins.

Napoli, D. J. (2006). *Ugly.* New York: Hyperion Books for Children.

Naylor, P. R. (1991). *Shiloh.* New York: Antheneum.

_____. (2006). *Roxie and the hooligans.* (A. Boiger, Illus.). New York: Atheneum.

Nelson, V. M. (2003). *Almost to freedom.* (C. Bootman, Illus.). Minneapolis, MN: Carolrhoda.

Nesbit, E. (2006). *Jack and the beanstalk.* (M. Tavares, Illus.). Cambridge, MA: Candlewick.

Nikola-Lisa, W. (2006). *How smart we are.* (S. Qualls, Illus.). New York: Lee & Low.

Nixon, J. L. (1987). *A family apart.* New York: Delacorte.

Noble, T. H. (2004). *The scarlet stockings spy.* (R. Papp, Illus.). Chelsea, MI: Sleeping Bear.

North, S. (1963). *Rascal.* New York: Dutton.

Norton, M. (1953). *The borrowers.* (B. & J. Krush, Illus.). New York: Harcourt.

Noyes, D. (2004). *Hana in the time of the tulips.* (B. Ibatouline, Illus.). Cambridge, MA: Candlewick.

Nye, N. S. (1995). *The tree is older than you are.* New York: Simon & Schuster.

O'Brien, R. C. (1971). *Mrs. Frisby and the rats of NIMH.* (Z. Bernstein, Illus.). New York: Atheneum.

O'Connor, J. (2006). *Fancy Nancy.* New York: HarperCollins.

_____. (2007). *Fancy Nancy and the Posh Puppy.* (R. P. Glasser, Illus.). New York: HarperCollins.

O'Dell, S. (1980). *Sarah Bishop.* Boston: Houghton Mifflin.

Offill, J. (2007). *17 things I'm not allowed to do anymore.* (N. Carpenter, Illus.). New York: Schwartz & Wade.

O'Malley, K. (2005). *Once upon a cool motorcycle dude.* (K. O'Malley, C. Heyer, & S. Goto, Illus.). New York: Walker & Co.

O'Neal, D., & Westengard, A. (2005). *The trouble with Henry: A tale of Walden Pond.* (S. D. Schindler, Illus.). Cambridge, MA: Candlewick.

O'Neill, A. (2002). *The recess queen.* (L. Huliska-Beith, Illus.). New York: Scholastic.

O'Neill, M. (1961). *Hailstones and halibut bones.* (L. Weisgard, Illus.). New York: Doubleday.

Osborne, M. P. (2000). *My brother's keeper: Virginia's Civil War diary (Book 1).* New York: Scholastic.

_____. (2002). *The one-eyed giant: Tales from the Odyssey.* (T. Howell, Illus.). New York: Hyperion.

Oswald, N. (2004). *Nothing here but stones.* New York: Holt.

Otten, C. F. (1997). *January rides the wind: A book of months.* (T. L. W. Doney, Illus.). New York: Lothrop, Lee, & Shepard.

Oughton, J. (1992). *How the stars fell into the sky: A Navajo legend.* (L. Desimini, Illus.). Boston: Houghton Mifflin.

Paolilli, P., & Brewer, D. (2001). *Silver seeds: A book of nature poems.* (S. Johnson & L. Fancher, Illus.). New York: Viking.

Paolini, C. (2002). *Eragon.* New York: Knopf.

_____. (2005). *Eldest.* New York: Knopf.

Parish, P. (1966). *Key to the treasure.* New York: Dell.

Park, B. (1995). *Mick Harte was here.* New York: Knopf.

_____. (2001). *Junie B., first grader (at last!).* (D. Brunkus, Illus.). New York: Random House.

Park, L. S. (2000). *The kite fighters.* New York: Random House.

Parkes, B., & Smith, J. (1997). *The enormous watermelon.* (M. Davy, Illus.). Melbourne, Australia: Mimosa Publications.

Parkinson, S. (2003). *Kathleen: The Celtic knot, 1937.* (T. Howell, Illus.). Middleton, WI: Pleasant Company.

Parr, T. (2005). *Reading makes you feel good.* Boston: Little, Brown.

Paterson, K. (1977). *Bridge to Terabithia.* (D. Diamond, Illus.). New York: HarperCollins.

_____. (1978). *The great Gilly Hopkins.* New York: Crowell.

_____. (2002). *The same stuff as stars*. New York: Clarion.

Pattou, E. (1998). *Fire arrow*. San Diego: Harcourt.

_____. (2003). *East*. Orlando, FL: Harcourt.

Paul, A. W. (1999). *All by herself: 14 girls who made a difference*. New York: Harcourt.

Paulsen, G. (1987). *Hatchet*. New York: Bradbury.

_____. (1996). *Brian's winter*. New York: Delacorte.

Pearce, P. (1959). *Tom's midnight garden*. (S. Einzig, Illus.). New York: HarperCollins.

Pearson, S. (2005). *Who swallowed Harold? And other poems about pets*. (D. Slomin, Illus.). New York: Marshall Cavendish.

Peck, R. (1997). *The ghost belonged to me*. New York: Puffin.

_____. (1998). *A long way from Chicago*. New York: Dial.

_____. (2000). *A year down yonder*. New York: Dial.

_____. (2001). *Fair weather*. New York: Dial.

Peck, R. N. (1974). *Soup*. (C. C. Gehm, Illus.). New York: Knopf.

Peddle, D. (2000). *Snow day*. New York: Doubleday.

Peet, B. (1970). *The Whingdingdilly*. Boston: Houghton Mifflin.

_____. (1971). *The caboose who got loose*. Boston: Houghton Mifflin.

_____. (1989). *Bill Peet: An autobiography*. Boston: Houghton Mifflin.

Pennypacker, S. (2007). *The talented Clementine*. New York: Hyperion.

Perez, L. K. (2002). *First day in grapes*. (R. Casilla, Illus.). New York: Lee & Low.

Peters, L. W. (2003). *Earthshake: Poems from the ground up*. (C. Felstead, Illus.). New York: Greenwillow.

Pfeffer, W. (2004). *Wiggling worms at work*. (S. Jenkins, Illus.). New York: HarperCollins.

Pienkowski, J. (2005). *Haunted house*. New York: Candlewick.

Pinkney, A. D. (2000). *Let it shine: Stories of black women freedom fighters*. (S. Alcorn, Illus.). San Diego: Harcourt.

Pinkney, J. (2000). *Aesop's fables*. New York: SeaStar.

Polacco, P. (1993). *The bee tree*. New York: Philomel.

_____. (1994). *Pink and Say*. New York: Philomel.

_____. (1998). *Thank you, Mr. Falker*. New York: Philomel.

Prelutsky, J. (1983). *The Random House book of poetry for children*. (A. Lobel, Illus.). New York: Random House.

_____. (1988). *Tyrannosaurus was a beast: Dinosaur poems* (A. Lobel, Illus.). New York: Greenwillow.

_____. (1993). *The dragons are singing tonight*. (P. Sis, Illus.). New York: Greenwillow.

_____. (2004). *If not for the cat: Haiku*. (T. Rand, Illus.). New York: Greenwillow.

_____. (2006). *Behold the bold umbrellaphant: And other poems*. (C. Berger, Illus.). New York: Greenwillow.

_____. (Ed.). (1991). *For laughing out loud: Poems to tickle your funnybone*. (M. Priceman, Illus.). New York: Knopf.

_____. (Ed.). (2006). *The beauty of the beast: Poems from the animal kingdom*. (M. So, Illus.). New York: Knopf.

Pringle, L. P. (1997). *An extraordinary life: The story of a monarch butterfly*. (B. Marshall, Illus.). New York: Orchard.

Pryor, B. (1999). *Joseph: 1861—A rumble of war*. (B. Dodson, Illus.). New York: HarperCollins.

_____. (2000a). *Joseph's choice: 1861*. (B. Dodson, Illus.). New York: HarperCollins.

_____. (2000b). *Thomas: 1778—Patriots on the run*. (B. Dodson, Illus.). New York: HarperTrophy.

Puttapipat, N. (2005). *The musicians of Bremen*. Cambridge, MA: Candlewick.

Rael, E. O. (1996). *What Zeesie saw on Delancey Street*. (M. Priceman, Illus.). New York: Simon & Schuster.

Rappaport, D. (2005). *The school is not white! A true story of the civil rights movement*. (C. James, Illus.). New York: Hyperion.

Raschka, C. (1993). *Yo! Yes?* New York: Orchard.

Rash, A. (2004). *Agent A to agent Z*. New York. Arthur A. Levine.

Raven, M. T. (2006). *Night boat to freedom*. (E. B. Lewis, Illus.). New York: Farrar, Straus, & Giroux.

Raven, N. (2007). *Beowolf: A tale of blood, heat, and ashes*. (J. Howe, Illus.). Cambridge, MA: Candlewick.

Rawls, W. (1996). *Where the red fern grows*. New York: Delacorte.

Ray, J. (1997). *Hansel and Gretel*. Cambridge, MA: Candlewick.

Recorvits, H. (2003). *My name is Yoon*. (G. Swiatkowska, Illus.). New York: Frances Foster.

Rex, A. (2006). *Frankenstein makes a sandwich*. Orlando: Harcourt.

Ringgold, F. (1991). *Tar beach*. New York: Crown.

_____. (1995). *Aunt Harriet's underground railroad in the sky*. New York: Knopf.

Roberts, S. (2003). *We all go traveling by*. (S. Bell, Illus.). Cambridge, MA: Barefoot Books.

Robertson, M. P. (2005). *The dragon snatcher*. New York: Dial.

Robinson, S. (2006). *Safe at home*. New York: Scholastic.

Rockwell, A. (2002). *They called her Molly Pitcher*. (C. von Buhler, Illus.). New York: Knopf.

Rockwell, A. F. (2002). *Becoming butterflies*. (M. Halsey, Illus.). New York: Walker & Company.

_____. (2005). *Honey in a hive*. (S. D. Schindler, Illus.). New York: HarperCollins.

Rockwell, T. (1973). *How to eat fried worms*. (E. McCully, Illus.). New York: F. Watts.

Rodman, M. A. (2006). *First grade stinks*. (B. Speigel, Illus.). Atlanta: Peachtree.

Roemer, H. B. (2004). *Come to my party and other shape poems*. (H. Takahashi, Illus.). New York: Henry Holt.

Rohmann, E. (1994). *Time Flies*. New York: Crown Books for Young Readers.

Root, P. (2001). *Rattletrap car*. (J. Barton, Illus.). Cambridge, MA: Candlewick.

Rosenthal, A. K. (2006). *Cookies: Bite-size life lessons*. New York: HarperCollins.

Rotner, S. (1996). *Action alphabet*. New York: Simon & Schuster/Atheneum.

Rowling, J. K. (1998). *Harry Potter and the sorcerer's stone*. (M. GrandPré, Illus.). New York: Scholastic.

_____. (2005). *Harry Potter and the half-blood prince*. (M. GrandPré, Illus.). New York: Scholastic.

Rubalcaba, J. (1998). *Place in the sun*. New York: Puffin.

Rubin, S. G. (2000). *Fireflies in the dark: The story of Friedl Dicker-Brandeis and the children of Terezin*. New York: Holiday House.

Ruckman, I. (1986). *Night of the twisters*. New York: Harper Trophy.

Rumford, J. (2004). *Sequoyah: The Cherokee man who gave his people writing*. Boston: Houghton Mifflin.

Rupp, R. (2005). *The return of the dragon*. Cambridge, MA: Candlewick.

Ryan, P. M. (1997). *A pinky is a baby mouse, and other baby animal names*. (D. deGroat, Illus.). New York: Hyperion.

_____. (1999). *Amelia and Eleanor go for a ride*. (B. Selznick, Illus.). New York: Scholastic.

_____. (2000). *Esperanza rising*. New York: Scholastic.

_____. (2001). *Hello ocean*. (M. Astrella, Illus.). Watertown, MA: Charlesbridge.

_____. (2003). *A box of friends*. (M. Whyte, Illus.). Columbus, OH: Gingham Dog.

_____. (2005). *Nacho and Lolita*. (C. Rueda, Illus.). New York: Scholastic.

Ryder, J. (2001). *The waterfall's gift*. (J. Watson, Illus.). San Francisco: Sierra Club Books.

Rylant, C. (1985). *The relatives came*. (S. Gammell, Illus.). New York: Bradbury.

_____. (1987). *Henry and Mudge: The first book of their adventures*. New York: Simon & Schuster.

_____. (1992). *Missing May*. New York: Orchard.

_____. (1994). *Mr. Putter and Tabby walk the dog*. (A. Howard, Illus.). San Diego: Harcourt Brace.

_____. (1997). *Poppleton*. (M. Teague, Illus.). New York: Blue Sky.

_____. (2005). *Henry and Mudge and the great grandpas*. New York: Simon & Schuster.

_____. (2006). *The journey: Stories of migration*. (L. Davis, Illus.). New York: Blue Sky.

_____. (2007). *Henry and Mudge and the big sleepover: The twenty-eighth book of their adventures*. New York: Simon & Schuster.

Sabuda, R. (2004). *America the beautiful*. New York: Simon & Schuster.

_____. (2005). *Winter's tale*. New York: Simon & Schuster.

Sachar, L. (1978). *Sideways stories from Wayside School.* (J. Brinckloe, Illus.). New York: Morrow.

_____. (1998). *Holes.* New York: Farrar, Straus, & Giroux.

Salley, C. (2002). *Epossumondas.* (J. Stevens, Illus.). San Diego: Harcourt.

San Souci, R. D. (1989). *The talking eggs.* (J. Pinkney, Illus.). New York: Dial.

_____. (2000). *Six foolish fishermen.* (D. Kennedy, Illus.). New York: Hyperion.

_____. (2003). *Little Pierre: A Cajun story from Louisiana.* (D. Catrow, Illus.). San Diego: Harcourt/Silver Whistle.

Sanderson, R. (2004). *The snow princess.* New York: Little, Brown.

Say, A. (1993). *Grandfather's journey.* Boston: Houghton Mifflin.

Sayre, A. P. (2005). *Stars beneath your bed: The surprising story of dust.* (A. Jonas, Illus.). New York: Greenwillow.

Schnur, S. (2002). *Winter: An alphabet acrostic.* (L. Evans, Illus.). New York: Clarion.

Schwartz, A. (1988). *Annabelle Swift, kindergartener.* New York: Orchard.

Scieszka, J. (1989). *The true story of the three little pigs.* (L. Smith, Illus.). New York: Viking.

_____. (1991). The *knights of the kitchen table.* (A. McCauley, Illus.). New York: Viking.

_____. (1998). *Summer reading is killing me.* (L. Smith, Illus.). New York: Viking.

_____. (2004). *Science verse.* (L. Smith, Illus.). New York: Viking.

_____. (2006). *Marco? Polo!* (A. McCauley, Illus.). New York: Viking.

Scruggs, A. (2000). *Jump rope magic.* (D. Diaz, Illus.). New York: Blue Sky.

Searchlight Films. (1993). *Eric Carle, picture writer.* New York: Philomel Books/Scholastic.

Selznick, B. (2007). *The invention of Hugo Cabret.* New York: Scholastic.

Seuss, Dr. (1957). *The cat in the hat.* New York: Random House.

Shannon, D. (1998). *No, David!* New York: Blue Sky Press.

_____. (1999). *David goes to school.* New York: Blue Sky Press.

_____. (2000). *The rain came down.* New York: Blue Sky Press.

_____. (2005). *Alice the fairy.* New York: Blue Sky Press.

Shannon, G. (2005). *White is for blueberry.* (L. Dronzek, Illus.). New York: Greenwillow.

_____. (Ed.). (1996). *Spring: A haiku story.* (M. Zeldis, Illus.). New York: Greenwillow.

Shaw, C. G. (1947). *It looked like spilt milk.* New York: Harper & Row.

Shaw, J. B. (2002). *Meet Kaya: An American girl.* (B. Farnsworth & S. McAliley, Illus.). Middleton, WI: Pleasant Company.

Shea, P. D. (1995). *The whispering cloth.* (A. Riggio, Illus.). Honesdale, PA: Boyds Mills.

Showers, P. (1991). *The listening walk.* (Aliki, Illus.). New York: HarperCollins.

Shreve, S. R. (2002). *Trout and me.* New York: Alfred A. Knopf.

Sidman, J. (2005). *Song of the water boatman & other pond poems.* (B. Pranage, Illus.). Boston: Houghton Mifflin.

_____. (2006a). *Butterfly eyes and other secrets of the meadow.* (B. Krommes, Illus.). Boston: Houghton Mifflin.

_____. (2006b). *Meow ruff: A story in concrete poetry.* (M. Berg, Illus.). Boston: Houghton Mifflin.

Siebert, D. (1989). *Heartland.* (W. Minor, Illus.). New York: Crowell.

_____. (2006). *Tour America: A journey through poems and art.* (S. T. Johnson, Illus.). New York: Chronicle.

Sierra, J. (2004). *Wild about books.* (M. Brown, Illus.). New York: Knopf.

Silverstein, S. (1974). *Where the sidewalk ends: The poems and drawings of Shel Silverstein.* New York: Harper & Row.

_____. (2005). *Runny babbit: A billy sook.* New York: HarperCollins.

Simon, S. (2003). *The moon.* New York: Simon & Schuster.

_____. (2005). *Amazing bats.* San Francisco, CA: Chronicle.

_____. (2006). *Planet Mars.* San Francisco, CA: Chronicle.

Singer, M. (1995). *A wasp is not a bee*. (P. O'Brien, Illus.). New York: Holt.

_____. (2006). *What stinks?* Plain City, OH: Darby Creek Publishing.

Singh, R. (1999). *Moon tales: Myths of the moon from around the world*. (D. Lush, Illus.). London: Bloomsbury.

Sinnott, S. (2003). *Extraordinary Asian Americans and Pacific Islanders*. New York: Scholastic.

Sis, P. (1996). *Starry messenger*. New York: Farrar, Straus, & Giroux.

Sleator, W. (2001). *Marco's millions*. New York: Dutton.

Smith, D. B. (1973). *A taste of blackberries*. (C. Robinson, Illus.). New York: Crowell.

Smith, Jr., C. R. (2003). *Hoop queens*. Cambridge, MA: Candlewick.

_____. (2004). *Hoop kings*. Cambridge, MA: Candlewick.

Sneve, V. D. H. (2003). *Enduring wisdom: Sayings from Native Americans*. (S. St. James, Illus.). New York: Holiday House.

Soto, G. (1995). *Canto familiar*. San Diego: Harcourt.

Soundworks Production. (1996). *Get to know Gerald McDermott*. Orlando, FL: Harcourt Brace.

Speare, E. G. (1983). *The sign of the beaver*. Boston: Houghton Mifflin.

Spinelli, E. (2004). *Feathers: Poems about birds*. (L. McCue, Illus.). New York: Henry Holt.

Spinelli, J. (1990). *Maniac Magee*. Boston: Little, Brown.

_____. (1997a). *The library card*. New York: Scholastic.

_____. (1997b). *Wringer*. New York: HarperCollins.

Spivak, S. (1997). *Grass sandals: The travels of Basho*. (Demi, Illus.). New York: Atheneum.

Squires, J. (2006). *The gingerbread cowboy*. (H. Berry, Illus.). New York: Laura Geringer.

Stanley, D. (1997). *Rumpelstiltskin's daughter*. New York: HarperCollins.

_____. (2002). *Saladin: Noble prince of Islam*. New York: HarperCollins.

Stanton K. (2007). *Papi's gift*. (R. K. Moreno, Illus.). Honesdale, PA: Boyds Mills Press.

Steptoe, J. (1987). *Mufaro's beautiful daughters: An African tale*. New York: Lothrop.

Steptoe, J. (Illus.). (1997). *In daddy's arms I am tall: African Americans celebrating fathers*. New York: Lee & Low.

Stevens, J. (1995). *Tops & bottoms*. San Diego: Harcourt.

Stevens, J., & Crummel, S. C. (2005). *The great fuzz frenzy*. San Diego: Harcourt.

Stewart, M. (2007). *Baboons*. Minneapolis, MN: Lerner.

Stinson, K. (2000). *King of the castle*. (K. Charko, Illus.). Toronto, Canada: Second Story Press.

Stolz, J. (2004). *The shadows of Ghadames*. New York: Delacorte.

Stuve-Bodeen, S. (2002). *Elizabeti's school*. (C. Hale, Illus.). New York: Lee & Low.

Sweet, M. (2005). *Carmine: A little more red*. Boston: Houghton Mifflin.

Taback, S. (1997). *There was an old lady who swallowed a fly*. New York: Viking.

Tafuri, N. (1984). *Have you seen my duckling?* New York: Greenwillow.

Tanaka, S. (2005). *A day that changed America: Earthquake!* (D. Craig, Illus.). New York: Hyperion.

Tang, G. (2003). *Math-terpieces*. New York: Scholastic.

_____. (2005). *Math potatoes*. New York: Scholastic.

Tavares, M. (2000). *Zachary's ball*. Cambridge, MA: Candlewick.

_____. (Illus.). (2006). *'Twas the night before Christmas: Account of a visit from St. Nicholas*. Cambridge, MA: Candlewick.

Taylor, S. (2004). *Boing!* (B. Ingman, Illus.). Cambridge, MA: Candlewick.

Teague, M. (2002). *Dear Mrs. LaRue: Letters from obedience school*. New York: Scholastic.

Thayer, J. (1989). *The popcorn dragon*. (L. McCue, Illus.). New York: Morrow.

Thimmesh, C. (2006). *Team moon: How 400,000 people landed Apollo 11 on the moon*. New York: Houghton Mifflin.

Thomas, J. C. (1998). *I have heard of a land*. (F. Cooper, Illus.). New York: HarperCollins.

Thomas, S. M. (2006). *Happy birthday, good knight.* (J. Plecas, Illus.). New York: Dutton.

Thomson, S. (2005). *Amazing sharks!* New York: HarperCollins.

Tolstoy, A. (2003). *The enormous turnip.* (S. Goto, Illus.). San Diego, CA: Harcourt.

Tomecek, S. (2004). *Moon.* (L. C. Guida, Illus.). Washington, D.C.: National Geographic Society.

Travers, P. L. (1934). *Mary Poppins.* (M. Shepard, Illus.). San Diego, CA: Harcourt.

Tunnell, M. O. (1997). *Mailing May.* (T. Rand, Illus.). New York: HarperCollins.

Tunnell, M. O., & Chilcoat, G. W. (1996). *The children of Topaz: The story of a Japanese-American internment camp based on a classroom diary.* New York: Holiday House.

Turkle, B. (1976). *Deep in the forest.* New York: Dutton.

Turner, A. (1992). *Katie's trunk.* New York: Simon & Schuster.

_____. (1997). *Dust for dinner.* (R. Barrett, Illus.). New York: HarperTrophy.

Udry, J. M. (1956). *A tree is nice.* (M. Simont, Illus.). New York: HarperCollins.

Uegaki, C. (2003). *Suki's kimono.* (S. Jorisch, Illus.). Tonawanda, NY: Kids Can Press.

Uhlberg, M. (2003). *The printer.* (H. Sorensen, Illus.). New York: Peachtree.

Vagin, V. (1998). *The enormous carrot.* New York: Scholastic.

Van Allsburg, C. (1981). *Jumanji.* Boston: Houghton Mifflin.

_____. (1983). *The wreck of the Zephyr.* Boston: Houghton Mifflin.

_____. (1984). *The mysteries of Harris Burdick.* Boston: Houghton Mifflin.

_____. (1988). *Two bad ants.* Boston: Houghton Mifflin.

_____. (2002). *Zathura.* Boston: Houghton Mifflin.

_____. (2006). *Probuditi!* Boston: Houghton Mifflin.

Van Draanen, W. (2001). *Flipped.* New York: Knopf.

Van Leeuwen, J. (1994). *Bound for Oregon.* New York: Dial.

Vaughan, M. (2003). *Up the learning tree.* (D. Blanks, Illus.). New York: Lee & Low.

Verniero, J. C. (2001). *One-hundred-and-one Asian read-aloud myths and legends.* New York: Black Dob & Leventhal.

Viorst, J. (1972). *Alexander and the terrible, horrible, no good, very bad day.* (R. Cruz, Illus.). New York: Atheneum.

_____. (1974). *Rosie and Michael.* (L. Tomei, Illus.). New York: Atheneum.

_____. (1988). *I'll fix Anthony.* New York: Aladdin Paperbacks.

_____. (1995). *The tenth good thing about Barney.* (E. Blegvad, Illus.). New York: Atheneum.

Volavkova, H. (Ed.). (1994). *. . . I never saw another butterfly: Children's drawings and poems from Terezin Concentration Camp, 1942–44.* New York: Random House.

Waber, B. (1972). *Ira sleeps over.* Boston: Houghton Mifflin.

_____. (1988). *Ira says goodbye.* Boston: Houghton Mifflin.

Walker, S. (2001). *Mary Anning: Fossil hunter.* Minneapolis, MN: Carolrhoda.

_____. (2004). *Sea horses.* Minneapolis: MN: Lerner.

_____. (2005). *Secrets of a Civil War submarine: Solving the mysteries of the* H. L. Hunley. Minneapolis, MN: Carolrhoda.

_____. (2006a). *Mystery fish.* (S. Gould, Illus.). Brookfield, CT: Millbrook Press.

_____. (2006b). *Shipwreck search: Discovery of the* H. L. Hunley. (E. Verstraete, Illus.). Brookfield, CT: Millbrook Press.

_____. (2007). *Rocks.* Minneapolis, MN: Lerner.

Walsh, E. S. (1991). *Mouse paint.* San Diego: Harcourt Brace.

Wattenberg, J. (2000). *Henny-Penny.* New York: Scholastic.

Waugh, S. (1994). *The Mennyms.* New York: Greenwillow.

Weatherford, C. B. (2006). *Moses: When Harriet Tubman led her people to freedom.* (K. Nelson, Illus.). New York: Jump at the Sun.

Whipple, L. (Ed.). (1989). *Eric Carle's animals, animals.* (E. Carle, Illus.). New York: Philomel.

White, E. B. (1952). *Charlotte's web.* (G. Williams, Illus.). New York: HarperCollins.

Wiesner, D. (1988). *Free fall*. New York: Lothrop, Lee, & Shepard.

_____. (1991). *Tuesday.* New York: Clarion.

_____. (1999). *Sector 7.* New York: Clarion.

_____. (2001). *The three pigs.* New York: Clarion.

_____. (2006). *Flotsam.* New York: Clarion.

Wilder, L. I. (1953). *Little house in the big woods.* New York: HarperCollins.

Wiles, D. (2001). *Freedom summer.* (J. Lagarrique, Illus.). New York: Atheneum.

_____. (2005). *Each little bird that sings.* San Diego: Harcourt.

Wilkinson, V. (1994). *Flies are fascinating.* Chicago: Children's Press.

Willems, M. (2004). *Knuffle bunny: A cautionary tale.* New York: Hyperion.

Williams, J. A. (2005). *How does the sun make weather?* Berkeley Heights, NJ: Enslow Publishers.

Williams, M. (2005a). *Brothers in hope: The story of the Lost Boys of Sudan.* (R. G. Christie, Illus.). New York: Lee & Low.

_____. (2005b). *Hooray for inventors!* Cambridge, MA: Candlewick.

Williams, V. B. (2001). *Amber was brave, Essie was smart.* New York: Greenwillow.

Wilson, G. (2001). *Ignis.* (P. Lynch, Illus.). Cambridge, MA: Candlewick.

Winter, J. (1989). *Follow the drinking gourd.* New York: Knopf.

_____. (2000). *The house that Jack built.* New York: Dial.

_____. (2005). *The librarian of Basra: A true story from Iraq.* San Diego: Harcourt.

Winthrop, E. (2005). *Squashed in the middle.* (P. Cummings, Illus.). New York: Henry Holt.

Wisniewski, D. (1992). *Sundiata, Lion King of Mali.* New York: Clarion.

_____. (1994). *The wave of the Sea-Wolf.* Boston: Houghton Mifflin.

Wojciechowski, S. (2005). *Beany and the meany.* (S. Natti, Illus.). Cambridge, MA: Candlewick.

Wood, A. (1984). *The napping house.* (D. Wood, Illus.). San Diego: Harcourt Brace Jovanovich.

_____. (1985). *King Bidgood's in the bathtub.* (D. Wood, Illus.). San Diego. Harcourt Brace.

_____. (1996). *The red racer.* New York: Simon & Schuster.

_____. (1998). *Sweet dream pie.* (M. Teague, Illus.). New York: Blue Sky Press.

_____. (2004). *Ten little fish.* (B. Wood, Illus.). New York: Blue Sky.

Wood, D. (1999). *Grandad's prayers of the earth.* (P. J. Lynch, Illus.). Cambridge, MA: Candlewick.

Woodruff, E. (1999). *The memory coat.* (M. Dooling, Illus.). New York: Scholastic.

_____. (2006). *Small beauties: The journey of Darcy Heart O'Hara.* (A. Rex, Illus.). New York: Knopf.

Woodson, J. (2004). *Coming on home soon.* (E. B. Lewis, Illus.). New York: Putnam.

Wright, B. R. (2006). *Princess for a week.* (J. Rogers, Illus.). New York: Holiday House.

Wright-Frierson, V. (1996). *A desert scrapbook: Dawn to dusk in the Sonoran Desert.* New York: Simon & Schuster.

Yep, L. (1996). *Ribbons.* New York: Putnam.

_____. (2002). *Spring Pearl: The last flower.* (K. Sano, Illus.). Middleton, WI: Pleasant Company.

Yin. (2001). *Coolies.* (C. K. Soentpiet, Illus.). New York: Philomel.

_____. (2006). *Brothers.* (C. K. Soentpiet, Illus.). New York: Philomel.

Yolen, J. (1988). *The devil's arithmetic.* New York: Viking/Kestrel.

_____. (1990). *Bird watch.* (T. Lewin, Illus.). New York: Philomel.

_____. (1992). *Briar Rose.* New York: Tor.

_____. (1992). *Encounter.* (D. Shannon, Illus.). San Diego: Harcourt.

_____. (1996). *Welcome to the sea of sand.* (L. Regan, Illus.). New York: Putnam.

_____. (2002). *Not one damsel in distress: World folktales for strong girls.* (S. Guevara, Illus.). New York: Silver Whistle.

_____. (2003). *Sword of the rightful king.* San Diego, CA: Harcourt.

Yolen, J., & Peters, A. F. (2007). *Here's a little poem: A first book of poetry.* (P. Dunbar, Illus.). Cambridge, MA: Candlewick.

Young, E. (1989). *Lon Po Po: A Red-Riding Hood story from China*. New York: Philomel.

_____. (1992). *Seven blind mice.* New York: Philomel.

Zelinsky, P. O. (1986). *Rumpelstiltskin*. New York: Dutton.

Zoehfeld, K. W. (2001). *Dinosaur parents, dinosaur young: Uncovering the mystery of dinosaur families.* (P. Carrick & B. Shillinglaw, Illus.). New York: Clarion.

_____. (2007). *Dinosaur tracks.* New York: HarperCollins.

Professional References Cited

Adams. M. J. (1990). *Beginning to read: Thinking and learning about print.* Urbana, IL: Center for the Study of Reading.

Allington, R. L. (1977). If they don't read, how they ever gonna get good? *Journal of Reading, 21,* 57-61.

_____. (2002). What I've learned about effective reading instruction from a decade of studying exemplary elementary classroom teachers. *Phi Delta Kappan, 83*(10), 740-747.

_____. (2005). Ideology is still trumping evidence. *Phi Delta Kappan, 86*(6), 462-469.

Alvermann, D. E. (2000). Classroom talk about texts: Is it dear, cheap, or a bargain at any price? In B. M. Taylor, M. F. Graves, & P. Van den Broek (Eds.), *Reading for meaning: Fostering comprehension in the middle grades* (pp. 136-151). Newark, DE: International Reading Association, & New York: Teacher's College Press.

Anderson, N. A. (2006). *Elementary children's literature: The basics for teachers and parents* (2nd ed.). Boston: Allyn & Bacon.

Anderson, R. C., Hiebert, E. H., Scott, J. A., & Wilkinson, I. A. G. (1985). *Becoming a nation of readers: The report of the Commission on Reading.* Washington, D.C.: National Institute of Education.

Anderson, R. C., & Pearson, P. D. (1984). A schema-theoretic view of basic processes in reading. In P. D. Pearson (Ed.), *Handbook of reading research, Vol. 1* (pp. 255-291). New York: Longman.

Atwell, N. (2007). *The reading zone.* New York: Scholastic.

Bainbridge, J., & Pantaleo, S. (2001). Filling in the text: Picture book reading in the middle years. *The New Advocate, 14*(4), 401-411.

Beck, C., Nelson-Faulkner, S., & Pierce, K. M. (2000). Historical fiction: Teaching tool or literary experience? *Language Arts, 77*(6), 546-555.

Beck, I. (1989). Reading and reasoning. *The Reading Teacher, 42*(9), 676-682.

Bettelheim, B. (1976). *The uses of enchantment.* New York: Knopf.

Bishop, R. S., & Hickman, J. (1992). Four or fourteen or forty: Picture books are for everyone. In S. Benedict & L. Carlisle (Eds.), *Beyond words: Picture books for older readers and writers* (pp.1-10). Portsmouth, NH: Heinemann.

Black, S. (2003). Harry Potter: A magical prescription for just about anyone. *Journal of adolescent and adult literacy, 46*(7), 540-544.

Block, C. C., & Pressley, M. (2002). What comprehension instruction could be. In M. Pressley & C. C. Block (Eds.), *Comprehension instruction* (pp. 383-392). New York: Guilford.

Bloom, B. (1956). *Taxonomy of educational objectives.* New York: David McKay.

Bogart, D. (Ed.). (2007). *Children's books in print* (38th ed.). New Providence, NJ: R. R. Bowker.

Calkins, L. M. (1994). *The art of teaching writing* (2nd ed.). Portsmouth, NH: Heinemann.

Campbell, J. (1968). *The hero with a thousand faces* (2nd ed.). Princeton, NJ: Princeton University Press.

Chaney, J. H. (1993). Alphabet books: Resources for learning. *The Reading Teacher, 47*(2), 96-104.

Chapman, V. G., & Sopko, D. (2003). Developing strategic use of combined-text trade books. *The Reading Teacher, 57*(3), 236-239.

Cramer, R. L. (2001). *Creative power: The nature and nurture of children's writing.* New York: Longman.

Cruz, M. C., & Pollock, K. B. (2004). Stepping into the wardrobe: A fantasy genre study. *Language Arts, 81*(3), 184-195.

Culham, R. (2003). *6 + 1 traits of writing: The complete guide (grades 3 and up).* New York: Scholastic.

_____. (2005). *6 + 1 traits of writing: The complete guide for the primary grades.* New York: Scholastic.

Cunningham, P. (2005). "If they don't read much, how they ever gonna get good?" *The Reading Teacher, 59*(1), 89-90.

Cunningham, P. M. (2005). *Phonics they use: Words for reading and writing* (4th ed.). New York: Pearson/Allyn & Bacon.

Darigan, D. L., Tunnell, M. O., & Jacobs, J. S. (2002). *Children's literature: Engaging teachers and children in good books.* Upper Saddle River, NJ: Merrill/Prentice Hall.

Dunn, M. A. (2000). Closing the book on social studies: Four classroom teachers go beyond the text. *The Social Studies, 91*(3), 132-136.

Dymock, S. (2005). Teaching expository text structure awareness. *The Reading Teacher, 59*(2), 177-182.

Eeds, M., & Hudelson, S. (1995). Literature as foundation for personal and classroom life. *Primary Voices K-6, 3*(2), 2-7.

Engelfried, S. (2001). The ABCs of ABCs: A look at 26 of the most innovative alphabet books around. *School Library Journal, 47*(1), 32-33.

Farland, D. (2006). Trade books and the human endeavor of science. *Science and Children, 44*(3), 35-37.

Farris, P. J., Fuhler, C. J., & Walther, M. P. (2004). *Teaching reading: A balanced approach for today's classrooms.* Boston: McGraw-Hill.

Fisher, C. J., & Natarella, M. A. (1982). Young children's preferences in poetry: A national survey of first, second and third graders. *Research in the Teaching of English, 16*(4), 339-354.

Fletcher, R. J. (2002). *Poetry matters: Writing a poem from the inside out.* New York: HarperCollins.

Fletcher, R., & Portalupi, J. (1998). *Craft lessons: Teaching writing K-8.* Portland, ME: Stenhouse.

_____. (2001). *Writing workshop: The essential guide.* Portsmouth, NH: Heinemann.

Fountas, I. C., & Pinnell, G. S. (1996). *Guided reading: Good first teaching for all children.* Portsmouth, NH: Heinemann.

_____. (1999). *Matching books to readers: Using leveled books in guided reading, K-3.* Portsmouth, NH: Heinemann.

_____. (2001). *Guiding readers and writers, grades 3-6: Teaching comprehension, genre, and content literacy.* Portsmouth, NH: Heinemann.

Freedman, R. (1992). Fact or fiction. In E. B. Freeman & D. G. Person (Eds.), *Using nonfiction tradebooks in the elementary classroom: From ants to zepplins* (pp. 2-10). Urbana, IL: National Council of Teachers of English.

Fuhler, C. J. (2000). *Teaching reading with multicultural books kids love.* Golden, CO: Fulcrum Publishers.

Fuhler, C. J., Farris, P. J., & Nelson, P. A. (2006). Building literacy skills across the curriculum: Forging connections with the past through artifacts. *Reading Teacher, 59*(7), 646-659.

Galda, L., Ash, G. E., & Cullinan, B. E. (2000). Children's literature. In M. L. Kamil, P. B. Mosenthal, P. D. Pearson, & R. Barr (Eds.), *Handbook of reading research*, Vol. III (pp. 361-379). Mahwah, NJ: Lawrence Erlbaum Associates.

Galda, L., & Cullinan, B. E. (2003). Literature for literacy. What research says about the benefits of using trade books in the classroom. In J. Flood, D. Lapp, J. R. Squire, & J. M. Jensen (Eds.), *Handbook of research on teaching the English language arts* (2nd ed.) (pp. 640-648). Old Tappan, NJ: Macmillan.

_____. (2006). *Literature and the child* (6th ed.). Belmont, CA: Wadsworth.

Gambrell, L. B. (1996). What research reveals about discussion. In L. B. Gambrell & L. F. Almasi (Eds.), *Lively discussion! Fostering engaged reading* (pp. 8-15). Newark, DE: International Reading Association.

Gangi, J. M. (2004). *Encountering children's literature: An arts approach.* Boston: Pearson Education, Inc.

Glazer, J. I., & Giorgis, C. (2005). *Literature for young children* (5th ed.). Upper Saddle River, NJ: Pearson.

Grandits, J. (2005). Concrete poetry and visual learning. *Book Links, 14*(5), 39-42.

Graves, D. H. (2003). *Writing: Teachers & children at work* (20th anniversary ed.). Portsmouth, NH: Heinemann.

_____. (2006). *Sea of faces: The importance of knowing your students.* Portsmouth, NH: Heinemann.

Hadaway, N. L., Vardell, S. M., & Young, T. A. (2001). Scaffolding oral language development through poetry for students learning English. *The Reading Teacher, 54*(8), 796-806.

Harvey, S. (2002). Nonfiction inquiry: Using real reading and writing to explore the world. *Language Arts, 80*(1), 12-22.

Harvey, S., & Goudvis, A. (2007). *Strategies that work: Teaching comprehension for understanding and engagement* (2nd ed.). Portland, ME: Stenhouse.

Heard, G. (1989). *For the good of the earth and sun: Teaching poetry*. Portsmouth, NH: Heinemann.

_____. (1995). *Writing toward home: Tales and lessons to find your way*. Portsmouth, NH: Heinemann.

_____. (1998*). Awakening the heart: Exploring poetry in elementary school*. Portsmouth, NH: Heinemann.

Hibbing, A. N., & Rankin-Erickson, J. L. (2003). A picture is worth a thousand words: Using visual images to improve comprehension in middle school struggling readers. *The Reading Teacher, 56*(8), 758-770).

Hillman, J. (1999). *Discovering children's literature* (2ⁿᵈ ed.). Upper Saddle River, NJ: Merrill.

_____. (2002). *Discovering children's literature* (3ʳᵈ ed.). Upper Saddle River, NJ: Merrill/Prentice Hall.

Hoyt, L. (1999). *Revisit, reflect, retell*. Portsmouth, NH: Heinemann.

_____. (2002). *Make it real: Strategies for success with informational texts*. Portsmouth, NH: Heinemann.

Huck, C. S. (1982). "I give you the end of a golden string." *Theory Into Practice, 21*(4), 315-325.

Huck, C. S., Kiefer, B. Z., Hepler, S., & Hickman, J. (2004). *Children's literature in the elementary school* (8ᵗʰ ed.). Boston: McGraw-Hill.

International Reading Association. (2000). Excellent reading teachers: A position statement. *The Reading Teacher, 54*(2), 235-240.

Jacobs, J., Mitchell, J., & Livingston, N. (2006). Children's books: U. S. children's literature award winners. *The Reading Teacher, 60*(4), 386-396.

Jacobs, J. S., & Tunnell, M. O. (2004). *Children's literature, briefly* (3ʳᵈ ed.). Upper Saddle River, NJ: Merrill/Prentice Hall.

Janeczko, P. B. (2005). *A kick in the head: An everyday guide to poetic forms*. (C. Raschka, Illus.). Cambridge, MA: Candlewick.

Janeczko, P. B. (Compiler). (2002). *Seeing the blue between: Advice and inspiration for young poets*. Cambridge, MA: Candlewick.

Jenks, C. K. (1992). Invitations from the librarian: Picture books for older children. In S. Benedict & L. Carlisle (Eds*.), Beyond words: Picture books for older readers and writers*. Portsmouth, NH: Heinemann.

Johnston, P. (2004). *Choice words: How our language affects children's learning*. Portland, ME: Stenhouse.

Kasten, W. C., Kristo, J. V., & McClure, A. A. (2005). *Living literature: Using children's literature to support reading and language arts*. Upper Saddle River, NJ: Pearson.

Kiefer, B. Z. (1995*). The potential of picturebooks: From visual literacy to aesthetic understanding*. Englewood Cliffs, NJ: Merrill.

Kiefer, B. Z., Hepler, S., & Hickman, J. (2007). *Charlotte Huck's children's literature* (9ᵗʰ ed.). Boston: McGraw-Hill.

Kurkjian, C., Livingston, N., & Cobb, V. (2006). Inquiring minds want to learn: The info on nonfiction and informational series books. *The Reading Teacher, 60*(1), 86-96.

Kurkjian, C., Livingston, N., Young, T., & Avi. (2006). Worlds of fantasy. *The Reading Teacher, 59*(5), 492-503.

Laminack, L. L. (2007). *Cracking open the author's craft: Teaching the art of writing*. New York: Scholastic.

Lamott, A. (1995). *Bird by bird: Some instructions on writing and life*. New York: Anchor Books.

Lehr, S. (1995). Fourth graders read, write, and talk about freedom. In S. Lehr (Ed.), *Battling dragons: Issues and controversy in children's literature*. Portsmouth, NH: Heinemann.

Leu, Jr., D. L., & Kinzer, C. K. (2003). *Effective literacy instruction, K–8* (5ᵗʰ ed.). Upper Saddle River, NJ: Merrill/Prentice Hall.

Levstick, L. (1993). "I wanted to be there": The impact of narrative on children's historical thinking. In M. O. Tunnell & R. Ammon (Eds.), *The story of ourselves: Teaching history through children's literature*. Portsmouth, NH: Heinemann.

Linaberger, M. (2004/2005). Poetry top 10: A foolproof formula for teaching poetry. *The Reading Teacher, 58*(4), 366-372.

Lukens, R. J. (2007). *A critical handbook of children's literature* (8ᵗʰ ed.). Boston: Allyn & Bacon.

Lynch-Brown, C., & Tomlinson, C. M. (2005). *Essentials of children's literature* (5ᵗʰ ed.). Boston: Allyn & Bacon.

Martinez, M. G., & McGee, L. M. (2000). Children's literature and reading instruction: Past, present, and future. *Reading Research Quarterly, 35*(1), 154-169.